Quality of Employment in Europe

Legal and Normative Perspectives

P.I.E. Peter Lang

Bruxelles · Bern · Berlin · Frankfurt am Main · New York · Oxford · Wien

Silvia Borelli & Pascale Vielle (eds.)

Quality of Employment in Europe

Legal and Normative Perspectives

"Work & Society"
No.74

This book has been published thanks to the European research project RECWOWE (Reconciling Work and Welfare in Europe), 2006-2011, co-funded by the European Commission, under 6th Framework Programme for Research – Socio-economic Sciences and Humanities (contract No. 028339-2) in the Directorate-General for Research.

Publié avec l'aide financière du Fonds de la Recherche Scientifique – FNRS.

Éditions scientifiques internationales
Brussels, 2012
1 avenue Maurice, B-1050 Brussels, Belgium
info@peterlang.com; www.peterlang.com

ISSN 1376-0955
ISBN 978-90-5201-888-1
D/2012/5678/91

Printed in Germany

Library of Congress Cataloging-in-Publication Data
Quality of employment in Europe : legal and normative perspectives / Silvia Borelli & Pascale Vielle (eds.). pages cm. -- (Work & society, ISSN 1376-0955 ; no.74) Includes bibliographical references and index.
ISBN 978-90-5201-888-1 (alk. paper)
1. Labor laws and legislation--European Union countries.
2. Work environment--European Union countries. I. Borelli, Silvia, editor of compilation. II. Vielle, Pascale, editor of compilation.
KJE2855.Q83 2012 331.2094--dc23 2012027869

CIP also available from the British Library.

Bibliographic information published by "Die Deutsche Nationalbibliothek".
"Die Deutsche Nationalbibliothek" lists this publication in the "Deutsche National-bibliografie"; detailed bibliographic data is available on the Internet at <http://dnb.d-nb.de>.

Table of Contents

INTRODUCTION

Legal and Normative Perspectives on Quality of Employment in Europe[1]

Pascale VIELLE
Professor of Social Law, University of Louvain

Silvia BORELLI
Researcher – Labour Law, University of Ferrara

I. Introduction

Since 2001, "quality of employment" is at the core of the political, academic and practical agenda, and feeds a wide-ranging debate. This collective work is an attempt to bring to this discussion an original normative and legal enlightenment. It is the result of a process of reflection carried out over two years within the "RECWOWE" (Reconciling work and welfare) international network of excellence.

Financed by the European Union within the sixth framework programme, RECWOWE ("Reconciling work and welfare") gathers together researchers from thirty research organisations in Europe, and aims at integrating the scientific activities devoted to the tensions that characterise relations between employment and social protection. One of the four main concerns of RECWOWE is the tension between quantity and quality of employment in Europe, which had led to a first work on quality of employment, already published by PIE Peter Lang[2]. Edited by A.-M. Guillen and S.A. Dahl, this first collective volume analysed a series of conceptual, methodological and substantial questions related to

[1] We are grateful to Gian Guido Balandi, Maria Jepsen, Marie-Ange Moreau, Jean-Jacques Paris and Greet Vermeylen for their stimulating and constructive discussion and comments at the Recwowe Final Conference, Brussels 15-17 June 2011.

[2] *Quality of Work in the European Union, Concept, Data and Debates from a Transnational Perspective*, Ana-M. Guillén, Svenn-Åge Dahl (eds.), Brussels, P.I.E. Peter Lang, Collection: Work & Society, vol. 67, 2009.

the quality of employment from sociological, economic and political angles.

This led to the proposal for a second work dedicated to the quality of employment. This concept had been approached in the European Union under the European Employment Strategy – emblematic of soft law –, but echoed the long European and national legal traditions of labour law. From the lawyers' point of view, the concept of quality of employment is embedded in the roots of social law (labour and social security law) emerging from the industrial revolution. It covers a range of fundamental aspects of employment relations, recognised in international, European and national social law. It consequently appeared necessary to confront the political concept of "quality of employment" with the "idea of social law"[3], in order to evaluate its normative relevance.

Treated in an interdisciplinary and international context, the project has a three-fold ambition. For the first time in a contemporary debate, a scientific work takes stock of the legal and normative understanding of the quality of employment in Europe. To this end, and through several topics, the authors try to grasp the relevance of the political concept of "quality" of employment compared to the concept of "social law", and question the way international, European and comparative law frame the concept of quality of employment. Moreover, this work aims to provide the conditions for an interdisciplinary dialogue enriched by a legal approach. Essentially this is a matter of making it possible for readers who are not lawyers to determine the importance of the law in the debate on quality of employment – which until now has paid little attention to a legal and normative approach – and to adapt the concepts and tools likely to advance scientific reflection. Lastly, the work proposes concrete and realistic paths for the improvement of European social law in order to fit in better with international and legal standards.

This study of the legal characteristics of quality of employment is not expected to be exhaustive. We have chosen some essential aspects (such as collective labour rights, equality and non-discrimination), but we had to omit others (such as health and safety at work). The research endorses a qualitative and normative standpoint. It aims to point out the cultural, historical, and legal contexts into which the quality of employment fits, and to formulate concrete tracks to reinforce the European social law in line with the concepts contained within the framework of the European Employment Strategy, but with respect to national and international legal traditions.

---

[3] To use Georges Gurvitch's expression in *L'idée de Droit social. Notion et système du droit social. Histoire doctrinale depuis le XVIIe siècle jusqu'à la fin du XIXe siècle*, Paris, Sirey, 1932.

In the following lines (and chapters), the authors will use the word "work" for whatever form of economic activity, including self-employment and undeclared work, performed by people. "Economic activity" is defined as an activity that aims at production, processing, packaging, selling, distribution, the purchase and consumption of goods and services (including intellectual property), as well as money or wealth, with a view to fulfilling some wants/needs on a commercial or self-reliant basis. "Employment" is meant to be an economic activity that is remunerated, undertaken for and/or under the direction and/or supervision of an employer. It also includes false self-employment such as undeclared work, since conditions of employment are *de facto* fulfilled. "Job" indicates a specific individual economic activity performed by an employee for an employer, under an employment contract (= a specific individual employment contract).

II. Taking Law Seriously

Also called the "Luxembourg Process", the European employment strategy (EES) was created in November 1997 at the European Council in Luxembourg. The aim was to reduce growing unemployment through an ambitious coordination process of national employment policies. This agreement led to the adoption of the "Employment Chapter" in the Treaty of Amsterdam. Based on well-known private and public management concepts (guidelines, best practices, benchmarking, action plans, recommendations etc.), the method endowed EU Commission and Member States with the possibility of a multilateral monitoring of employment policies.

The original Lisbon Strategy, launched in 2000 as a response to the challenges of globalisation and ageing, extended the main features to new policy domains – the so-called "open method of coordination" (OMC). The European Council defined the objective of the strategy for the EU in the following terms: "*to become the most dynamic and competitive knowledge-based economy in the world by 2010 capable of sustainable economic growth with more and* better *jobs and greater social cohesion and respect for the environment*".

At the Laeken Summit in 2001, Member States agreed on a multidimensional definition of "quality of employment", with a set of indicators, allowing the assessment of ten dimensions of employment quality (see Caillaud, Ghailani and Pena-Casas in this book). However the attention given to quality of employment waned with time, leaving more and more room for the objective of "quantity of jobs", partly viewed as contradictory with strong legal protection for employment. This longstanding trend was recently reinforced by the EU Commission in its Communication "EU 2020" (see hereafter).

At the same time, the Treaty of Lisbon signed in 2009 clearly expressed the aims of the European Union in art. 3, par. 3 TEU, specifying that the establishment of an internal market shall be pursued together with "*the sustainable development of Europe based on balanced economic growth and price stability, a highly competitive social market economy, aiming at full employment and* social progress, *and a* high level of protection *and improvement of the quality of the environment*". In addition, the European Union shall "*combat social exclusion and discrimination, and shall promote social justice and protection, equality between women and men, solidarity between generations and protection of the rights of the child*". Moreover, art. 9 TFEU echoes art. 3 TEU and requires that "*in defining and implementing its policies and activities, the Union shall take into account requirements linked to the promotion of a* high level of employment, the guarantee of adequate social protection, the fight against social exclusion, and a high level of education, training and protection of human health". The common values of the European Union are nowadays listed in the European Charter of Fundamental Rights, considered as part of the Treaty. Art. 6 also provides for the Union to accede to the European Convention for the Protection of Human Rights and Fundamental Freedoms. Negotiations for accession were carried out with the Council of Europe in July 2010. As the Preamble to the European Charter of Fundamental Rights specifies, the preservation and the development of these common values need "*to strengthen the protection of fundamental rights*".

These important changes within the institutional and legal Framework at EU level shed a new light on the debate of quality of employment. As the book clearly shows, if the Union intends to ensure full implementation of the Treaty of Lisbon, it will have to review the notion of "quality of employment" in line with common legal principles, well established at national as well as at international level. In this brief introduction, we would like to draw attention to two important aspects, dealing with the governance of quality of employment, that from now on will have to be taken seriously by EU authorities when establishing social policies. The first concerns the articulation between fundamental social rights, labour hard law, and soft law. The second concerns the articulation between economic and social governance.

A. Constructing Quality of Employment on Soft Law?

In the fields of employment and social protection, encouragement by the Treaty of Amsterdam to implement the convergence process (soft law) was initially interpreted as a welcome rebalancing of EU competences. Indeed, the economic dimension of the Treaty had partly been strengthened by the Single European Act and the Treaty of Maastricht that had paved the way to economic and monetary union based on criteria arising from orthodox economic concepts (inflation, public deficit, public debt), on the one hand, and by the same Treaty of Amsterdam that introduced the "subsidiarity principle" which made it even more unlikely to develop autonomous European social policies, on the other hand.

The brief history of soft law has not fulfilled the ambition of a new balance between social and economic EU policies – that was put forward by the Lisbon Declaration in 2000 and the Laeken Declaration in 2001. Within just five years, the first has become subservient to the second, both from an institutional perspective (integrating formal and procedural guidelines for employment in the Broad guidelines for economic policies – BGEPs) and a substantive perspective (reinforcement of quantitative objectives to the detriment of quality objectives, under the Economic Policy Committee's stronger leadership on the EES and OMC). In any event, one could question from the outset the relevance of social policies governed in the same way as economic policies, and immediately cast in the form of quantifiable targets. The form seemed doomed to over-determining the substance. This trend appears to be moreover confirmed by the recent evolution of economic governance (see hereafter).

At the same time, the construction of a comprehensive corpus of social rights at work remains to be achieved in Europe. If non-discrimination emerges as an exception, being one of the rare social fields where EU provisions go beyond most of the ILO standards (see Carlson, Canazza, Garcia-Izquierdo and Ramos-Villagrasa), European social law today seems rather like a patchwork colander, where many rights have slipped away, including the most fundamental, such as freedom of association or the right to collective bargaining (see Dorssemont). A few months before the implementation of the Treaty of Lisbon, the Laval, Viking and some subsequent cases confirmed what many European social lawyers had feared: in the absence of recognition and guarantee of fundamental social rights by the European Treaties (still recognised as among the most fundamental by the International Labor Organization and all Member States), the Court of Justice, according to its teleological approach, tackles the right to collective bargaining or the right to strike as restrictions to economic freedoms guaranteed by the Treaty. It therefore submits these expressions of fundamental social rights to a test of compliance with the Treaty, and even assesses whether they are necessary, proportionate and adequate to achieve the goals they seek. The legal order that henceforth applies to citizens of Member States subordinates their more fundamental social rights to the economic objectives of the Treaty. This shows that, as long as it is not translated into hard law, "quality of employment" will go unheeded in the European Union.

At ILO level, the governance of "Decent work agenda" seems to have taken the opposite direction. We may recall that all EU Member States are also members of the ILO and, for this reason, have adhered to this ILO concept. In an attempt to understand why the EU mostly failed to implement concrete quality of employment, it may be interesting to turn to the way the ILO determined the notion of "decent work" and its governance.

The Decent Work concept was formulated by the ILO's constituent members – governments, employers and workers – and is conceived as an agenda for the working community. It provides support through integrated Decent Work Country Programs developed in coordination with its constituent members. Putting the Decent Work Agenda into practice is achieved through the implementation of the ILO's four "inseparable, interrelated and mutually supportive" strategic objectives[4], where gender equality is a crosscutting objective:

- Creating Jobs – an economy that generates opportunities for investment, entrepreneurship, skills' development, job creation and sustainable livelihoods.
- Guaranteeing rights at work – to obtain recognition and respect for the rights of workers. All workers, in particular disadvantaged or poor workers, need representation, participation, and laws that work in their interest.
- Extending social protection – to promote both inclusion and productivity by ensuring that women and men enjoy working conditions that are safe, allow adequate free time and rest, take into account family and social values, provide for adequate compensation in case of loss of or reduced income and permit access to adequate healthcare.
- Promoting social dialogue – the involvement of strong and independent workers' and employers' organisations is central to increasing productivity, avoiding disputes at work, and building a cohesive society.

There are several differences between the ILO strategy of "decent work" and the EU approach to "quality of employment". One major distinction lies in the fundamental aims of the strategy (general objectives count! See Caillaud and Bonvin *et al.*): where in the context of the Lisbon Strategy, the OMC and EES (and even "quality of employment")

---

[4] *ILO Declaration on Social Justice for a Fair Globalization*, adopted by the Conference at its 97th session, 2008.

were supposed to serve ultimate economic objectives, "decent work", on the contrary, "*is based on the understanding that work is a source of personal dignity, family stability, peace in the community, democracies that deliver for people, and economic growth that expands opportunities for productive jobs and enterprise development*"[5].

In terms of governance, the main distinction concerns the significance attached to legal rights at work. The Decent Work Agenda is based on a full range of conventions and recommendations defining minimal common standards in labour law (see Caillaud, Ghailani and Peña-Casas). This corpus of legal instruments and its implementation constitutes the second axis of the strategy (after the "jobs creation" axis). Although embedding all the conventions and recommendations adopted since the ILO's foundation, this priority must be considered in line with the Declaration for the Universal Protection of Workers' Rights. Indeed, confronted to a crisis of ratifications and effectiveness, the ILO adopted in 1998 a Declaration committing Member States to respect and promote principles and rights in four categories, whether or not they have ratified the relevant Conventions. These categories are:

- freedom of association and the effective recognition of the right to collective bargaining,
- the elimination of forced or compulsory labour,
- the abolition of child labour and
- the elimination of discrimination in respect of employment and occupation.

In the Decent Work Agenda, social protection – embedded in a series of conventions, but not incorporated in the 1998 Declaration – is considered as the third axis of the strategy. Although proclaimed as one of the fundamental rights in the 1998 Declaration, social dialogue is conceived as another major axis, whereas non-discrimination – also recognised in several conventions and recommendations – is recalled as a transversal dimension – following the "double trail approach" recommended by feminist literature, for instance.

---

[5] As described on the ILO Website (http://www.ilo.org/global/about-the-ilo/decent-work-agenda/lang--en/index.htm – 15/06/11).

Hierarchy of social rights in the decent work agenda

1. Freedom of association + collective bargaining	1998 Declaration + Axis 4 DWA
2. Gender equality	1998 Declaration + transversal Axis DWA
3a. Elimination of forced or compulsory labour	1998 Declaration
3b. Abolition of child labour	1998 Declaration
3c. Non Discrimination	1998 Declaration
4. Extension of social protection	Axis 3 + Axis 2 DWA (Conv. 102)
5. Other rights at work	Axe 2 DWA (all conventions)

In other words, the Decent Work Agenda places fundamental social rights at the core of the strategy, giving ultimate priority to collective social rights and to non-discrimination. Among other rights at work, the right to social protection has a particular importance, with a whole axis dedicated to it.

To summarise, the whole Decent Work strategy aims to improve the effectiveness of social rights at work, through the reinforcement of control mechanisms and soft law.

In the absence of a clear and compulsory fundamental rights' framework, on the one hand, and of sufficient institutional competences in the field of labour law on the other, EU could have built on the experience of the 1989 Community Charter of Fundamental Social Rights for Workers that establishes the major principles on which the European labour law model is based. In fact, whereas the Charter only had a symbolic significance, the Delors Commission took this opportunity to draw up an action plan that led to the adoption of several directives in the field of labour law. Along the same lines, with a stronger European and national will, the EES and OMC could have led to a social agenda conducive to the adoption of hard law. Today, the Treaty of Lisbon opens avenues for a renewed articulation between fundamental social rights, labour law and soft law in the EU. While the Treaty henceforth integrates fundamental rights (including a range of social rights) and requires the accession of the EU to the European Convention for the Protection of Human Rights and Fundamental Freedoms, it also reformulates the Union main objectives (art. 3 TEU) and instruments (i.a. the horizontal social clause: art. 9 TFEU), redirecting the European policies and actions towards social goals. Within this new framework, the EU institutions could propose an architecture for social policies, rooted in fundamental social rights, supplemented by a hard law comprehensive range of instruments providing workers with rights at work, substantiated with soft law techniques.

B. *Employment Strategy in the Context of European Economic Governance: Encompassing Labour Law while Developing Employment Policies*

Adopted after the Treaty of Lisbon, in response to the economic and financial crisis, the new EU Economic Governance, as defined in the Europe 2020 strategy, comprises a range of policy initiatives.

- First of all, the Commission proposed to create a *European Semester* to coordinate *ex ante* the EU and euro zone budgetary and economic policies. The European Council endorsed the priorities for fiscal consolidation and structural reform, which means "*restoring sound budgets and fiscal sustainability, reducing unemployment through labour market reforms and making new efforts to enhance growth*"[6]. The EU Semester starts with the Annual Growth Survey (published in January)[7], in which the Commission provides an analysis on the basis of the progress towards the Europe 2020 targets. At the Spring European Council meeting, Member States adopt conclusions providing EU guidance on the Stability and Convergence Programs (SCPs) and on the National Reform Programs (NRPs). These two documents should be sent in April to the European Commission for assessment. Based on recommendations from the Commission[8], the European Council conveys, in June/July, its opinion on Stability and Convergence Programs and Countries' specific policy guidance. The conclusion of the first European Semester marks the opening of a "national semester". In the second semester of the year, the Member States should discuss how to incorporate European Guidance into their budgets and national decision-making.
- The Economic and Financial Affairs Council and the Employment, Social Policy, Health and Consumer Affairs Council adopt, respectively, the *broad guidelines for the economic policies* and the *guidelines for the employment policies* of the Member States[9]. These integrated guidelines are one of the main tools of the Europe 2020 strategy.

---

6 *European Council Conclusion*, 24/25 March 2011, EUCO 10/11, p. 3.

7 The *Annual Growth Survey 2012* (COM(2011) 815 final) has been adopted the 23rd of November 2011 in order to ensure ample time for it to be considered by the Member States and EU Institutions.

8 See Communication from the Commission, *Concluding the first European semester of economic policy coordination: Guidance for national policies in 2011-2012*, COM(2011) 400 final.

9 *The Employment guidelines for 2010* were adopted in October 2010, in principle, for a duration of four years. The guidelines for 2011 have been maintained unchanged

- A third process, activated by the Member States in line with and to strengthen existing EU economic governance, concerns the reform of the Stability and Growth Pact. The new *Euro-plus Pact* will cover "*priority policy areas that are essential for fostering competitiveness and convergence*", avoiding harmful imbalances[10]. In these areas, "*common objectives will be agreed upon at the Heads of State or Government level*". Each Member State should decide its own policy-mix and undertake specific measures to reach these goals. The implementation of commitments and progress toward the common policy objectives will be indicated in the Stability and Convergence Programs and in the National Reform Programs and will be monitored politically by the Heads of State or Government, "*on the basis of a series of indicators covering competitiveness, employment, fiscal sustainability and financial stability*".
- In April 2011, the European Commission adopted the "*Single Market Act. Twelve levers to boost growth and strengthen confidence. Working together to create new growth*"[11]. Like other policies included in the EU Economic Governance, the Single Market Act is aimed at delivering growth and employment and promoting competitiveness. The Commission has identified twelve levers and will present legislative proposals for the implementation of this key action in 2011. The Parliament and Council should adopt an initial series of priority measures to relaunch the single market by the end of 2012. At the same time, it will take stock of the progress of the Action Plan and will present a program for the next stage.
- In the wake of financial crisis, the Member States agreed on a package of economic and budgetary recommendations sets priorities and measures to reinforce financial governance and stability in the Eurozone. This includes the *Six Pack* that amends and strengthens the Stability and Growth Pact (SGP), introduces a new Excessive Imbalances Procedure and lays down new requirements for Member States' national budgetary frameworks. On the basis of the *Six Pack*, the Commission has proposed two new *Regulations* aimed at further strengthening the coordination and the surveillance of budgetary processes for all euro area Member States, as well as a *Green Paper on presenting op-*

(*Council's Decision of 19 May 2011 on the employment guidelines of the Member States for 2011*, 2011/308/UE).

10 The Euro Plus Pact aims to: foster competitiveness, foster employment, contribute further to the sustainability of public finances and reinforce financial stability.

11 COM(2011) 206 final.

tions for euro Stability Bonds. Therefore, the surveillance tools agreed as part of the *Six Pack* are to be used within the framework of the European Semester. In particular, the two proposals require the Member States to publish and present to the Commission their draft budgetary plans in advance of their adoption by the national parliaments. The Commission will examine them and will address an opinion to a Member State if these plans do not appear to be in line with the obligations under the Stability and Growth Pact and the recommendations from the European semester in the budgetary area[12].

These new four instruments of EU Economic Governance assert economic objectives as the prime aim of European Integration. Consequently, European Employment Policies sustain and promote *Employability* by increasing labour market participation, reducing structural unemployment and promoting social inclusion[13]. In this perspective, and notwithstanding the new Treaty, labour law is commonly considered by economic policies as a restriction on economic freedoms and employment protection legislation is accused of creating labour market rigidity and of preventing increased participation in the labour market[14]. Moreover, all the indicators aimed at measuring social goals are quantitative[15]

12 If the Commission issues an opinion stating that the plans are not in line with the SGP and the Member State does not take corrective action, the Commission can use this when deciding whether to place the Member State in an Excessive Deficit Procedure (EDP). The new monitoring requirements allow assessments to be made about the content and direction of fiscal policy at any point while a Member State is in an EDP. If a risk of non-compliance with the deadline to correct the excessive deficit exists, the Commission can address a recommendation to the Member State. The Member States experiencing severe difficulties with regard to their financial stability or in receipt of financial assistance are submitted to even more strengthened monitoring and surveillance procedures. In these cases, the Commission may propose the Council to recommend that the Member State concerned seek financial assistance and that a macro-economic adjustment programme be prepared. The Regulation also introduces a new procedure that will apply to the preparation and adoption of any future macroeconomic adjustment procedures. It sets out how financial assistance granted outside the framework of the Union (such as through the EFSF and IMF), fits with the Treaty.

13 *Council Decision on guidelines for the employment policies of the Member States*, 12 October 2010.

14 Communication from the Commission, *Annual Growth Survey: advancing the EU's comprehensive response to the crisis*, COM(2011) 11 final, and *Annual Growth Survey 2012*, COM(2011) 815 final, p. 11. On this topic see: A. Supiot, "Justice sociale et libération du commerce international", *Droit social*, 2010, p. 133.

15 The Commission has also suggested to "*review the EU definition and common indicators of quality of work, and make them more operational for the evaluation and benchmarking of Member State policies*" (Communication from the Commission, *An Agenda for new skills and jobs: A European contribution towards full employment*, COM(2010) 682 final, p. 15).

so that the performance of each State can be easily calculated (i.e. nation branding or government by indicators), which tends to favor more competition between social legal systems (i.e. normative Darwinism)[16]. The new economic governance has clearly incorporated Employment Policies[17].

Beyond fundamental rights at work, this new governance framework will adversely affect several aspects of quality of employment, such as some essential features of labour contract, equality at work, social protection, wages, social dialogue and collective labour rights.

The Europe 2020 Strategy is aimed at directing the EU economy towards smart, sustainable and inclusive growth, intended as the achievement of some "social" targets: a 75% employment rate for women and men aged 20-64 by 2020; reduction of school drop-out rates to less than 10% and at least 40% of 30-34 year-olds completing third level education; at least 20 million fewer people in or at risk of poverty and social exclusion. In this context, two flagship initiatives are launched: the Agenda for new skills and jobs (Communication from the Commission, *An Agenda for new skills and jobs: A European contribution towards full employment*, COM(2010) 682 final)[18] and the European Platform Against Poverty. The first aims at modernising labour markets in order to raise employment levels, to reduce unemployment, to raise labour productivity and to ensure the sustainability of the social model. The second intends to guarantee respect for the fundamental rights of people experiencing poverty and social exclusion.

Fundamental rights are only mentioned in the platform against poverty. Consequently, social protection is reduced to the fight against

---

16 "*Le concept de gouvernance porte à considérer le chiffre non comme un cadre, mais comme un but de l'action, ou plus exactement comme un moteur de la réaction puisque chaque acteur privé ou public est censé, non plus agir, mais rétroagir aux signaux chiffrés qui lui parviennent afin d'améliorer sa performance*" (A. Supiot, *L'esprit de Philadelphie, la justice sociale face au marché total*, Paris, Seuil, 2010, p. 84).

17 On this topic see: *Social developments in the European Union 2010*, C. Degryse and D. Natali (eds.), Brussels, Ose-Etui, 2011; A. Dufresne, "Les grandes orientations de politiques économiques: un tournant institutionnel, quels changements substantiels", *Revue Belge de Sécurité Sociale*, 2001, p. 92; A.L. de Val Tena, "La polìtica de empleo en la Uniòn Europea: de la estretegia de Lisboa a la estrategia 'Europa 2020'", *Temas Laborales* 106/2010, p. 99.

18 The Agenda's priorities will be revised in 2014 and adapted to the new Multiannual Financial Framework. "*Till then, it will report on progress in the Annual Growth Survey with Europe 2020 strategy*" (Communication from the Commission, *An Agenda for new skills and jobs: A European contribution towards full employment*, COM(2010) 682 final, p. 21).

poverty (i.e. social exclusion)[19]. The main imperative is a rapid reduction in unemployment: "*This means first and foremost removing institutional obstacles that prevent proper functioning of Member States' labor market*"[20]. Therefore, social protection is reduced to the sole objective of social inclusion[21] and there is no mention of the quality of jobs created. On the contrary, flexible working arrangements and open-ended contracts are supported (see Deumer)[22]. Enhancing greater internal flexibility should ease the reconciliation of work and private life and contribute to women's employment[23]. There is no requirement to accommodate work-life balance to the extent feasible in the employment relationship for both parents (see Carlson, Canazza, Garcìa-Izquierdo and Ramos-Villagrasa). No consideration is given to the variability and predictability of working time, both important elements for working time balance[24]. No attention is paid to the risk of segregation that teleworking and flexitime (expressly supported by the Commission) could generate.

The use of open-ended contractual arrangements with a gradual increase in protection of rights should diminish the existing divisions between atypical and permanent contracts[25]. It does not matter if the adaptation (alteration) of Employment Protection Legislation (EPL) increases the precariousness of labour market, transforming standard workers into unstable workers. No consideration is given to the requirement to prevent the status of employees becoming insecure, testified by the large number of cases pursued before national and European courts by atypical workers (see Borelli). The reduction of EPL is necessary to increase any form of labour market participation[26].

---

19 B. Vanhercke, "Is the 'Social Dimension of Europe 2020' an Oxymoron?", in *Social developments in the European Union 2010*, *op. cit.*, p. 141.

20 *Joint Employment Report*, adopted by the Council (EPSCO), 8 March 2011, p. 9.

21 B. Vanhercke, "Is the 'Social Dimension of Europe 2020' an Oxymoron?", *op. cit.*

22 On the contrary, the Report of the Director-General of ILO, *A New Era of Social Justice* (International Labour Conference, 100th Session 2011), underlines that "*flexible labour markets*" are "*a crucial characteristic of inefficient growth*", being associated with "*greater job precariousness, the de-linking of labour incomes and productivity developments and weaker incentives to invest in worker skills*". Moreover, "*systematic deregulation has not contributed to higher levels of investment in real economy*".

23 *Annex 3. Annual Growth Survey, Draft Joint Employment Report*, COM(2011) 11 final, p. 12.

24 *Work-Life Balance in Europe. The Role of Job Quality*, Sonja Drobnic and Ana-M. Guillén (eds.), Palgrave Macmillan, 2011.

25 *Annex 3. Annual Growth Survey, Draft Joint Employment Report*, COM(2011) 11 final, p. 13.

26 Communication from the Commission, *Concluding the first European semester of economic policy coordination: Guidance for national policies in 2011-2012*, COM(2011) 400 final, p. 7.

Moreover, unemployment benefits are claimed to be reassessed in order to ensure that they provide incentives to work (i.e. policies to make work pay)[27]. By inviting Member States to reform unemployment benefit systems, the European Institutions do not take into account the definition of suitable employment as accepted by the Member States and do not consider the difficulty that the geographical mobility of labour can create. Therefore, there is a risk that Member States gradually enlarge the notion of suitable of employment, or even worse, abandon it in favor of the notion of "reinsertion in the labour market" (see Dermine and Caillaud).

The leading concept of "austerity" prescribes a rigorous fiscal consolidation. In particular, all Member States "*should keep public expenditure growth firmly below the rate of medium term trend GDP growth*". Member States in excessive deficit procedure should also "*set out the expenditure pact and the broad measures they intend to take in order to eliminate their excessive deficits*"[28]. Labour market reforms should be most cost-effective and should contribute to the sustainability of social protection systems[29]. In that context, "*further efforts to reduce early retirement schemes and increase the retirement age need to be pursued to increase the participation of older workers in employment*"[30]. In particular, the sustainability of social protection systems will be assessed on the basis of the "*sustainability gap indicators*" that measure whether debt levels are sustainable based on the current policies and taking into account demographic factors[31].

Moreover, Euro Plus Pact imposes a monitoring of unit labour costs in order to assess whether wages are evolving in line with productivity[32].

---

27 *Annex 3. Annual Growth Survey, Draft Joint Employment Report*, COM(2011) 11 final, p. 13.

28 Communication from the Commission, *Annual Growth Survey: advancing the EU's comprehensive response to the crisis*, COM(2011) 11 final.

29 As underlined in the *Joint Employment Report*, adopted by the Council (EPSCO), 8 March 2011, there is a wide variety of national shares in social expenditure and a great diversity in the capacity of Member States to meet the rising demand for social protection.

30 *Joint Employment Report*, adopted by the Council (EPSCO), 8 March 2011; see also Communication from the Commission, *Concluding the first European semester of economic policy coordination: Guidance for national policies in 2011-2012*, COM(2011) 400 final.

31 Euro Plus Pact, *Stronger Economic Policy Coordination for Competitiveness and Convergence*.

32 The necessity to improve "*the responsiveness of wage setting processes to market developments in conjunction with the social partners*", so that "*wages properly reflect labour productivity in the medium term and ensure the EU's competitiveness position vis-à-vis the rest of the world and inside the EU and Member States*" is underlined in the *Joint Employment Report*, adopted by the Council (EPSCO), 8 March

To reach this objective, the Member States should "*review the wage setting arrangements, and, where necessary, the degree of centralization in the bargaining process, and the indexation mechanisms*". The measures to adjust wage-setting mechanisms threaten not only the indexation systems, but also the autonomy of the social partners. Even if the Member States do respect "*national traditions of social dialogue and industrial relations*", the importance given to decentralised collective agreements alters the structure of collective bargaining.

In fact, the autonomy of the social partners has already been seriously compromised by some recent decisions by the European Court of Justice (see Dorssemont). In *Laval*[33], for example, the Court has interpreted art. 56 TFUE and Directive 96/71 as preventing a trade union, from attempting, by means of collective action, to force a provider of services established in another Member State to enter into negotiations with it and to sign a collective agreement the terms of which lay down more favorable conditions than those resulting from the legislative provisions that implement art. 3 of the Directive or relate to matters not referred to in art. 3.

Moreover the incorporation of Employment Policies in the EU Economic Governance has displaced the competence to adopt or modify Labour Law. For instance, legislation aimed at improving and reinforcing the transposition, implementation and enforcement of the Posting of Workers Directive, together with legislation aimed at clarifying the exercise of freedom of establishment and the freedom to provide services alongside fundamental social rights, has been included in the key actions that the DG Internal Market and Services will enhance in 2011. This means avoiding the legislative procedure of art. 154 and 155 TFEU, and setting aside social partners.

Social dialogue is considered to be effective and important when austerity measures must be decided, as only a division of efforts will guarantee socially acceptable and successful reforms[34]. However, social partners are facing a Hobson's choice: they should accept the Europe 2020 strategy and find negotiated solutions to pursue its aims, without modifying the type of economic governance that the European Union imposes.

2011 and in the Communication from the Commission, *Concluding the first European semester of economic policy coordination: Guidance for national policies in 2011-2012*, COM(2011) 400 final, p. 6.

33 ECJ, 18 December 2007, C-341/05.

34 *Annex 3. Annual Growth Survey, Draft Joint Employment Report*, COM(2011) 11 final.

Again, the marginality of social partners in the current European Economic policies is demonstrated by their role in enhancing the Single Market Act. They have "*the opportunity to present their positions on issues relating to economic and social cohesion*", but they do not figure among the institutions that are party to the development of the Single Market. Moreover, in listening the Single Market players, the Commission has mentioned "citizens and business". In the Economic context, "citizens" more often means "consumers" than "workers"[35].

III. Policy Recommendations

This book illustrates the importance of restoring a *precise distinction between values, objectives and means* in the European Union[36].

In terms of values, the international approach of decent work (ILO) and a comparative perspective show that quality of employment is primarily a matter of fundamental substantial and subjective social rights. The EU has to seek a new architecture for employment quality, rooted in fundamental rights. All the new possibilities offered by the Treaty of Lisbon must be exploited to ensure the efficiency of social rights: implementation of the Charter of fundamental rights, EU adhesion to the European Convention of human rights but also to the ILO – which leads to automatic adhesion to fundamental social rights –, to the European social charter of the Council of Europe, and other relevant international instruments (including CEDAW and others at the UN level). As stated in the Report of the ILO Director-General, *A New Era of Social Justice* (International Labour Conference, 100th Session 2011), fundamental principles and rights at work "*provide the basic framework for market forces to operate efficiently and fairly*"[37].

Still, from the point of view of values, the concept of *Employability* should be replaced by the concept of *Capability*, i.e. the freedom to choose our lives (or the freedom that a person actually has to do or be things that he or she may value doing or being)[38]. Therefore, increasing

---

35 European Parliament, "*Delivering a single market to consumers and citizens*", A7-0132/2010.

36 See A. Supiot, *L'esprit de Philadelphie*, *op. cit.*

37 The Report mentions the *Declaration concerning the aims and purposes of the International Labour Organisation*, adopted in Philadelphia in 1944, that declares: "*all national and international policies and measures, in particular those of an economic and financial character, should be judged in this light and accepted only in so far as they may be held to promote and not to hinder the achievement of this fundamental objective*", the fundamental objective being the right of all human beings "*to pursue both their material well-being and their spiritual development in conditions of freedom and dignity, of economic security and equal opportunity*".

38 A. Sen, *The Idea of Justice*, London, Penguin, 2009, p. 232.

employment level should be considered as a positive outcome only if the jobs created improve the actual lifetime opportunities for workers (see Bonvin, Cianferoni, Widmer).

As already mentioned, the social *objectives* of the EU are listed in art. 3 par. 3 TEU. Art 9 TFEU echoes art 3 par. 3, giving the EU institutions and Member States more concrete guidelines to reach these objectives. It has to be fully implemented in order to assess the impact of EU policies on quality of employment[39]. Horizontal social clause assigns social objectives to all policies and actions of the Union. It must be imposed in all fields (including the "hardest" economic fields) and to all EU institutions – the Commission and the Council, of course, but also the European Parliament and the Court of Justice. In the field of hard law, many emblematic social features of what might be called the "European social model"[40] would be protected from the grip of economic law. In the area of soft law, operated properly, the horizontal social clause could allow an emancipation of the Lisbon process and of a "quality of employment" strategy towards economic convergence criteria, or even a compatibility assessment of economic areas in regard with the social purposes of the Treaty.

However, the institutions and social actors should propose and enhance institutional mechanisms capable of ensuring effectiveness of fundamental rights and social values. For instance, more improvement in the social dimension would be assured if DG Employment, Social Affairs and Inclusion, European Economic and Social Committee, national Ministers of labour and social protection, as well as social partners, were actively involved in formulating legislative proposals. It would be unreasonable to expect the European social partners to be consulted to modify, for example, the Working Time Directive (as art. 154 and 155 require), but not to regulate the right to take collective action in the context of freedom of establishment and the freedom to provide services.

With respect to *means*, a catalogue of rights and freedoms at work which constitute "quality of employment in Europe" should be estab-

39 A "High level of employment" must be understood from a quantitative as well as from a qualitative point of view. See P. Vielle, "How the Horizontal Social Clause can be made to work: the lessons of gender mainstreaming", in *The Lisbon Treaty and Social Europe*, N. Bruun, K. Lörcher, I. Schömann (eds.), Oxford, Hart Publishing, 2012.

40 To ensure that the legislative proposals concerning the internal market include a reference to social policies and social rights, an impact assessment will accompany each proposal of the Commission (*Single Market Act. Twelve levers to boost growth and strengthen confidence. "Working together to create new growth"* (COM(2011) 206 final, p. 5).

lished. In fact, although the Treaty of Lisbon henceforth clearly promotes fundamental social rights, the "hard law" framework of social rights at work still remains incomplete at EU level, compared to national traditions and national commitments towards the ILO and the Council of Europe (Strasbourg). This catalogue should include the four universally acknowledged social rights listed in the ILO Declaration, and be extended to the commonly agreed corpus of social rights in the EU (on the basis of the EU "social acquis", of the Charter of fundamental rights of EU and of the relevant instruments of the Council of Europe). It would constitute the "spinal column" of an EU strategy of quality of employment, supplemented by soft law. The decent work approach should be mainstreamed in the EU policy framework, firstly as a key element of its external dimension, but also as a component of EU internal policies, as a complementary and supportive approach towards the improvement of quality of work and also employment policies (Caillaud, Ghailani, Peña-Casas).

In so far as "*the indivisible, universal values of human dignity, freedom, equality and solidarity*" should be pursued, employment policies should be considered as an alternative mechanism to enhance substantial rights. To this end, they should be considered as a complement – by no means a substitute or an opponent – to "hard" labour law (Bonvin, Cianferoni, Widmer). "Decent work" at ILO level shows the efficiency of a soft law strategy built on the roots of fundamental social rights. In this perspective, EES and OMC must be reviewed in line with the rights that are or will be recognised at EU level. These rights must shape the list of criteria for "quality of employment", but also the way they are conceived through indicators (and not the reverse).

The policies defined in the context of EU Economic Governance identify the *means* by which one of the *objectives* of the European Union may be achieved. These means must respect the *values* of European Union and guarantee the fulfillment of the other *objectives* listed in art. 3 TEU (or, at least, they must not hinder the fulfillment of the latter)[41]. The recent revision of economic governance in Europe shows the limits of social soft law, which from now on is going to be more and more shaped by economic considerations and objectives. If the EU still pretends to build a "European social model", it has to protect "quality of employment" from economic governance. A catalogue of social rights at

41 Gottardi D., "Tutela del lavoro e concorrenza tra imprese nell'ordinamento dell'Unione europea", *Giornale di diritto del lavoro e delle relazioni industriali*, 2010, p. 509. As stated by A. Supiot, "*dans cette perspective, la libération du commerce n'est plus une fin en soi, mais seulement l'un des moyens possibles de poursuivre cet objectif de justice sociale*" ("Justice sociale et libération du commerce international", *op. cit.*, p. 137).

work and a quality of employment strategy anchored in a fundamental rights framework would contribute to the emancipation of the social arena and would fit in with art. 3 par. 3 of the Lisbon Treaty and the "capabilities" approach.

In order to promote "job quality", regulations should not only define substantial rights, but also procedural rights and negotiation (Bonvin, Cianferoni, Widmer)[42]. Social partners' autonomy should be respected, in line with art. 152 TFEU. Accordingly, collective agreements can never be considered as an obstacle to economic freedom, but rather as a normal consequence of the right to collective bargaining (art. 28 Charter of Fundamental Rights of the European Union)[43]. In the capability perspective, the power to do something (conferred by the right to negotiate) comes with responsibility for what we do (in this instance, the duty to respect the collective agreement). Duties emanate from the exercise of power, as a consequence of the choices[44] we make.

Finally, the distinction between short-term and long-term reforms has to be rejected[45]. It disguises the intention to reform Labour Law *now so* as to promote flexible contractual arrangements and less regulated labour market, and to improve (maybe) *in the future* social protection for employees in flexible jobs. Up to now, this strategy only allowed an increasing so called "Matthew Effect"[46]: "*les réformes conduites au nom de l'adaptation [du Droit du travail] aux besoins des marchés n'ont nullement conduit à supprimer les 'acquis' de l'État providence, mais bien plutôt à rogner ou supprimer les protections là où elles étaient le plus nécessaire tandis qu'elles continuent de s'empiler en haut de l'échelle salariale*"[47].

42 A. Supiot (*L'esprit de Philadelphie*, *op. cit.*, p. 140) refers to "*capacité collective*", that is either the individual freedom to organise and act collectively to defend our own social and economic interests (liberté syndicale et droit d'action collective), or the power of organisations to negotiate and conclude collective agreements (droit de négotiation collective).

43 As stated in the Report of the Director-General of the ILO, *A New Era of Social Justice* (International Labour Conference, 100th Session 2011), freedom of association and the right to collective bargaining are necessary in order to avoid market incomes deviating from productivity trends.

44 A. Sen, *The Idea of Justice*, *op. cit.*, p. 19.

45 For a recent proposal to reconcile short-term and long-term considerations, see Vandenbroucke, F., Hemerijck, A. and Palier, B. *The EU Needs a Social Investment Pact*, OSE Paper Series, Opinion paper No. 5, May 2011, that suggest embedding the social investment strategy in budgetary policy and financial regulation, i.e. "short-term macroeconomic governance serves long-term social investment".

46 Dovis P. – Saraceno C., *I nuovi poveri: politiche per le disuguaglianze*, Turin, Codice, 2011.

47 Supiot, *L'esprit de Philadelphie*, *op. cit.*, p. 56.

IV. Presentation of the Chapters

The book is subdivided into four parts. The first part points out the theoretical bases on which social law is founded and given legitimacy as a paramount instrument for quality of employment. It analyses the conformity of the political and legal European framework with these fundamental norms. The contribution of *Pascal Caillaud, Dalila Ghailani, Ramón Peña-Casas* compares the main elements in the definition of job quality within the European framework and the concept of decent work developed by the International Labor Organization (ILO), highlighting the high degree of convergence of both approaches. The second part is dedicated to the legal dimension of several areas of job quality, as reflected in European hard and soft laws and also ILO conventions, and considers the role of EU and international regulations in promoting fundamental social rights.

In his chapter, *Jérôme Deumer* makes a critical assessment of the definition which has been given by the European Commission to the concept of quality of work and flexicurity, and aims at assessing whether these goals could be reconciled in the same social policy. Indeed, since the beginning of the 1990s, the improvement in quality of work has been considered as the priority of social agenda of several international organisations, including the European Union. At the same time, numerous discussions have been held on the implementation of a policy of flexicurity which aims to increase the flexibility of employment relations whilst securing the professional path of workers.

Even the social doctrines of the Catholic Church have an essential place in the installation of a normative framework for quality of employment. As underlined by *Pascal Caillaud*, the moral and religious nature of the precepts has not prevented the Social Teaching of the Catholic Church from expanding its influence on major international organisations. Its rules on finding the "common good" can be detected in ILO policies to promote decent work in the quest for "common welfare" (Article III of the Declaration of Philadelphia) or in EU policies on "quality employment" in the quest for the "welfare of workers".

The second part of the book returns to some of the most critical aspects of the quality of employment: the employee concepts, the development of atypical forms of work, freedom of association and the effective right to collective bargaining. The ILO Decent Work Agenda, as well as European Employment Strategy focus not only on the creation of jobs, but also on the creation of jobs of an acceptable quality. It is therefore important to consider the type of work contract. *Silvia Borelli's* contribution examines the employee concepts developed by European Court of Justice and the criteria for the interpretation of these concepts. The author underlines the importance of establishing a common set of transparent, coherent and objective indicators within any employment relationship.

In the next chapter, the EU's strategies to avoid the risk of segmentation of the labour market are taken into account. On the one hand, EU law sets broad definitions for an employee, part-time worker, fixed-time worker and temporary agency worker; on the other hand, it prohibits discrimination between atypical workers and comparable standard employees. The recent proposal on economically dependent self-employment is also considered.

Filip Dorssemont examines whether the Commission's understanding of concepts of decent work and quality in work takes sufficient recognition of freedom of association and freedom of collective bargaining, as a lever to promote better and decent jobs. Furthermore, it examines to what extent the European Court of Justice recognises and respects both freedoms, in face of the necessity to protect and promote fundamental economic freedom.

The third and the fourth parts of the volume analyse from various angles two substantial dimensions of the quality of employment: the role of social protection and the prohibition of discrimination. The contributions of *Elise Dermine* and *Pascal Caillaud* focus on the concept of suitable employment. In the first chapter, the framework incorporating the different dimensions that shape a job of quality is compared with the international framing (ILO, Council of Europe and EU) of the concept of suitable employment, to assess whether the framing includes the necessary safeguards to ensure that a suitable job plays a part as a springboard into jobs of quality. *Pascal Caillaud*, in his turn, examines whether the concept of a valid or reasonable offer of employment, existing in French legislation, can be considered as the informal interpretation of the concept of suitable employment. The author also underlines that a valid offer does not have the same characteristics as a reasonable offer of employment: in the second case, the job seeker's obligation not to refuse a job, is qualified by the nature and the characteristics of the employment offered, the geographical area and the expected wage.

The fourth part further demonstrates the concern for a legal and qualitative implementation of quality of employment concept. *Laura Carlson* highlights the necessity of considering work-life balance as an aspect of quality of work. Moving away from a gender concept in parenting is necessary to achieve equality in the workplace between women and men. Combining family and work is the next step in this process, which entails employers considering the need to accommodate the requirements of both parents in reconciling work and family.

The contribution of *Christine Canazza* examines the quality of work framework as a major aspect to be taken into account within the active ageing strategy and with special regard to the principle of age discrimination. After demonstrating that the struggle against discrimination is a significant aspect of quality of work, the paper focuses on the importance of these objectives to achieve the goals of the European Employment Strategy in terms of an active ageing policy.

Antonio L. García-Izquierdo and *Ramos-Villagrasa* review the European equal opportunities law, stressing the wide gap existing between such legislation and job access for women. As a solution, the authors suggest following the organisational justice approach and incorporating it in the legal provisions as a mean to improve equality between women and men.

In conclusion, *Jean-Michel Bonvin, Nicola Cianferoni and Frédéric Widmer* explore the place of law, in a globalised context, in the regulation of the labour market, firstly identifying the main changes that are currently challenging job quality. Then, the authors focus on some actual strategies that have been developed and suggest alternative conceptions inspired by the capability and *capacitas* frameworks. In this context, a combination of substantial and procedural rights is needed to promote job quality.

PART I

THEORETICAL & INTERNATIONAL FRAMEWORK

Conceptual and Legal Framework for Quality of Work and Employment in International Institutions – The European Union and the International Labour Organisation

Pascal CAILLAUD
Researcher – Law and Social Change (UMR-CNRS 6297)
Maison des Sciences de l'Homme Ange Guépin – University of Nantes

Dalila GHAILANI
Researcher – European Social Observatory (OSE)

Ramón PEÑA-CASAS
Researcher – European Social Observatory (OSE)

I. Introduction

The multifaceted concept of "job quality" has only recently appeared in the rhetoric of international organisations. At the start of this millennium, both the European Union (EU) and the International Labour Organisation (ILO) of the United Nations (UN) included among their policy objectives similar concerns about improving "job quality" or promoting "decent work". This was followed by an intense institutional process for the conception and operation of its notions. The aim of this chapter is to explore the international concepts of "job quality" according to two complementary and intertwined perspectives: the policy and legal dimension.

As policy concepts, "job quality" and "decent work" reflect a (relative) consensus between Member States on their significance in a policy with commonly agreed objectives. In procedural terms, their complex nature and implementation by means of indicators includes a process to monitor and compare the progress in the agenda to improve job quality or promote decent work. From this viewpoint, both approaches have the characteristics of a "soft law" approach towards governance, such as the

Open Method of Co-ordination (OMC). In a broader policy perspective, the EU and ILO/UN concepts are both presented as strategies to accommodate the new constraints of globalisation in a socially fair manner. However, as policy concepts, "job quality" and "decent work" are also deeply anchored in a legal context underpinning the institutions originating these concepts. Thus, they also reflect a legal apprehension about the concepts incorporated in their policy definitions.

The first section of this chapter is dedicated to the policy dimension of "job quality"/ "decent work". A systematic review and comparison of the sub-dimensions characterising the concept shows that both approaches are very convergent in terms of policy perspective. This comparative approach highlights a selection of the dimensions of "job quality"/"decent work" for which it is possible to establish a clear relationship with the legal framework at institutional level. The second section reviews the way these dimensions are defined from a legal perspective for both institutions and discusses some of the issues raised by this legal approach to the qualitative aspects of work.

II. Setting the Framework: Employment Quality Dimensions in International Institutions

A. European Union: "Job Quality"

The definition and measurement of "job quality" has been on the EU agenda since the qualitative dimension of policies became a pivotal element of the Lisbon Strategy at the beginning of the millennium, in the nascent cooperation between Member States on employment and social policies[1]. This cooperation was fostered by the introduction of "soft law" methods of governance such as the "Open Method of Coordination" (OMC), developed by the EU in order to promote coordination in the policies of Member States (subsidiarity), such as employment and social policies.

[1] We lack space here to include in our review the work being undertaken by the European Foundation for the Improvement of Living and Working Conditions (EUROFOUND), regarding the definition of the quality of work and employment from an integrated perspective, but we should stress its importance. This work is closely related to the EU process to define "job quality" which began under the 2001 Belgian presidency of the EU. The conceptual framework developed by EUROFOUND has four main dimensions: (a) ensuring career and employment security; (b) maintaining and promoting the health and well-being of workers; (c) developing skills and experience; (d) reconciling working and non-working life (EUROFOUND 2002 and 2006).

1. "Job Quality" in the EU Policy Agenda

Under the original Lisbon Strategy, Europe was aiming notably to create both more and *better* jobs in the context of a globalised knowledge economy. It should be stressed here that the initial Lisbon Strategy encompassed a holistic approach to quality. The notion of quality was supposed to relate to all aspects of the economy and society, including the quality of social policy in its entirety but also training and industrial relations policies. This is why the Stockholm European Council, in 2001, established the qualitative dimension of employment as a general horizontal objective in the Employment Guidelines of the European Employment Strategy (EES), meaning that all the guidelines should be evaluated from a quality perspective, as was already the case for other horizontal issues such as gender equality or non-discrimination. A set of around 40 indicators was adopted at the Laeken European Council in December 2001 to monitor "job quality" in the framework of the EES. Also in 2001, the European Commission issued its first Communication setting out the conceptual framework for "job quality" (European Commission, 2001).

From a policy perspective this period could be depicted as the "golden age" of "job quality" in the European policy arena. Since 2005, after the mid-term "streamlining" of the Lisbon Strategy and its revamping as the narrowly focused Growth and Jobs Strategy, the issue of "job quality" has been relegated to the background of the EU social policy agenda. Nevertheless, due to a "lock-in effect", whereby once a concept has appeared in the European policy field and has been approved by the European institutions it cannot easily disappear, so "job quality" still remains in the European debate. From 2005 to 2010, "job quality" was still one of the pillars of the EES and of the Growth and Jobs Strategy, but its understanding has substantially changed in policy terms. Good quality jobs are no longer presented as a crucial element to foster the well-being of European citizens and workers or as the European Social Model(s), but are increasingly interpreted in terms of job productivity to sustain economic growth and financial attractiveness for job creation to foster employment participation (Peña-Casas, 2010). The recent agreement on the content of the new mid-term strategy for the EU (Europe 2020) and the Employment Integrated Guidelines confirm this declining interest in "job quality" in the EU. The dimensions of the initial concept are still present but have been reduced in the framework of a general lesser priority for "inclusive growth", aimed at improving social cohesion and also the effective functioning of labour markets (European Commission, 2010a), and are evoked as one of the components of a specific Employment Guideline aimed at developing a skilled workforce in response to labour market needs, promoting job quality and lifelong learning (European Commission, 2010b).

In the framework of the Europe 2020 flagship initiative on New Skills for New Jobs, the Commission announced its intention to review the definition of QWE in 2011 (European Commission, 2010c). According to a note in the context of the conceptual review of QWE undertaken by the European Employment Committee, the Commission proposes a narrower definition based on four characteristics of what constitutes a good quality job; these are: to provide adequate earnings,; offer opportunities to upgrade skills, lifelong learning and career progression; to ensure safe and healthy working conditions; and to combine a high level of both security and flexibility, including flexible arrangements allowing for the reconciliation of work and private life (European Commission, 2010d). Note the proximity of these dimensions with the conceptual framework underpinning the flexicurity paradigm (see Chapter II by J. Deumer in this book).

2. *Dimensions of Quality of Work and Quality of Employment*

The conceptual framework for "job quality" in Europe was introduced by the abovementioned 2001 Communication. The Commission identified ten key dimensions associated with key policy objectives and standards (see Table 1). There is no space here to enter into a precise description of all these dimensions and associated indicators, but we need to stress certain elements that are of utmost importance to clarify the links between policy and the legal dimensions of the concept[2].

The first is the key distinction made in the Communication between aspects of "job quality" concerning the job characteristics themselves (objective and intrinsic characteristics, including: job satisfaction, remuneration, non-pay rewards, working time, skills, training and prospects for career advancement, job content, match between job and worker characteristics) and those related to the work and wider labour market context (gender equality, health and safety, flexibility and security, access to jobs, work-life balance, social dialogue and worker involvement, diversity and non-discrimination). This distinction is essential as it clearly separates two aspects that are interconnected but which nevertheless differ in terms of their concept and also legal perspective. If we have used up to now the expression "job quality", it is important to distinguish aspects related to *quality of work (QW)* from those regarding *quality of employment (QE)*, with employment being understood here as the policy and legal dimensions of labour market functioning. Such a

[2] For a detailed comparative assessment of the EU conceptual frameworks and indicators, see Peña-Casas 2010.

distinction is also apparent in the conceptual frameworks of other international institutions, at least implicitly. This is why from now on reference will be made to the different concepts used by institutions under the term *quality of work and employment (QWE)*.

A second important distinction to be made is the difference between the conceptual dimensions of QWE and the indicators used in their monitoring. The choice of indicator does not necessarily nor adequately reflect the policy objectives of QWE, as it is constrained by data availability issues, as well as policy considerations. The monitoring indicators require common agreement on their use in a policy process, especially at EU level. This is for instance the case with wages or social dialogue indicators, on which there is a lack of consensus among the policy stakeholders regarding the validity of the available indicators. The comparative approach of this chapter focuses on the conceptual and policy dimensions of QWE, as it enables a better understanding of the legal framework.

The following table, taken from the 2001 Communication, very well illustrates the relationships between the ten dimensions of QWE, the key policy objectives of the EU/EES and the instruments that can be mobilised to achieve these objectives.

Table 1. EU dimensions of QWE, related policy objectives and main instruments

DIMENSIONS	KEY POLICY OBJECTIVES AND STANDARDS	MAIN INSTRUMENTS
1. Intrinsic job quality	Jobs ought to be intrinsically satisfying, compatible with a person's skills and abilities, and provide appropriate levels of income.	EU and MS economic and social policies in general, BEPG, EES, Social Partners
2. Skills, lifelong learning, and career development	People ought to be able to develop their potential abilities to the full through appropriate support for life-long learning.	Education and life-long learning policies, legal framework, including mutual recognition of qualifications
3. Gender equality	Labour markets should offer equal opportunity for men and women in respect of equivalent value jobs, and in terms of lifetime careers.	EES, legislation, social partners, action programmes
4. Health and safety at work	It has to be ensured that working conditions are safe, healthy and supportive – in both physical and psychological terms – of sustainable participation and employment.	New health and safety strategy, including legislation backed by monitoring and benchmarking, social partners

5. Flexibility and security	An appropriate balance between flexibility and security is called for to encourage positive attitudes to change at the workplace and in the labour market. This requires appropriate support for those who lose their jobs or are seeking an alternative, as well as encouragement for the full use of abilities and flexible career choices through appropriate support for occupational and geographical mobility.	Open method of coordination, taxation, legislation, social partners, transferability of supplementary pension rights, information and agency support + EES
6. Inclusion and access to the labour market	Access to and inclusion in labour markets should be increased, including those entering the labour market for the first time or after a period of unemployment or inactivity, and to allow them to stay in the labour market.	EES, Public employment services at EU level, European Social Fund, corporate social responsibility, work on local development
7. Work organisation and work-life balance	Working arrangements, especially those concerning working time, together with support services should allow an appropriate balance between working life and life outside work.	EES, legislation, social partners
8. Social dialogue and worker involvement	All workers should be informed about and involved in the development of their companies and their working life.	Social partners cooperation, legislation
9. Diversity and non-discrimination	All workers should be treated equally without discrimination in terms of age, disability, ethnic origin, religion or sexual orientation.	EES, social partners, action programmes, ESF (EQUAL)
10. Overall work performance	High levels of labour productivity and high living standards across all regions of the Community	Economic policies and structural policies

Source: European Commission, 2001

The second column incorporates policy objectives, mainly those of the EES and more basic legal standards, such as gender equality, non-discrimination or workers' rights[3]. The third column shows the wide

---

[3] It should be recalled here that the policy objectives of the EES in 2001 were already encompassing a "mainstream" perspective on gender and non-discrimination. Quality was supposed to be the third mainstream concern, as attested by the introduction of quality as a cross-cutting dimension in the Guidelines of the EES at that time. These objectives are in one form or another still present in the current EES, although widespread in a more limited number of guidelines or new concepts, such as "flexicurity" (see Chapter II by J. Deumer in this book).

spectrum of instruments available to foster QWE in Europe. It is a complex mix of hard and soft law. EU hard law consists of primary law such as treaties and secondary law such as directives as well as the rulings of the European Court of Justice that are binding on Member States. Hard law defines the EU competency for action, the fields where it can impose binding legislation and policy on its Member States. In contrast, soft law is a broader notion and consists of different policy documents, recommendations and declarations that rely on the power of persuasion, the spreading of good practices and softer instruments. Soft law can however be powerful in terms of setting trends as highlighted by Beveridge, who cautions against constructing too strong a dichotomy between hard and soft law (Beveridge, 2008).

B. *International Labour Organisation: Decent Work*

The Decent Work Agenda of the International Labour Organisation (ILO) was initiated in 1999, thus at the same time as the EU was introducing its QWE framework. Following the 1998 Declaration on Fundamental Principles and Rights at Work, the ILO introduced the concept of Decent Work (DW) as "the converging focus" of all the ILO's four strategic objectives: the promotion of rights at work, of employment, social protection and social dialogue (ILO, 1999). DW is understood in terms of equal rights and opportunities for all, encompassing the "capability approach" promoted by the UN in its human development agenda. DW sums up the aspirations of people for their working lives – their aspirations for advancement and income; rights, voice and recognition; family stability and personal development; and fairness and gender equality (on the capabilities perspective, see also Chapter XII by Bonvin *et al.* in this book).

1. Decent Work in the International Policy Agenda

DW has been gaining momentum in the UN policy agenda. The ILO DW agenda is increasingly being integrated into the UN Millennium Development Goals. Decent work is considered as a crucial means to reduce poverty and for achieving equitable, inclusive and sustainable development. At the UN World Summit in September 2005, more than 150 countries agreed to place full and productive employment and decent work at the heart of relevant national and international policies and to spell out the central role of decent work in development strategies and poverty reduction. The ILO Declaration on Social Justice for a Fair Globalisation endorses the Decent Work Agenda as a primary objective in the ILO's work and recommends that Member States consider establishing appropriate indicators or statistics, if necessary with ILO assistance, to monitor and evaluate progress made (ILO, 2008a). The ILO

DW agenda was also discussed at the "High Level Segment" of the UN Economic and Social Council (ECOSOC) meeting in Geneva on 3-5 July 2010, underscoring once again the fundamental contribution of DW towards achieving the Millennium Development Goals. The UN has included the DW framework in the assessment structure for the Millennium Development Goals (ILO, 2009a).

2. Dimensions of Decent Work

Ever since its introduction in 1999, the definition of the conceptual dimensions of decent work and adequate monitoring indicators have been the subject of on-going work by specialised bodies within the ILO, such as the International Conference of Labour Statisticians. There has also been a good deal of international cooperation on this matter[4]. This has led to the proposal for a common framework for measuring and monitoring DW, accompanied by a detailed list of indicators (ILO, 2008b). This framework is currently being used by the ILO to conduct pilot studies on DW in several countries. As far as European countries are concerned, a study has already been conducted on Austria (ILO, 2009b). The conceptual framework of DW is composed of eleven dimensions based on the four fundamental objectives promoted by the ILO: (1) fundamental principles and rights at work and international labour standards; (2) employment and income opportunities; (3) social protection and social security; (4) social dialogue and tripartism. The eleven dimensions are as follows (the numbers between brackets referring to the four fundamental objectives):

1. Employment opportunities (1 + 2)
2. Adequate earnings and productive work (1 + 3)
3. Decent hours (1 + 3)
4. Combination of work, family and personal life (1 + 3)
5. Work that should be abolished (1 + 3)
6. Stability and security of work (1, 2 + 3)
7. Equal opportunity and treatment in employment (1, 2 + 3)

---

4 See notably the work undertaken by the taskforce for the measurement of quality of employment under the auspices of the UN Economic Commission for Europe (UNECE). In order to encourage the measurement and reporting of QWE in the group of countries under its competency (56 countries forming the UN "region" of Europe), this taskforce has gathered together several national and international statistical bodies since 2003. It stresses notably the high degree of convergence existing between EU and ILO conceptual frameworks. It proposes a "convergent" framework based on seven main dimensions of QWE: safety and ethics of employment; income and benefits from employment; working hours and balancing work and non-working life; security of employment and social protection; social dialogue; skills' development and training; workplace relationships and work motivation (UNECE, 2010).

8. Safe work environment (1 + 3)
9. Social security (1 + 3)
10. Social dialogue, workers' and employers' representation (1 + 4)
11. Economic and social context for decent work

C. Comparison of EU and ILO Conceptual Frameworks

The comparative exercise of these different institutional frameworks of QWE demonstrates their high degree of convergence and overlap. Both institutions provide a conceptual framework mixing issues related to QW and QE, thus creating a wider perspective on QWE. In the following table the EU QWE framework is compared with the DW framework. As mentioned previously, here our comparative approach is limited to the main areas in both frameworks, since policy objectives and fundamental principles are expressed at this level, rather than through the chosen indicators which are subject to technical constraints.

Table 2. Comparison and concordance between different QW frameworks

EU QWE DIMENSIONS	UN / ILO DECENT WORK DIMENSIONS
1. Intrinsic job quality (appropriate levels of income + adequate skills + satisfying job).	2. Adequate earnings and productive work
2. Skills, lifelong learning, and career development	2. Adequate earnings and productive work
3. Gender equality	7. Equal opportunities and fair treatment in employment
4. Health and safety at work	8. Safe work environment
5. Flexibility and security	6. Stability and security of work + 9. Social security
6. Inclusion and access to the labour market	1. Employment opportunities 7. Equal opportunities and fair treatment in employment
7. Work organisation and work-life balance	2. Decent hours 4. Combining work, family and personal life
8. Social dialogue and worker involvement	10. Social dialogue, workers' and employers' representation
9. Diversity and non-discrimination	7. Equal opportunities and fair treatment in employment
10. Overall work performance (High levels of labour productivity and high living standards across all regions of the Community)	1. Employment opportunities + 11. Economic and social context of decent work

Source: the author's compilation

There are some differences between the frameworks. The issues of child and forced labour are not incorporated in the EU framework, mainly because it is not a policy issue in the EU, since all EU member states have ratified the European Convention on Human Rights (Article 4). The question of social protection is explicitly mentioned in the ILO framework, but is not a specific dimension in the EU framework, although dimension 5 on flexibility and security includes the coverage and access to social protection as a condition of security. Another difference, which is more astonishing, is the absence in the ILO framework of an explicit reference to the fundamental matters of training and lifelong learning. However, skills' acquisition and development are implicit in "productive work" (dimension 2).

Apart from these differences, there is a high degree of convergence between the two frameworks. The first case of convergence lies in the common preoccupation with strengthening the social dimension of globalisation. The EU has put in its Renewed Social Agenda of 2008 and also in its meta-strategies the need to reinforce the cohesion of internal and external policies (mainly trade and development) to contribute to a fairer globalisation. A second factor of convergence lies in the series of principles in the EU and UN agendas. Both policy agendas encompass a framework for action in favour of more and better jobs, managing change, social cohesion and equal opportunities. The values promoted through the ILO and notably its DW agenda are also at the core of the so-called "European Social Model", characterised by a focus on the right to productive and freely chosen work, in which rights are protected, which generates an adequate income, with adequate social protection and in which there is an emphasis on equal opportunities. All this should happen in a democratic process guaranteed by tripartism and social dialogue.

Furthermore, the EU has also committed itself to promote the DW agenda *within* and *outside* the Union. The 2006 Communication on "Decent Work for all" highlights the role that the EU must play in the promotion of the DW agenda at international level: by supporting the setting of policy agendas and standards at multilateral level, developing bilateral relations and exchanges on these issues with partner countries and regions, as well as integrating decent work objectives into the EU's trade and development policies (European Commission, 2006). However, the promotion of DW has been more apparent outside the EU than within. The internal EU agenda on QWE appears totally disconnected from the external agenda on DW. It is striking that, at one and the same time, the EU supports the DW agenda in its external policies while internally it places QWE on the back burner of its meta-strategies. Needless to say, the credibility of the EU's role in promoting DW at a global level depends largely on the EU's ability to achieve its own objective of delivering more quality jobs in Europe.

As mentioned previously, there is another point in common between the ILO and EU frameworks. Both are defined for use in the context of a policy exercise. The concepts and indicators developed by both international institutions are intended for use in a governance process, with the characteristics of what is defined in the EU as a "soft law" process. The agreement on common objectives and monitoring indicators in the context of a comparative reporting procedure, implying a form of peer review/pressure, are at the core of the ILO Decent Work Agenda and the EU holistic approach to "job quality" under the Lisbon Strategy and, more precisely, with the EES as an OMC.

III. Legal Aspects of Job Quality Dimensions

Table 1, as presented above, highlights the complexity of the multidimensional perspective on QWE, and consequently the diversity of the legal tools that are to be considered and mobilised to improve effectively QWE in Europe, as either "hard law" or "soft law" processes. In this section, we review some of the EU and the ILO dimensions of QWE from the viewpoint of their legal basis in their own institutional frameworks. As it is not possible to cover all aspects of QWE in this chapter, we are focusing on some dimensions related to essential QWE issues and incorporated in both EU and ILO frameworks. This section will be limited to the analysis of job quality under hard and soft law, described by Supiot (2006) as a divergence between *Dura Lex* and *Soft Law* on one hand and the matter of fundamental social rights on the other.

A. Hard Law v Soft Law

1. At the EU Level

a. The Legislative "acquis"

As a complement to Member States' action, the EU has overtime built up a solid legislative "*acquis*" in various domains regarding employment quality. The European Coal and Steel Community (ECSC) of 1951 and the Rome Treaty of 1957 already contained articles concerning such issues as health and safety, working conditions, worker representation and equal pay for men and women. In 1974, the Social Action Programme[5] incorporated over thirty measures in the areas of health and safety at work, minimum wages, working hours, employee participation,

5 Council Resolution of 21 January 1974 concerning a Social Action Programme, OJ C 13, 13 December 1974, p. 1-4.

etc. The first reference in an EU framework to the issue of employment quality is found in the first main objective of the programme, aimed at the attainment of full and *better* employment in the Community[6]. During the same period, the EU created dedicated institutions to foster an exchange of knowledge and the debate on various topics related to job quality, starting with the European Foundation for the Improvement of Living and Working Conditions (EUROFOUND) and the European Centre for the Development of Vocational Training (CEDEFOP), both in 1975, and later the European Agency for Safety and Health at Work in 1996. Furthermore, since the Maastricht Treaty in 1992, there is also an institutionalised European social dialogue between various industries and sectors. The major part of the European "*acquis communautaire*" covering various important aspects of job quality such as working conditions, health and safety and, more widely, gender equality and non-discrimination, was established during this period.

It is not possible in the restricted space of this chapter to review the extensive scope of EU hard law covering all aspects of employment quality. Hence we will focus upon the three main spheres evoked previously: equality and non-discrimination, health and safety at work and employment security and social protection.

EU efforts regarding equal treatment and non-discrimination have led to the adoption of several directives. A large body of European legislative texts is dedicated to equality between women and men. This is mainly covered in various Treaty provisions and Directives concerning access to employment, equal pay, protection during maternity, parental leave, social security and occupational social security, the burden of proof in discrimination cases and self-employment[7] (for a

6 The second main objective involves the improvement in living and working conditions, while the third is a precursor to the instigation, nearly twenty years later, of an European Social Dialogue, aiming at an increased involvement of management and labour in the economic and social decisions of the Community, Addison, J. (2009), *In the Beginning, there Was Social Policy: Developments in Social Policy in the European Union from 1972 through 2008*, The Rimini Centre for Economic Analysis, PR 01-09.

7 Council Directive 75/117/EEC of 10 February 1975 on the approximation of the laws of the Member States relating to the application of the principle of equal pay for men and women, OJ 1975, L 45/19; Council Directive 76/207/EEC of 9 February 1976 on the implementation of the principle of equal treatment for men and women as regards access to employment, vocational training and promotion and working conditions, OJ 1976 L39/40; Council Directive 79/7/EEC of 19 December 1978 on the progressive implementation of the principle of equal treatment for men and women in matters of social security, OJ 1979 L 6/24; Council Directive 86/378/EEC of 24 July 1986 on the implementation of the principle of equal treatment for men and women in occupational social security schemes, OJ 1986, L224/40; Council Directive 86/378/EEC of 24 July 1986 on the implementation of the principle of equal treatment for men

further analysis of the legal developments on gender equality and reconciling work and family life, see Laura Carlson's chapter in this book). These directives are far from perfect to ensure real quality of work. The Pregnant Workers' Directive applies exclusively to issues relating to dismissal and excludes pay-related matters. It does not include the right of a woman to return to her job or an equivalent job at the end of her maternity leave and it excludes employees on short-term and temporary contracts. Under the parental leave directive, the leave entitlement is limited to parents of children below the age of eight and ignores the needs of parents of older children and parents on leave are not granted financial compensation (Caracciolo *et al.*, 2010). Based on Article 13 of the EU Treaty, in 2000, the European Union enacted two directives protecting people in the EU from discrimination on grounds of race and ethnic origin (the Racial Equality Directive), and on grounds of religion or belief, disability, age or sexual orientation (the Employment Framework Directive)[8]. They define a set of principles that offers every individual in the EU a common minimum level of legal protection against discrimination and is specially relevant to issues of age (see Christine Canazza' chapter in this book on "Quality of Employment within the Active Ageing Strategy").

Secure employment and equal access to social protection are two major elements of quality of employment and are also at the heart of the EU debate on the implementation of flexicurity policies (see Chapter II by Deumer in this book). If the EU's main legislative action on social security relates to harmonisation issues to further the single market and freedom of circulation for European citizens and workers[9], we should mention here the Directives promoting equal access to social protection schemes[10], regardless of gender or individual characteristics as men-

---

and women in occupational social security schemes, OJ 1986, L224/40; Council Directive 92/85/EEC of 19 October 1992 on the introduction of measures to encourage improvements in the health and safety at work of pregnant workers and workers who have recently given birth or are breastfeeding, OJ 1992 L 348/1.

8 Council Directive 2000/43/EC of 29 June 2000 implementing the principle of equal treatment between persons irrespective of racial or ethnic origin, OJ L 180/22; Council Directive 2000/78/EC of 27 November 2000 establishing a general framework for equal treatment in employment and occupation, OJ 2000 L 303/16.

9 European Parliament and Council, Regulation (EC) No. 883/2004 of the European Parliament and of the Council of 29 April 2004 on the coordination of social security systems, OJ 2004 L 166, 30.4.2004, p. 1-123.

10 Council Directive 79/7/EEC of 19 December 1978 on the progressive implementation of the principle of equal treatment for men and women in matters of social security, OJ 1979 L 6/24; Council Directive 86/378/EEC of 24 July 1986 on the implementation of the principle of equal treatment for men and women in occupational social security schemes, OJ 1986, L224/40; Council Directive 86/378/EEC of 24 July

tioned above, but also for the type of work performed by individuals. In response to the increasing use of non standard employment contracts in the 1980s and 1990s, EU legislation has provided a legal framework for non standard employment contracts, recognising that workers under such contracts experience lower quality working conditions than permanent workers (Bercusson, 2009). The European sectoral social dialogue produced two framework agreements which became directives for part-time and fixed term work[11]. The first one aims at eliminating discrimination against part-time workers and improving the quality of part-time work and at promoting the development of part-time work on a voluntary basis. This Directive is far from ideal as part-time work is generally not associated with high-quality jobs, and until this is the case, any improvement in the quality of part-time work will remain an illusion (Barnard, 2006). The Fixed-Term Work Directive aims at improving the quality of fixed-term work by ensuring the application of the principle of non-discrimination and by establishing a framework to prevent abuse from the use of successive fixed-term employment contracts or relationships[12]. The Directive on Temporary Agency Work endorses the principle of equal treatment between temporary agency workers and permanent workers by the employer undertaking, subject to certain limitations and exemptions (see Silvia Borelli's chapter on atypical work in this book). As for the gender equality directives, these directives are also not ideal. The part-time directive applies only to part-timers who have an employment contract or employment relationship as defined by the law, collective agreement or current practice. Some atypical workers are thus excluded from the application of non-discrimination rights because they do not have an employment contract and are qualified as self-employed. The fixed-term Directive excludes the self-employed and temporary workers. Only workers employed in the same establishment, under the same applicable collective agreement, the same national legislation, collective agreement or practice are able to claim favourable treatment whereas not all employment relationships can be easily traced back to any single arrangement.

1986 on the implementation of the principle of equal treatment for men and women in occupational social security schemes, OJ 1986, L224/40.

11 Council Directive 97/81/EC concerning the framework agreement on part time work concluded by UNICE, CEEP and ETUC, OJ 1997, L14/9; Council of the European Union (1999), Council Directive 1999/70/EC of 28 June 1999 concerning the framework agreement on fixed-term work conducted by ETUC, UNICE and CEEP, OJ 1999, L 175/43; European Parliament and Council of the European Union (2008), Directive 2008/104/EC of the European Parliament and of Council of 19 November on temporary agency work, OJ (2008), L327/9.

12 On 16 July 2002, the European Social Partners ETUC, UNICE, UEAPME and CEEP signed a framework agreement on telework which did not become a directive.

EU law provides also a certain protection for workers in relation to their employment situation. With regard to the rights and the protection of employees, a large number of EU directives have been adopted since the 1970s and then subsequently revised. These directives aim on one hand to protect employees from unfair or unjustified dismissal and, on the other, to provide a common framework for information and the participation of employees in their employment conditions. These two aspects are strongly interrelated. The Employer's Insolvency Directive[13] protects workers' rights to immediate or future old-age benefits, including survivors' benefits, under supplementary company or inter-company pension schemes outside the national statutory social security schemes in the event of insolvency while the Collective Redundancies Directive[14] affords greater protection to workers in the event of collective redundancies. The Transfer of Undertakings Directive[15], replacing the previous Directive 77/187/EEC, ensures, as far as possible, that the employment relationship remains unchanged for the transferee and that the workers are not placed in a less favourable position solely as a result of the transfer. The Information Consultation Directive[16] establishes a general framework for informing and consulting employees. Employee information and consultation covers three areas relating to economic, financial and strategic developments, the structure and foreseeable development of employment and related measures and decisions likely to lead to substantial changes in work organisation or contractual relations (Bedrac, 2006).

A healthy and safe working environment is an essential feature of quality of employment. Health and Safety at work represents one of the most important advances in the social policy of the European Union. A solid corpus of legislation has been adopted to cover the maximum number of risks with the minimum number of regulations. The *Europe-*

13 Council of the European Communities (1980), Council Directive 80/987/EEC of 20 October 1980 on the approximation of the laws of the Member States relating to the protection of employees in the event of their employer's insolvency, OJ 1980, L 283/23.

14 Council of the European Union (1998), Council Directive 98/59/EC of 20 July 1998 on the approximation of the laws of the Member States relating to collective redundancies, OJ 1998, L 225/16.

15 Council of the European Union (2001), Council Directive 2001/23/EC of 12 March 2001 on the approximation of the laws of the Member States relating to safeguarding of employees' rights in the event of transfers of undertakings, businesses or part of undertakings or businesses, OJ 2001, L 82/16.

16 Council and European Parliament (2002), Directive 2002/14/EC of the Council and the European Parliament of 11 March 2002 establishing a general framework for informing and consulting employees in the European Community, OJ 2002, L 80/29.

an Framework Directive on Safety and Health at Work[17] adopted in 1989 guarantees minimum health and safety requirements throughout Europe and to ensure a higher degree of protection for workers at work, through the implementation of preventive measures to guard against accidents at work and occupational diseases. A series of individual directives focusing on specific aspects of health and safety at work were adopted on the basis of the Framework Directive (Hennion *et al.*, 2010, Nayer *et al.*, 2007). Among these individual directives, one should be specially mentioned, the so-called *Working time Directive*[18], one of the main instruments for improving workers' conditions. This Directive lays down minimum health and safety requirements for the organisation of working time (minimum daily rest periods, weekly and annual leave, breaks or weekly maximum working time as well as for specific aspects of night work, shift work and work patterns).

b. The Soft law processes

However, legislation at EU level is not always adequate. Soft instruments such as policy coordination, the operation of good practices, implementation of guides, frameworks for action, codes of conduct and recommendations can help shape a consensus and create the right conditions for action at national or company level (European Commission, 2010c). This recourse to soft law to complement, and even sometimes to substitute, hard law has become increasingly prevalent at EU level since the end of the 1990s. Indeed, even in fields such as gender equality, non-discrimination or health and safety, for which a strong legal corpus already exists, implementation is often complemented by soft law tools. For instance, "The Community Strategy 2007-2012 on Health and Safety at Work" outlines the options for further action to make workplaces across Europe healthier and safer (European Commission, 2007). The Strategy for Equality between Men and Women 2010-2015 is another example of traditional soft law that sets out the policy priorities of the Commission on gender equality including the gender pay gap (European Commission, 2010e).

As explained previously, "job quality" appears in the EU picture through the Lisbon Strategy and more particularly through one of the new forms of soft law governance, such as the EES. Equal opportunity is one of the four pillars of the EES, alongside employability, entrepre-

---

17 Council of the European Communities (1989), Council Directive 89/391/EEC of 12 June 1989 on the introduction of measures to encourage improvements in the health and safety of workers at work, OJ 1989, L 183/1.

18 Council Directive 93/104/EC of 23 November 1993 concerning specific aspects of the organisation of working time, OJ L307/18, now Directive 2003/88/EC, OJ 2003, L 299/9.

neurship and adaptability. Equal opportunity included tackling the gender (pay) gap, facilitating reconciliation between work and family life and encouraging the return to work after absence. Under the EES, atypical jobs are perceived as opportunities for the creation of new employment in response to the employer's need for greater flexibility, as well as the employees' desire to reconcile work with their family life, while at the same time retaining employment security. This promotion of work "flexibilisation" by the EES was later reinforced and given a prominent position in the current EES (Keune and Jepsen, 2007). The question of flexicurity is discussed in more detail in Chapter II of this book, so we will just briefly recall here the complexity of harmonising the worker's need for protection and security with the employer's need for flexibility. Encouraging flexibility in employment with a high level of social security can only be carried out if employees are given a real chance to stay in the job market and to advance in their employment and if some specific obligations are imposed on employers (Fredman, 2004). Many Member States are questioning whether the approach to flexicurity in general is well-founded, particularly with reference to reconciliation (Huiskamp and Vos, 2007). The issue of the legal protection of workers is also covered by the debate on flexicurity.

Job quality[19] is still among the objectives of the Europe 2020 Strategy to increase productivity and workers' participation in employment. Job quality is evoked in the context of the pillar dedicated to "inclusive growth", aimed at social cohesion and especially the effective functioning of labour markets "*(...) through investing in successful transitions, appropriate skills development, rising job quality and fighting segmentation, structural unemployment and inactivity while ensuring adequate, sustainable social protection and active inclusion to reduce poverty (...)*" (European Commission, 2010a).

Job quality is also mentioned in the seventh guideline for the Employment Policies of the Member States entitled "Increasing labour market participation of women and men, reducing structural unemployment and promoting job quality". Accordingly, the quality of jobs and employment conditions should be addressed and Member States should undertake action to fight poverty wages, promote occupational health and safety and ensure adequate social security for those on fixed-term contracts and the self-employed (European Commission, 2010b).

One of the "flagship initiatives" of the Europe 2020 Strategy also deals more explicitly with employment aspects, and in particular job quality (European Commission, 2010c). To increase participation in

---

19 For an in-depth analysis see Marlier, E. and Natali, D. (eds.) with Van Dam, R. (2010), *Europe 2020: Towards a more social EU?*, Brussels, P.I.E. Peter Lang.

employment, the European Commission proposes to boost action across four main areas: reducing segmentation and supporting transitions (new momentum for flexicurity), equipping people with the right skills for employment, improving job quality and working conditions, and creating jobs. Several of the proposed measures are related to the 'simplification' and 'adaptation' of employment legislation and the '*acquis communautaire*' in several areas of job quality, notably working conditions and health and safety at work. The Commission encourages the use of 'soft' instruments (comparative analysis, policy coordination, the operation of good practices, benchmarking, implementing guides, frameworks for action, codes of conduct and recommendations) to complement this approach. In the context of this flagship initiative, the Commission also announced its intention to review and streamline the policy concept on quality of work, in cooperation with the Member States and social partners. This report is expected to contribute to the debate by clarifying the multidimensional concept of job quality, not only from an academic perspective but also from close interaction between current European policy and legal frameworks.

c. Soft Versus Hard Law?

Soft law refers to EU measures that are not binding on those they address. It is essential to distinguish soft law's lack of a legally binding effect from its potential impact in practice. As highlighted by Trubek *et al.* (2005), soft law may be "harder" than we think. It may impact on policy development and practice precisely because of its lack of legal effect. Soft law tends to be used in the EU context where Member States are unable to agree on the hard law measure which is legally binding or where the EU lacks the competence to adopt hard law measures. According to Sciarra *et al.* (2004), the Member States and EU institutions are thus able to adopt EU policy proposals, while leaving their implementation optional for those Member States who do not wish to be so bound. They are thus an obvious temptation for the Commission when faced with resistance from some Member States which threaten to block policy proposals. Soft law may be seen as a more flexible instrument to achieve policy objectives.

For example, the legal strategy of the EES has been questioned. Guidelines have been criticised on a number of grounds as pointed out by Zappala (2003). They are soft law instruments. Non-binding EU guidelines may not lead Member States to change their national employment policies. There is also a fear that non-binding guidelines are a tempting substitute model for EU social and labour regulation, allowing for more Member States' autonomy compared to the binding "hard law" legislative application. However, the Employment Guidelines have had some effect on EU labour legislation. The Directive on race and ethnic discrimination was an element of the overall EES aiming to create a labour market that promotes entry by minority groups. The Preamble to the Directive refers to the 2000 Employment Guidelines. Similarly, a relationship between equal opportunities as a pillar of the EES and EU Labour law is established. The former Directive on Parental leave 96/34, with its explicit aim to be a "means of reconciling work and family life and promoting equal opportunities and treatment between women and men" could be regarded as part of the equal opportunities pillar of the EES. As explained by Bercusson (2009), the relationship between the *acquis* and the EES is a two-way street. The *acquis* is a legally binding framework of labour regulation which limits the scope and nature of the policies adopted under the EES. At the same time, the EES expanded the scope of the *acquis* by inspiring new regulations aimed at achieving the objectives of the EES, but based on the social chapter of the Treaty, among other provisions.

Thus, the debate on the opposition or the complementarity between hard and soft law within the EU policy framework is still on-going, and probably will be for the long term. Currently, it seems that the introduction of new hard law relating to job quality dimensions has become complex given the increased number of EU Member States and the relative blocking of European Social Dialogue in recent years, at least at the inter-professional level. The Lisbon Treaty has given more legislative powers to the European Parliament, but this has not yet really been translated into effective action, and the tensions between European institutions (Parliament, Commission, Council) are at their greatest when it comes to discussing hard law issues. As mentioned, there is not much to be expected from the ECJ either, as it tends to interpret EU law mainly according to competition and single market perspectives.

2. At the ILO Level

The status accorded to ILO standards has been the subject of much attention since the launch of the Decent Work Agenda.

According to the ILO Director General report, "normative action is an indispensable tool to make decent work a reality" because it should help to clarify its meaning. Indeed, the ILO standards (Conventions and Recommendations)[20] "provide an authoritative answer to the question of what decent work implies in concrete terms as regards the preconditions (fundamental principles and rights), its content (work that meets certain criteria on quality and security) and the means for achieving it (social dialogue)". Moreover, this legislative activity is also a decisive indicator

---

20 Report of the Director-General: Reducing the decent work deficit – a global challenge, Report 1(A), 89th session, June 2001.

of progress towards the achievement of ILO objectives, through its system of monitoring the implementation of Conventions ratified and for encouraging compliance with Recommendations.

However, although essential, normative action is not considered sufficient to ensure the promotion of decent work. Indeed, "decent work is universal in concept and its components are interdependent", while the ILO's normative action is "voluntary and necessarily fragmented in practice, as it seeks to break down the general objectives of the Constitution into a certain number of specific problems to which it offers concrete solutions"[21]. Therefore, the standards do not ensure immediate and consistent progress, no more than they can secure their universal application in all countries and business sectors.

To overcome this difficulty, the promotion of the decent work agenda was initially based on developing a "decent work pilot program", a pilot experiment of the ILO Policy involving eight members[22]. The objective of this program was to put into operation the concept of decent work in ILO Member States of the, through the establishment of practical methods to promote integrated approaches to this policy at national levels. The objective of this program is to test the relevance of an integrated approach, for achieving the goals and priorities in ILO constituent Member States (ILO, 2006).

In a second phase, based on the results of this pilot program, country programs (DWCPs) were developed. Their content varied from one country to another, depending on national circumstances, the commitments of the ILO global priorities as identified by the strategic framework, program and the budget of the Regional Agenda for Decent Work[23]. Each DWCP is therefore an analysis of national problems, the determination of a limited number of priorities, the setting of program objectives per country, the definition of a plan for implementing and evaluating performance in order to adjust strategies to obtain better results by each country (ILO, 2008c).

The strategy to promote the decent work agenda is therefore based on three stages. Initially, it was defined as a world model of qualitative

---

21 Report of the Director-General: Reducing the decent work deficit – a global challenge, Report 1(A), 89th session, June 2001.

22 Bahrain, Bangladesh, Denmark, Ghana, Kazakhstan, Morocco, Panama and the Philippines.

23 As of 31 January 2010 there were 44 active Decent Work Country Programmes. Eleven Decent Work Country Programmes ended before the end of 2009 and another 12 will end in 2010. Over 80 programmes are currently under development. Six country programmes have already been evaluated: Argentina, Indonesia, Jordan, Philippines, Ukraine and Zambia; http://www.ilo.org/wcmsp5/groups/publiced_norm/relconf/documents/meetingdocument/wcms_123396.pdf.

and quantitative indicators that can be used to measure progress in achieving decent work objectives in each country (Cf. II.2). Besides this series of key indicators common to all countries, the indicators of decent work must also take into account the circumstances and priorities of each country. The objective is to achieve a model that is applicable at the international level and adaptable according to differing national situations. The second stage is to perform a series of statistical data and qualitative information relating to specific indicators of decent work. The ILO Member States must collect this information using their own statistical methods or administrative data-collection processes, such as databases set up by the labour inspection services. Qualitative indicators, such as those produced by social dialogue, could be based on a textual analysis of authoritative reports, including reports submitted to and produced by the ILO supervisory system, local surveys or administrative data. Finally, the inclusion in country profiles of decent work indicators and statistics will provide specific information on each country as well as a global picture of the agenda's implementation (ILO, 2008b).

It would be difficult not to measure this procedure against the open EU's method of coordination to produce a definition of common objectives, common indicators and national plans using a common reporting system. But, unlike the European procedure, the last part of the ILO procedure is more delicate and problematic, involving injunctions or recommendations to the countries. Does the ILO have the legal means to force the Member States to make any progress?

The importance given to the right to measure the progress towards decent work reflects the ambivalence of the role of the legal standard. Absent from the legal model used for the promotion of decent work (reports, agendas, etc.), legal standards ultimately reappear as a tool to measure progress made by ILO Member States in the national implementation of this policy.

Two components must be distinguished in the ILO legal framework to implement the decent work agenda. The first component concerns the concrete implementation of the decent work agenda. This focuses upon the minimum workers' rights as stipulated in the international standards of work and a correlation was thus established by the ILO between the categories of indicators on decent work and information on the national legislations on work. How can the ILO make an appreciation and correlate this type of information? In international comparisons, the ratification by the countries of ILO conventions gives the best indication of the current legislation and the regulation of work. However, ratification may be an insufficient indicator of implementation and its effect on work standards. Information on the legal framework of work must relate to legislation and the scope of application, as well as to implementation of the right in jurisprudence. Such information must be regularly updated (ILO, 2008b). In its report on "the measurement of decent work", the *ad hoc* tripartite meeting of experts put forward a model for the organisation of information on labour laws and the decent work legal framework. Conventions were thus measured against this model, for which the ILO conventions appeared relevant. Curiously, whereas one might have expected a large number of conventions to figure within the categories of indicators listed, the tripartite meeting accepted only a small number of them (17), which were intended to measure the States' efforts to implement the agenda in their legislation (Cf. Infra. IV.2.2 – Table 3). However, with a total of 188 ILO Conventions issued since the organisation was created, it would seem that many more than those mentioned in the report of the tripartite meeting of experts could be expected to be recalled during any analysis of the legal framework for quality of work.

One of the criticisms made against the classical ILO normative action was its disparate development in the form of separate and autonomous instruments for each of the organisation's objectives, quite, independently of one another (Maupain, 2008). The aim of the Decent Work concept was initially to provide a concise overview of the objectives and programs of the ILO (Bonnechère, 2007) which has enabled some authors to speak of a "new integrated normative approach" (Maupain, 2008). The adoption of the "Declaration on Social Justice for a Fair Globalization" by the International Labour Conference, 10 June 2008, had the specific objective of strengthening the ILO's capacity for action whilst providing a legal platform for the Decent Work Agenda (Drouin, Duplessis, 2010). Although there are many references to Decent Work in the body of the Declaration itself, it is surprising that this concept is lacking in the title of the Declaration. This suppression is due to the fact that for the employers' organisations, the concept of Decent Work is not consensually defined, and it must also be defined at national level (Drouin, Duplessis, 2010).

Another criticism is also made because of recourse to a Declaration establishing a standard with a dubious obligatory nature. Recourse in the form of a declaration is not an innovation in ILO courses of action; the 1944 Philadelphia Declaration on the aims and purposes of the International Labour Organisation, the 1963 Declaration concerning the Policy of Apartheid in South Africa (abrogated in 1991), the 1998 Declaration on "Fundamental Principles and Rights at Work" (Cf. IV.2.2) and the 2008 Declaration on "Social Justice for a Fair Globalisation" are four such examples. It aims to renew the ILO's message without modifying its constitutional texts (Maupain, 2008).

If not ratified (Wisskichen, 2005), a declaration should not be perceived as a normative instrument but as a "formal and solemn instrument suitable for rare occasions when principles of lasting importance are being enunciated"[24]: it is an "exceptional form which goes beyond the organisation and reaches the whole world (…), used by the ILO to "recognise, guarantee and protect rights and principles that are untouchable" (ILC Record proceedings in 1964 quoted by Maupain, 2008).

The interest of these declarations is based on a "new approach of the normative question", management by objectives, (Supiot, 2006) whose effectiveness is not measured only by the ratification of conventions, but also by the procedures created as a follow-up. For the 1998 Declaration on Fundamental Principles and Rights at Work, in order to guarantee the effectiveness of the obligations included in the declaration, a follow-up procedure was set up; each Member State that has not ratified one or more of these Conventions is asked every year to report on the status of the relevant rights and principles within their borders, and stating any impediment to ratification.

This mechanism tries to solve the problem of the weak ratification of fundamental conventions (Servais, 2004) related to the "normative self-service" (Supiot, 2006) authorised by the system of ratification in the ILO constitution.

The perceptions of this use of soft law are divergent. Some authors (Maupain, 2008) see it as a tool to overcome the inefficiency of the ILO's legal control mechanisms. Others (including Duplessis, in 2007) note that soft law is emerging as a social and legal response to the growing complexity of international orders, but suggest a risk of dissolution of labour law and the body of standards developed since the origins of the ILO. However, this strategy has also been considered as a confirmation of the abandonment of the ILO normative action in the form of hard law (Alston, 2004) even if, for other authors (e.g. Maupain, 2005), the recourse to a declaration, like that on "Fundamental Principles and Rights at Work", in 2008, allowed a definite progression in the ratification of conventions since the Declaration was adopted.

B. Promoting Fundamental Social Rights

1. The European Charters

Fundamental rights in the EU legal order have been developed by the European Court of Justice as a result of the awareness by national constitutional courts in respect of fundamental rights protected by EU Member States' national legislation. The need for general principles of EU law to include protection for fundamental rights is driven by the

[24] Memorandum of the United Nations Office of Legal Affairs, E/CN.4/L.610 (1962), 2 April 1962.

consequences in the doctrine of supremacy for EU Law and for national constitutions to protect such rights. As pointed out by Bercusson (in 2006), the evidence of these past struggles is to be found in Treaty provisions, rulings of the ECJ and in many resolutions and declarations issued by EU institutions.

The most important solemn declaration on the quality of employment was the Community Charter of the Fundamental Social Rights of Workers, adopted on 9 December 1989 in a declaration by all Member States, with the exception of the United Kingdom. The Community Charter established the main principles on which the European labour law model was based and influenced the development of the European social model in the following decade. Under this Charter, the Community has to make provision for the fundamental social rights of workers as follows: Freedom of movement (Articles 1 to 3); Employment and remuneration (Articles 4 to 6); Improvement of living and working conditions (Articles 7 to 9); Social protection (Article 10); Freedom of association and collective bargaining (Articles 11 to 14); Vocational training (Article 15); Equal treatment for men and women (Article 16); Information and consultation and participation for workers (Articles 17 to 18); Health protection and safety at the workplace (Article 19); Protection of children and adolescents (Articles 20 to 23); Elderly persons (Articles 24 to 25); Disabled persons (Article 26). The Charter represents a commitment by the Member States to a set of social policy and labour law objectives (Hennion *et al.*, 2010).

The legal status of the Community Charter is that of a political declaration since, due to the opposition of the UK Government, the Charter could not be integrated in the EC Treaty in 1989 (Bercusson, 1990). However, it had three effects and legal consequences. Firstly, the 1989 Charter is mentioned in the preamble to the Treaty on European Union and in Article 136 of the EC Treaty[25]. Secondly, as a form of soft law, the Charter may be used by the European Court of Justice as an interpretative guide in litigation concerning social and labour rights. Such litigation could take the form of legal action by way of preliminary references by national courts (Article 267 TFEU) challenging Member States' implementation of Union law, which arguably violates the fundamental social rights of workers in the Charter (Kravaritou, 2009).

[25] "The Community and the Member States, having in mind fundamental social rights such as those set out in the European Social Charter signed at Turin on 19 October 1961 and the 1989 Community Charter of the Fundamental Social Rights of Workers. Article 151 of the Social Chapter of the TFEU explicitly refers to it: "*The Union and the Member States, having in mind fundamental social rights such as those set out ... in the 1989 Community Charter of the Fundamental Social Rights of Workers*".

Thirdly, following the declaration of the Community Charter, the European Commission adopted a Social Action Programme[26] to implement the Charter.

Despite its declaratory nature, the Charter was influential in the launching of initiatives in employment and industrial relations policy, which during the 1990s produced a number of directives relevant to employment quality[27]. However, it should be mentioned that social rights at EU level, also developed in the context of the progressive institutional process of European integration. The consideration of fundamental rights relating to working conditions, and particularly to working time, is driven by the possibilities that these procedural institutional changes allow. The passage from unanimity to a qualified majority procedure of voting, introduced since the Single Act in 1986, has allowed the EU to introduce a wide range of directives, notably in the field of workers' health and safety. The establishment by the Maastricht Treaty of an institutionalised European Social Dialogue and social partner organisations able to conclude common agreements has also opened up a new pathway for the development of Directives in several other fields relating to employment quality (Addison, 2009). As noted by Bercusson (2000), the Directives on parental leave and part-time work are outcomes of the provisions of the Employment Title, which promote the adaptability of working time, one of the pillars of the future EES Guidelines, with the fundamental right to sex equality that involves reconciliation between work and family life. The Community Charter has also inspired the introduction of a qualitative perspective in the shaping of the original European Employment Strategy (EES), the first OMC soft law process introduced in 1997 and, more broadly, on the affirmed qualitative and rights-based perspective of the Lisbon Strategy, at least in its initial vision in the early 2000s.

---

26 European Commission, Communication from the Commission concerning its Action Programme relating to the implementation of the Community Charter of Basic Social Rights for Workers, COM(89) 568 final, 29 November 1989.

27 Among these we could highlight: the pregnant workers Directive (1992) providing maternity leave, dismissal protection, preservation of employment rights and provision of risk assessments; the 1993 Working Time Directive establishing the 48-hour week, rest periods, annual paid leave and regulation of night work; the directives based on the framework agreements on parental leave (1996), the part-time work Directive (1997), the fixed-term work Directive (1999), the 1994 European Works Council Directive, the directive on posted workers (1996) guaranteeing host country conditions to posted workers, on atypical workers (health and safety), a directive requiring agency workers and those on fixed term contracts to be informed of job risks and trained appropriately, the employers' duty to inform employees of the conditions applicable to any contract or employment relationship, and the protection of young people at work.

The Community Charter anticipated the potential of individual fundamental employment rights in the Charter of Fundamental Rights of the European Union, adopted in Nice in December 2000[28]. The EU Charter includes a large number of fundamental trade union rights and social and labour standards. One of its stated objectives was to make fundamental rights more visible, relevant and important to EU citizens (Ellis, 2010). In the EU Charter, social and economic rights are recognised as having the same status as civil and political rights. The consequence is that fundamental rights upheld by the European Court may afford greater or more extensive protection (Kravaritou, 2009).

The EU Charter refers explicitly to a range of individual fundamental and collective rights related to employment quality in its multidimensional perspective[29]. However, if these fundamental social rights are recognised they are poorly protected and implemented.

The first grey area lies in the limitations included in the EU Treaties and the Charter itself regarding the scope and implementation. Article 6(1) of TFEU provides that "*The Union recognises the rights, freedoms and principles set out in the Charter of fundamental rights of the European union of 7 December 2000, as adapted at Strasbourg on 12 December 2007 which shall have the same legal value as the Treaties*". The impact of the Charter will be limited as the total legal effect of the Charter is itself extremely moderated by the provisions of Title VII governing its interpretation and application (Ellis, 2010). The third indent of Article 6(1) of the TFEU requires the Charter to be interpreted in accordance with this Title. There is no question of the Charter creat-

---

28 Charter of Fundamental Rights of the European Union, proclaimed at the meeting of the European Council held in Nice from 7 to 9 December 2000 and adopted by the Commission, the Council and the Member States, OJ C364/01 of 18 December 2000.

29 The Title I on Dignity includes an article on the prohibition of slavery and forced labour (Art. 5). In Title II dedicated to freedoms, we would mention the freedom of thought, conscience and religion (Art. 10), freedom of assembly and association (Art. 12), freedom of access to vocational training (Art. 14), freedom to choose an occupation and to engage in work (Art. 15). Title III concerns equality rights, and particularly the fundamental principles of non-discrimination (Art. 21), equality between men and women (Art. 23) and also the right to an occupational integration for disabled persons (Art. 26). Title IV, dedicated to solidarity, evokes several rights important for employment quality: the right to information and consultation within the undertaking (Art. 27), right to collective bargaining and action (Art. 28), access to free placement services (Art. 29), protection against unjustified dismissal (Art. 30), right to fair and just working conditions which respect health, safety and dignity (Art. 31), the prohibition of child labour and the protection of young workers (Art. 32), protection from dismissal for maternity reasons and to paid maternity and parental leave (Art. 33), and the right to social security and social assistance in the event of industrial accidents and loss of employment (Art. 34).

ing new free-standing rights because Article 51(1) limits those it addressees:

> The provisions of this Charter are addressed to the institutions, bodies, offices and agencies of the Union with due regard for the principle of subsidiarity and to the Member States only when they are implementing Union law. They shall therefore respect the rights, observe the principles and promote the application thereof in accordance with their respective powers and respecting the limits of the powers of the Union as conferred on it in the Treaties.

The Charter thus provides assistance with interpretation of Union legislation and Member States' implementation measures, and may also provide an argument supporting any challenge to such acts, but this is the legal extent of its power (De Schutter, 2010). The second indent of Article 6(1) of the TFEU states firmly that the '*provisions of the Charter shall not extend in any way the competences of the Union as defined in the Treaties*'. Moreover, Article 51(2) reiterates that the Charter does not extend the field of application of EU law beyond the powers of the Union, establish any new power or task for the Union, nor modify powers and tasks as defined in the Treaties. This provision poses a central problem as there is no EU competence to promote many of the Charter's rights. To that extent the EU and related Member States' activities may fall outside the scope of the Charter (Groussot and Pech, 2010). One example very well illustrates well this lack of harmony. Article 153(5) TFEU (137(6) of the EC Treaty) explicitly excludes the right of association and the right to strike, but freedom of association and the right to take collective active action are explicitly guaranteed in Articles 12 and 28 of the Charter. The central problem is the clash between limited EU competence and the EU Charter's fundamental rights. If fundamental rights are subject to any competence, it seriously undermines the concept of fundamental human rights. Values elevated by the EU to the status of fundamental human rights are only protected within the limits of EU competence, and the EU must ignore fundamental human rights where they come up against the limitation of its competence (Bercusson, 2008). Article 52(2) emphasises that rights recognised by the Charter for which provision is made in the Treaties must be exercised within the limits set out in the Treaties (Garcia, 2002).

A second important grey area for implementation of the Charter is linked to the derogations negotiated by certain Member States. Poland and the UK secured a Protocol on the application of the Charter for their countries. Its most important stipulation concerns 'justiciability'; the Charter does not extend the capability of the European Court of Justice or of Polish or UK courts to find that the national laws of these two Member States are inconsistent with the Charter. The Protocol does not, apparently, preclude such courts from giving an extensive interpretation of national laws in recognition of rights protected by the Charter. Poland therefore established Declaration 61, stating that the Charter "does not affect in any way the right of Member States to legislate in the sphere of public morality, family law, as well as the protection of human dignity and respect for human physical and moral integrity". As noted by Ellis (2010), all this makes it unlikely that the courts of the other Member States will interpret the Charter very rigorously since to do so would be to disadvantage themselves whilst creating an advantage for Poland and the UK.

Moreover, the Charters of the European Union, whilst guaranteeing special rights, cannot guarantee nor safeguard all fundamental rights equally. These texts do not offer the same guarantees as the national legal orders in several specific domains that are crucial for employment quality. This is the case with the right to work or to social security in respect of new categories of workers. The protection of these rights has not yet been adapted to cover flexible jobs, temporary work, part-time employment or low paid jobs, categories that are created by the climate of a globalised economy and cross-border labour relations which are not protected by law. This has negative consequences, not only on social rights arising from labour but also on other fundamental rights, including the right to social security. They are both linked as the rights of underemployed workers, part-time workers or those with flexible jobs are threatened and weakened. Although the charters recognise these rights *stricto sensu*, the real issue is their effective implementation in the EU legal framework. The narrow scope of EU policy on employment and economic growths, clearly set as the overriding objectives for the EU in the new Europe 2020 Strategy, has been underpinned by a narrow legal focus on economic freedoms to the detriment of the social dimension (Kravaritou, 2009). It has been argued that the ECJ, by reference to the Charter in its rulings, could be an important vector for the implementation of fundamental rights in the EU legal order. However, the recent evolution of ECJ rulings does not really support this perspective. Both *Viking* and *Laval* rulings[30], even before ratification of the Charter, referred to article 28 and not only did they subordinate the right to strike to economic freedoms but they also applied their own criteria to assess the legality of the strike, ignoring any reference to national rules, and even constitutional rules concerning these criteria (Ghailani, 2008; Dorssemont, 2009).

[30] Case 438/05, *International Transport Workers' Federation, Finnish Seamen's Union v Viking line ABP*, 11 December 2007; Case c-341/05, *Laval und Partneri*, 18 December 2007.

The *Rüffert*[31] judgment is also worrying. The case was about whether public authorities, when awarding contracts for work, have the right to demand that tendering companies commit themselves to pay wages to all workers including posted workers in line with rates in collective agreements applicable in the place where the work is being carried out. It does not recognise the rights of Member States and public authorities to use public procurement instruments to counter unfair competition on wages and working conditions of workers by cross-border service providers, as these would not be compatible with the Posting Directive. Nor does it recognise the rights of trade unions to demand that equal wages and working conditions and the observance of collective agreed standards be applied to migrant workers in line with workers from the place of work, regardless of nationality, beyond the minimum standards recognised by the Posting Directive (Ghailani, 2009). As pointed out by Aliprantis (2010), the ideology of economic liberalism and not that of the European economic treaties, is at the origin of this evolution which won the case in the Court of Justice. This ideology sees social rights as incompatible with economic freedoms, freedom of the market and competition. We would like to refer to Filip Dorssemont's chapter which deals with this issue in further detail.

In the negative perspective of the evolution of the hard law process, in terms of improving the legal dimensions of employment, could a soft law procedure come to the rescue for the implementation of fundamental rights? Social rights guaranteed by the Treaty could be used to put pressure on the Commission to make proposals for their implementation through the establishment of an action programme. The threat of the European Court invoking the doctrine of direct effect in the absence of such implementation measures would be an incentive to Community legislative action (Bercusson, 2009). It should be mentioned that in 2009 the European Economic and Social Committee adopted an opinion on "A new European Social Action Programme"[32]. The EESC stressed the need for a new European Social Programme so EU social developments could keep pace with economic and market developments. The programme should specifically address policy areas such as the quality of life, fundamental rights, employment and work of high quality, social solidarity (…). Guaranteeing fundamental rights was identified as a key priority: the principles and provisions of the Charter of Fundamental Rights should help guide and encourage EU social policy developments and actions. This opinion was unfortunately not taken up by the European Commission.

---

31 Case C-346/06, *Dirk Rüffert v land Niedersachsen*, 8 April 2008.

32 EESC (2008), Opinion of the European Economic and Social Committee on A new European Social Action Programme, SOC/295, 9 July 2008.

In addition to these legally binding declarations, the EU has also recently set up softer tools to reinforce implementation of fundamental rights. The Fundamental Rights Agency (FRA) was set up by Regulation 168/2007[33] to provide assistance and independent expertise relating to fundamental rights, in the domain of Community law. The FRA's activities serve to promote fundamental rights and to support the EU institutions and Member States in raising the level of protection for everyone in the European Union. To achieve this objective, the Agency collects data on fundamental rights, conducts research and analysis, provides independent advice to policy-makers, networks with human rights stakeholders, and finally it develops communication activities to communicate the results of its work and to raise awareness of fundamental rights. It publishes an annual report on fundamental rights issues covering all the areas in which the agency is active, and highlighting examples of good practices.

The European Commission also adopted in 2010 a "Strategy for the Effective Implementation of the Charter of Fundamental Rights by the European Union" (European Commission, 2010f). In this Strategy, the Commission announced its intention to present an annual report monitoring progress on the enforcement of the Charter in areas where the EU has powers to act. The first report was issued on 30 March 2011 by the European Commission.

2. *ILO Declaration on Fundamental Principles and Rights at Work*

In order to respond to the evolution of economic globalisation (Maupain, 2005), in 1998, the ILO adopted, a Declaration on "Fundamental Principles and Rights at Work"[34]. This Declaration commits all Member States to respect and promote principles and rights in four categories, whether or not they have ratified the relevant Conventions, and makes it clear that these rights are universal. These categories and conventions are:

- freedom of association and the effective recognition of the right to collective bargaining: C87 Freedom of Association and Protection of the Right to Organise Convention, 1948 and C98 Right to Organise and Collective Bargaining Convention, 1949;

[33] Council Regulation (EC) No. 168/2007 of 15 February 2007 establishing a European Union Agency for Fundamental Rights, OJ L 53/1.

[34] Adopted by the International Labour Conference at its 86th Session, Geneva, 18 June 1998 (Annex revised 15 June 2010).

- the elimination of forced or compulsory labour: C29 Forced Labour Convention, 1930 and C105 Abolition of Forced Labour Convention, 1957;
- the abolition of child labour: C138 Minimum Age Convention, 1973 and C182 Worst Forms of Child Labour Convention, 1999;
- the elimination of discrimination in respect of employment and occupation. C100 Equal Remuneration Convention, 1951 and C111 Discrimination (Employment and Occupation) Convention, 1958.

We will not deal again with the obligatory nature of this declaration and its follow-up procedure, and the doctrinal debates that it caused (Alston, 2004; Maupain, 2005; Drouin and Duplessis, 2010). At this stage, it would appear important, and by means of a legal analysis of the quality of employment, to compare the standards considered as "fundamental" by the 1998 declaration with those retained by the Tripartite Meeting of Experts on the Measurement of Decent Work, as legal indicators of the progress made by Members States in the promotion of decent work (Table 3).

Table 3

Substantive element of the Decent Work Agenda	Ratification of ILO Conventions	ILO's Fundamental Conventions (1998 declaration)
Employment opportunities – Government commitment to full employment – Unemployment insurance	C.122[35] C.102[36]	
Adequate earnings and productive work – Statutory minimum wage	C.131[37]	
Decent hours – Maximum hours of work.	C.1[38]	
Combination of work, family and personal life – Maternity leave	C.183[39]	
Work that should be abolished – Child labour	C.138[40]-C.182[41]	C.138-C.182

[35] Employment Policy Convention, 1964.

[36] Convention concerning minimum standards of social security, 1952.

[37] Minimum Wage Fixing Convention, 1970.

[38] Hours of Work Convention, 1919.

[39] Maternity Protection Convention, 2000.

[40] Minimum Age Convention, 1973.

[41] Worst Form of Child Labour Convention, 1999.

– Forced labour	C.29[42]-C.105[43]	C.29-C.105
Stability and security of work	(no legal indicator suggested)	
Equal opportunity and treatment in employment – Anti-discrimination law based on sex of worker – Anti-discrimination law based on race, ethnicity, religion or national origin	C.100[44]-C.111[45] C.100-C.111	C.100-C.111 C.100-C.111
Safe work environment – Occupational safety and health insurance – Labour inspection	C.155[46] – C.102 C.81[47] – C.129[48]	
Social security – Pension. – Incapacity for work due to sickness – Incapacity for work due to invalidity	C.102 C.102 C.102	
Social dialogue, workers' and employers' representation – Freedom of association and right to organise – Collective bargaining right – Tripartite consultations	C.87[49] C.98[50] C.144[51]	C87 C98

(Source: ILO, "Measurement of decent work: Discussion paper for the Tripartite Meeting of Experts on the Measurement of Decent Work", Geneva, 8-10 September 2008)

Thus it may be noted that of the ten major elements of the Decent Work Agenda, only four appear in the Declaration of 1998. How can the variation in standards be justified? Is there in the proclamation of the fundamental character of the rights of the 1998 Declaration an implicit risk that the others will be considered as secondary rights and relegated to a normative accessory role (Supiot, 2006)? One explanation for the low number of conventions selected lies in the origin of this Declara-

---

42 Forced Labour Convention, 1930.

43 Abolition of Forced Labour Convention, 1935.

44 Equal Remuneration Convention, 1951.

45 Discrimination in respect of Employment and Occupation Convention, 1958.

46 Occupational Safety and Health Convention, 1981.

47 Labour Inspection Convention, 1947.

48 Labour Inspection in Agriculture Convention, 1969.

49 Freedom of Association and Protection of the Right to Organise Convention, 1948.

50 Right to Organise and Collective Bargaining Convention, 1949.

51 Tripartite consultations to promote the Implementation of International Labour Standards Convention, 1976.

tion. As an initiative by the employers' group in 1997, it acts primarily to establish a link between international trade and standards of work and to promote fundamental rights without the application of commercial sanctions against the States which do not respect them (Drouin, Duplessis, 2010). The 2008 Declaration which refers in Article 1-a to the principles and rights set out in the ILO Constitution and the Philadelphia Declaration, can be seen as the introduction of an international social public order (Supiot, 2006) and not just the diminution of the ILO's normative capacity (Alston, 2004).

If both the Decent Work Agenda and the 1998 Declaration on Fundamental Rights also mention collective bargaining and discrimination, the fact is that neither social security, nor the general protection for workers' health and safety appear in the 1998 Declaration. Why should Social security not be considered as a fundamental right? On this issue, the 1998 Declaration seems to have less authority than the requirements of the Decent Work Agenda. But is it conceivable that fundamental rights should have fewer requirements than decent work? This restrictive and rigorous interpretation should be moderated.

On the one hand, to include only eight conventions of the 1998 Declaration amounts to not taking account of the whole of the ILO constitutional context. In its Resolution and Conclusions on social security (ILO, 2001), the International Labour Conference recalled that social security is a basic human right. It may be considered that the 1998 Declaration covers only rights at work and the social security aspect is outside its framework, though its fundamental nature had already been affirmed by the 1944 Philadelphia Declaration (Supiot, 2006).

On the other hand, it can also be considered that the policy of the ILO is a progressive process which aims to enlarge the scope of conventions which any Member State must respect as a condition of its membership of the ILO, since the 1998 Declaration, continuing with the Decent Work Agenda then the 2008 Declaration. The Convention 102, which is the basic convention covering the minimum standards for social security, is the only one of the six ILO conventions on social security which defines the nine traditional branches of social security and establishes minimum standards for every one of these branches. The ratification of the Convention 102 seems to be the legal tool for measuring decent work in three major elements of the Decent Work Agenda: social security (pension, incapacity for work due to sickness, incapacity for work due to invalidity), employment opportunities (unemployment insurance) and a safe work environment (occupational safety and health insurance).

The 2008 "Declaration on Social Justice for a Fair Globalisation" is dedicated to social security as being one of the most important considerations of the ILO. Although this Declaration does not explicitly proclaim fundamental rights, it recognises that the promotion of employment, social protection, social dialogue, and rights at work, are "inseparable, interrelated and mutually supportive" in the commitments and the efforts of the Member States and ILO action. More recently, in the "Global Jobs Pact", adopted on 19 June 2009, the International Labour Conference asked Members countries to incorporate adequate social protection for everybody, in accordance with basic social protection including: access to health care, income security for the elderly and persons with disabilities, child benefits and income security, combined with public employment guarantee schemes for the unemployed and working poor.

Conclusive Remarks

The comparison of the conceptual frameworks of job quality developed in the EU and the ILO shows that beyond slight differences on particular aspects, such as e.g. children's labour, there is a convergence in the approaches of both institutions. Although expressed from different policy perspectives and scopes, there is a common embedding in fundamental human and workers' rights arising from both legal backgrounds. This could be expected as international, and particularly ILO, conventions are endorsed by the EU member states and often underpin the EU legal framework. The values promoted by the ILO through the decent work agenda and the preoccupation of strengthening the social dimension of globalisation are also supported by the EU in its external policy dimension, and within the EU through the values characterising the European Social Model. The policy agendas of the ILO and the EU encompass similar frameworks for action in favour of more and better jobs, managing change, social cohesion and equal opportunities. However, if the perspective of improving job quality, and more broadly social quality, is still present, to a certain extent, in the new EU meta-strategy for the next decade (Europe 2020), this is obviously not an overarching priority, as the focus is more than ever on economic and budgetary perspectives and the creation of more but not necessarily better jobs.

The EU conceptual framework of job quality needs to be redefined, as acknowledged by the EU Commission in its flagship initiative on New Skills for New Jobs framing the Europe 2020 Strategy. The complementarities with the ILO Decent Work approach could be highlighted and deepened in this perspective. It is necessary to mainstream the decent work approach in the EU policy framework, first as a key-dimension of its external policy, but also as a component of its internal policies, as a complementary and supporting approach towards the improvement of quality of work and employment policies. The credibility of the EU at the international level in promoting DW depends largely on its ability to achieve its own objective of delivering more quality jobs in Europe. There is a need to (re)mainstream job quality in the EU internal policy agenda if Europe wants to sustainably cope with the succession of economic crises affecting the world. Beyond this, there is also pressing need for the EU to (re)introduce a social quality perspective in the European integration, focused on the improvement of well-being of European citizens (as stated in the Treaties). This is what European citizens are expecting from the EU, but out of sight in the obsessive focus on economic and monetary integration of Europe.

Over time, the EU has built up a solid legislative *acquis* in various domains regarding employment quality such as working conditions, health and safety and, more widely, gender equality and non-discrimination. However, legislation at EU level is not always adequate and soft instruments such as policy coordination can help shape a consensus and create the right conditions for action at national or company level. This recourse to soft law to complement, and sometimes to substitute, hard law has become increasingly prevalent at EU level since the end of the 1990, even in fields such as gender equality, non-discrimination or health and safety, for which a strong legal corpus already exists.

This intensive recourse to soft law raised a strong debate on the opposition or the complementarity between hard and soft law within the EU policy framework. As explained in this chapter, "job quality" appears in the EU landscape through the Lisbon Strategy and more particularly through one of the new forms of soft law governance, the EES. The relationship between the *acquis* and the EES is a two-way street. The *acquis* is a legally binding framework of labour regulation which limits the scope and nature of the policies adopted under the EES. At the same time, the EES expanded the scope of the *acquis* by inspiring new regulations aimed at achieving the objectives of the EES, which are based on the social chapter of the Treaty, among other provisions. This debate is still on-going, and probably will be for a long time. The introduction of new hard law relating to job quality dimensions has become complex given the increased number of EU Member States and the relative blocking of European Social Dialogue in recent years, at least at the inter-professional level. The Lisbon Treaty has given more legislative powers to the European Parliament, but this has not exactly yet been translated into effective action, and the tensions between European institutions are reaching a peak when it comes to discussing hard law issues.

Such tensions also appear in the action of the ILO on decent work, which is indeed based on ambivalence issues as well. Here, the focus is on to the normative action, which is essential for measuring progress of

Member States in achieving the goals set by the ILO through the number and the importance of the conventions ratified by each state. However, this same normative action is found to be insufficient. Due to a lack of interdependence between the various conventions developed by the ILO, disadvantages which are of voluntary and fragmented character become apparent/are disclosed.

The use of soft law has been rendered necessary to compensate for the insufficiency of the normative action in policy domains where legal competences are typically at national (or subnational) levels. However, the point where the comparison between the action of the ILO on decent work and the European policy on job quality finds an end, is precisely this lack of binding tools for global institutions as they do not possess the legal capacity to force member states to progress in the promotion of decent work. Although these new ILO instruments are viewed as being insufficient, it seems paradoxically that they actually do reappear in MS national policy making. The action of promoting decent work has enabled the ILO to launch a new normative approach, through the use of legal instruments such as solemn Declarations.

The discussions arising from the action of the European Union on job quality on whether hard and soft law are of opposing or complementing character, are also reflected at the ILO regarding issues of compensating the low number of ratifications and the risk of dissolution of labour law and the body of standards developed since the origins of the ILO.

Reconciling "Quality of Employment" with the Principles of "Flexicurity"

Jérôme DEUMER

Attorney – Member of the Brussels Bar

Introduction

Ways of improving quality of work are key issues since the economic crisis of the 1970s. The oil shock of 1973 marked the end of "The Glorious Thirty" and led to inflation and economic slowdown, causing an increase in unemployment rates all around the world. Then, governments introduced a range of policies intended to relaunch economic growth and decided to put in place measures aimed at making employment more flexible, such as working time reduction and promotion of atypical jobs, in such a way as to bring about improvement in the redistribution of work and resolve the unemployment issue[1]. However, the measures undertaken in this context can be suspected of decreasing the quality of jobs and more generally, of having a negative impact on the quality of the workers' life.

The crisis that started in 1973 lasted a while, notably because of the competition from the post-Soviet States and the transition to the single market that resulted from the Single European Act adopted in 1986. Therefore, in the middle of the 1990s, several international organisations, including the European Union, started to initiate debates about job insecurity, and, more generally, about the quality of jobs and the right way to render work and human dignity compatible. Promoting quality of employment has been a growing concern of the European Union since then. It is now a central concept of the European Employment Strategy, which was adopted at the Luxembourg summit in 1997 with the aim of

---

1 V. Canals, *Formation-insertion et transformation de la relation salariale*, coll. Logiques économiques, Paris, L'Harmattan, 2001, p. 37 et s.

creating more and better jobs throughout the Union, in order to counter increasing unemployment rates[2].

In parallel with these developments, the "flexicurity" wave started breaking on Continental Europe and it seemed to announce the end of the "classical" labour law we have known since the industrial revolution. In June 2007, the European Commission published a Communication on common principles of so-called "flexicurity" in which this concept was defined as "*an integrated strategy to enhance, at the same time, flexibility and security in the labour market*", revolving around flexible and reliable contractual arrangements, comprehensive lifelong learning, effective active labour market policies and modern social security systems[3]. But the Commission's approach to flexicurity led to much criticism because of the fact it would run counter to job protection and stability[4].

Over the past decade, the concepts of flexicurity and that of job quality have become central pillars of European social policy. However, considering the criticism levied at the flexicurity approach of the Commission (part II), one could wonder whether both concepts can be conciliated in the same social policy. In this framework, it might appear necessary to review the concept of "quality", which is at the core of the European Employment Strategy (part III), in order to point out the main features of both concepts, redefine them and assess whether they can be combined in a single European social policy (IV).

Flexicurity: a Tool for the Renewal of the European Social Model

The concept of "flexicurity" appeared in the 1990s in order to qualify the social reforms that had been put in place in Denmark and in the Netherlands. Originally, the concept did not relate to a political awareness as such but rather to the results of negotiations between political and social partners on the reform of the organisation and structure of the labour market.

The neologism "flexicurity" appeared to qualify this new social policy whose aim is to conciliate the flexibility and security of the labour market. The two components should in principle reinforce one another rather than being opposed to each other.

---

2 European Commission, Communication, *Employment and social policies: a framework for investing in quality*, COM(2001) 313 final.

3 European Commission, Communication, *Towards common principles of flexicurity: more and better jobs through flexibility and security*, COM(2007) 359 final, p. 5.

4 European Trade Union Confederation, *"Flexicurity" Communication: ETUC insists on smart labour market reforms*, Press release, 27 June 2007.

At a European level, the concept is to be found for the first time in 2006 in an official paper of the Commission. In its Green Paper entitled "*Modernising labour law to meet the challenges of the 21st century*", the Commission painted the picture of a labour law which is inadequate to meet current economic necessities and called for more flexible regulations. The modernisation of labour law will, according to the Commission, be effected through the implementation of the principles of flexicurity[5]. These principles were proposed by the Commission in a Communication in June 2007[6], and approved by the Council in December 2007.

However, ever since the beginning of the Luxembourg process (that started with the adoption of the European Employment Strategy in 1997), the European willingness to reform the labour market by allying flexibility with job security already existed. Flexicurity, presented by the Commission in 2007 as a new concept ready to revolutionise our vision of the European social model, had already been germinating at European level since the end of the 1990s[7].

Nowadays, flexicurity remains at the heart of the Union's social policy, especially at the level of the leadership of the Commission and the Council, who stressed in the most recent employment guidelines the need for the Member States to "integrate the flexicurity principles endorsed by the European Council into their labour market policies"[8].

The European Definition of Flexicurity

Following the economic down-turn of recent years, the Commission holds that the implementation of flexicurity-inspired policy would enable the Union to achieve the objectives of the Lisbon strategy[9] and to maintain or even to improve its competiveness while at the same time preserving its social model.

---

5 European Commission, Green paper, *Modernising labour law to meet the challenges of the 21st century*, COM(2006) 708 final.

6 European Commission, Communication, *Towards common principles of flexicurity: more and better jobs through flexibility and security*, COM(2007) 359 final.

7 See the conclusions of the Extraordinary European Council Meeting on Employment held in Luxembourg on 20 and 21 November 1997, especially point 70: "*the social partners are invited to negotiate, at the appropriate levels, in particular at sectoral and enterprise levels, agreements to modernize the organization of work, including flexible working arrangements, with the aim of making undertakings productive and competitive and achieving the required balance between flexibility and security*".

8 Guideline No. 7, annex to the Council decision of 21 October 2010 on guidelines for the employment policies of the Member States (2010/707/EU), OJEU L 308, 24 November 2010, p. 46.

9 That is "*to become the most competitive and dynamic knowledge-based economy in the world capable of sustainable economic growth with more and better jobs and greater social cohesion*".

To this end, flexicurity shall be understood as a global political strategy aimed at improving not only flexibility on the labour market, work organisation or employment relationships but also workers' security of employment and income.

According to the Commission, in view of the increase in flexibility in employment relations which has been rendered necessary by the globalisation of the economy, workers currently need a new type of security which would enable them to remain in the labour market and to accommodate the changes they face. This new kind of security should not be limited to a particular job but should rather concern the transition between different jobs. The main goal is no longer employment security but rather employability security.

But the Commission states that measures encouraging flexibility in the labour market and improving the level of security will not be effective if workers do not obtain the means to adapt to changes, to remain in the labour market and to progress in their professional life. This is the reason why the Commission also puts the emphasis on active policies on the labour market, the promotion of education, training and lifelong learning, the improvement in personalised support services to help people get into work, the encouragement of equality of opportunities for all and gender equality[10].

The Commission's definition of flexicurity is perfectly in line with the debates within the OECD (Organisation for Economic Co-operation and Development) in recent years. This organisation has also had the opportunity to consider flexicurity, with a view to conciliating the employment flexibility required by employers and the employment security sought by workers. On this issue, the OECD promotes more flexible employment relations, which could be compensated by appropriate social protection. The OECD also considers that enhanced job security should be envisaged on a much wider basis and not be limited to strengthening employment protection regulations[11].

Shortcomings of the European Definition of Flexicurity

An analysis of the 2007 Commission Communication has led numerous scholars to consider the Commission's view to be partisan, because it is based on the negative assumption that labour law is not

10 See the communication of the European Commission "*Towards common principles of flexicurity: more and better jobs through flexibility and security*", *op. cit.*

11 See Organisation for Economic Co-operation and Development, "Employment protection regulation and labour market performance", *OECD Employment Outlook*, 2004, p. 61-125; Organisation for Economic Co-operation and Development, "Addressing the globalization paradox", *OECD Employment Outlook*, 2007, p. 11-15.

adapted to the current economic situation and leads to inflexibility for employers[12]. If the general outlines of the Commission's Communication may seem attractive, several points of criticisms may be levied at this – biased – conception of flexicurity.

A Definition Centered on Flexibility

Trade unions considered this conception of flexicurity as reflecting the Commission's willingness to reform the European social model by requiring more flexibility from workers, without guaranteeing them any security[13].

In this respect, two observations can be made.

Firstly, the assumption according to which labour law is now a constraint for employers and harmful to economic growth is wrong. In fact, we have experienced in the last few decades an increase in the flexibility of employment relations due to contractual arrangements concerning working time as well as contracts on the term of employment (fixed-term contracts, part-time work, temporary work, etc.), with a purely economic purpose[14].

In the 1980s, policies for the redistribution of working time favoured atypical jobs, either fixed-term contracts or part-time work. Regulations on variable working time and on new flexible working arrangements have also permitted a better redistribution of the available working time. However, in the 1990s, flexibility also invaded the employment contract itself, including open-ended full-time contracts. We have observed the insertion into employment contracts of specific provisions concerning the definition of the function, workplace, working time, working arrangement, salary, etc. These elements enabled employers to make internal flexibility possible by linking the worker's employment with the economic risks of the business, and to protect themselves against a slowdown in economic growth[15].

The preceding considerations lead us to our second and more fundamental observation: the priority given to more flexible employment relations goes against the European willingness to improve quality of

---

12 J.-F. Macours, "La flexicurité: panacée européenne à la crise de l'emploi?", *Actualités en droit social européen*, Brussels, Larcier, 2010, p. 122.

13 European Trade Union Confederation, *"Flexicurity" Communication: ETUC insists on smart labour market reforms*, Press release, 27 June 2007.

14 A. Cieslar, A. Nayer, B. Smeesters, *Le droit à l'épanouissement de l'être humain au travail: métamorphoses du droit social*, Brussels, Bruylant, 2007, p. 41-43 and 574-576.

15 C. Bessy, "La diversité des contrats de travail", *La qualité de l'emploi*, Centre d'études de l'emploi, Paris, La Découverte, coll. Repères, 2006, p. 64.

work. According to the Commission, an increase in flexibility should lead to an increase in the quality of work, without reducing workers' job security. However, much criticism is made of this assumption, since one can see from the increasing level of flexibility evidence of greater insecurity and a mediocre quality. Hence, some argue that more flexible employment relations would work against security and stability for workers[16].

In the context of the debates on the implementation of the flexicurity concept, the effects of the increase in atypical contracts and internal flexibility make it necessary to consider if and how quality of work has been impaired. Indeed, the Commission's definition of flexicurity, centered on the necessity to implement flexible employment relations, hardly seems compatible with a willingness to improve quality of work. Besides, the Commission's call for more flexible forms of employment does not seem justified.

Disregard of the Social Protection Aspect

As mentioned before, the European flexicurity concept is based mainly on the Dutch and Danish approaches to the labour market which were put in place at the beginning of the 1990s.

The Danish model of the "golden triangle" is based on flexible employment protection regulations, the improvement of social protection including unemployment benefits and active policies for the labour market. The Commission considers that Members States should draw on the Danish model in order to engage in legislative reforms in the field of labour and social security law. But at the same time, the Commission remains silent on an extremely important element of this model: such a model is only practicable if accompanied by massive public investment in education and social protection[17]. This criticism has also been levelled by the European Parliament[18].

For many commentators on the 2007 Communication, the "vague and imprecise call" of the Commission to ensure adequate social protec-

---

[16] See A. Cieslar, A. Nayer, B. Smeesters, *op. cit.*, p. 43. The authors state that the absence of stability and the implementation of flexible employment relations at all costs may have important consequences on a worker's health and more generally on his professional fulfillment.

[17] Vielle, P., "Flexicurity: redefining the security of European citizens", OSE Policy Paper No. 1, Brussels, October 2007, 13 p.

[18] Resolution of 6 July 2010 on atypical contracts, secured professional paths, flexicurity and new forms of social dialogue (2009/2220(INI)), *O.J.* C351E, pp. 39-48.

tion is a matter of regret, and will always translate in practice into slimmer protection and a decrease in unemployment benefits[19].

A Reductive Definition

The Commission and the OECD have expressed a similar "economic" vision of flexicurity. They both consider that the primary purpose of this new model is to improve economic growth and not an immediate or better organisation of social relations.

In this sense, the Commission takes the view that a worker is merely looking for employment security, whereas flexibility represents an economic lever available to the employer.

This assumption is wrong and leads to a reductive definition. On the one hand, flexibility in the employment relationship is not necessarily a drawback for the worker. On the other hand, employers are also demanding more flexibility and some kind of economic security[20].

Therefore, it would be preferable to acquire a better view of the worker's needs and acknowledge that his/her job should offer him/her not only material security but also sufficient flexibility and a better work-life balance.

Follow-up and Current Situation

Since the 2007 Communication, the concept of flexicurity has slightly evolved with the "Mission for flexicurity" launched by the Commission following a request from the Council. This "mission" has in practice led to an assessment of the flexicurity measures put in place in five Member States and resulted in a final report in December 2008 in which the importance of social partners in the implementation of flexicurity was recalled[21].

This report also refers to the difficulty with respect to implementing flexicurity measures in a climate of economic crisis. In fact, the question could be asked if flexibility and security can be combined during such an economic crisis situation?

Indeed, the economic crisis has led to an important increase in unemployment rates in most Union countries, more rapidly where policies

---

19 M. Keune, "Flexicurité: le nouveau remède aux problèmes du marché européen du travail", Bilan social de l'Union européenne 2007, Brussels, ETUI-REHS, 2008, p. 175, quoted by J.-F. Macours, *op. cit.*, p. 115.

20 This more correct approach to flexicurity is adopted by L. Duclos and J.-Y. Kerbourc'h in working paper No. 10 of the Conseil d'Orientation pour l'Emploi with the title *Organisation du marché du travail et "flexicurité" à la française*, Paris, 2006, 96 p.

21 Report of the Mission for flexicurity, 12 December 2008, 17047/1/08.

of flexibility had already been implemented[22]. At the same time, austerity measures have been put in place and public investment reduced. Yet, securing professional career opportunities requires strong social protection and investments in workers' education. The consequences of a flexicurity policy could then be challenged in a situation of economic crisis, where government budget considerations render impossible the maintenance of strong social protection[23].

At the present time, the Commission still makes flexicurity its hobbyhorse in order to improve the European social model. This was recalled during the consultation process on the new Lisbon Strategy[24].

Improving Quality of Work

Quality of work was originally defined as a goal of economic policy, opposed to the creation of poor quality jobs with low wages. The concept became in 2001 one of the main concerns of the social partners and a key issue in the public debates on employment[25].

The European Definition of "Quality of Work"

The work undertaken in 2001 by the Commission resulted in the identification of the 10 dimensions of the "quality of work", which were approved by the Council after the Laeken summit of December 2001. For each of these ten dimensions, the Commission has identified the key instruments and statistical indicators which should render it possible to assess improvements in this field (see Caillaud, Ghailani and Peña-Casas in this book). We briefly summarise those ten dimensions hereafter[26].

Intrinsic job quality: in order to ensure higher employment rates, the Commission holds that jobs should be attractive enough and be such that workers are able to envisage career perspectives.

Skills, lifelong learning and career development: according to the Commission, it is time to invest in the education and training of workers

22 J.-F. Macours, *op. cit.*, p. 123.

23 *Ibid.*

24 European Commission, Working document, Consultation on the future "EU 2020" strategy, COM(2009) 647 final. See also Guideline No. 7, annex to the Council decision of 21 October 2010 on guidelines for the employment policies of the Member States (2010/707/EU), *O.J.*, L 308, 24 November 2010, p. 46.

25 L. Davoine, C. Erhel, "La qualité de l'emploi: une mise en perspective européenne", *La qualité de l'emploi*, Centre d'études de l'emploi, Paris, La Découverte, coll. Repères, 2006, p. 16.

26 The criteria and indicators of the quality of work have been defined and are to be found in the European Commission's Communications COM(2001) 313 of 20 June 2001 and COM(2003) 728 of 26 November 2003.

"*with a view to promote productivity, competitiveness and active ageing*"[27].

Gender equality: considering that gender discrimination is still present, the Commission recalls that this dimension is strongly linked to the other dimensions of quality and calls for the involvement of all actors in the fight against gender discrimination.

Health and safety at work: in order to fight the economic consequences of accidents at work and occupational diseases, the Commission insists on the importance of improving health and safety at work. It is indeed essential to keep people in work, taking into account the ageing of the population and the ensuing necessary intergenerational solidarity.

Flexibility and security: because of globalisation, according to the Commission it is primordial to encourage positive attitudes towards more flexible working relations, to foster workers' mobility, while at the same time guaranteeing them appropriate support and integration in the labour market. The voluntary and involuntary precarious jobs, in the form of atypical employment contracts, will be taken into account in order to assess the level of security.

Inclusion and access to the labour market: this dimension relates to improved access to the labour market for all workers willing to work.

Work organisation and work-life balance: the Commission insists on the necessity to integrate more flexibility into working time and work organisation, the necessity to put in place services enabling parents to have a professional life, the importance to conciliate flexibility and security and the necessity for workers to adapt themselves to changes in the undertaking thanks to lifelong learning.

Social dialogue and worker involvement: not only do social dialogue and worker involvement cover the conclusion of collective bargaining agreements, they also refer to mechanisms of information and consultation for workers and their involvement in committees within the undertaking.

Diversity and non-discrimination: equality and non-discrimination between workers is an essential pillar of European law. These principles concern all categories of workers, the final purpose being for undertakings to maximise the productivity of all their workers and to benefit from their diversity.

Overall economic performance and productivity: the Commission considers that positive links are to be identified between quality of

---

27 European Commission, Communication, *Improving quality in work: a review of recent progress*, COM(2003) 728 final, p. 10.

work, high productivity rates and the overall economic performance of the labour market.

Shortcomings of the European Definition of "Quality of Work"

Many points of criticisms may be directed against the European definition of the suggested dimensions of the quality of work. The aim of this chapter is not to present an exhaustive view of this criticism, but merely to highlight the relevant difficulties in the context of the current debate and the possibility to conciliate improvements in the quality of work with the implementation of a flexicurity-based social policy[28].

Flexibility of jobs versus security of employment

In order to assess whether and how the European definition could be improved, a first and global comparison with the International Labour Organisation's definition of "decent work" renders it possible to highlight some shortcomings of the European definition[29]. Without going back on the "decent work" concept, we would like to mention here that precise dimensions and indicators on the fundamental dimensions of work have already been proposed in 2002 in order to refine the concept of "decent work"[30].

Based on those criteria, a first analysis of the European definition of the "quality of work" highlights the fact that some dimensions are only partially treated by the Commission (quality and intensity of education, indicators of working conditions, etc.), whilst other elements are totally omitted, such as the level of salary, the intensity of work or income security. The "social protection" feature is also absent, except for atypical jobs. The absence of indicators to assess the level of social dialogue and worker involvement, and the lesser priority given to the "health and safety" aspect will also be noted.

---

28 On the use of indicators and a criticism of the indicators themselves, see R. Peña-Casas, "Monitoring quality of work and employment in the European Union. Conceptual frameworks and indicators", in A.-M. Guillén and S.-A. Dahl (eds.), *Quality of Work in the European Union – Concept, Data and Debates from a Transnational Perspective*, Brussels, P.I.E. Peter Lang, 2009, p. 41-85.

29 For a wider and deeper comparison of these concepts, see the contribution of P. Caillaud, D. Ghaliani and R. Peña-Casas to this book on the conceptual and legal framework for job quality in the European Union.

30 See International Labour Organisation, International Labour Office, General Report, 17th ICLS, ICLS/17/2003/1, Geneva, November 2003; R. Anker *et al.*, "Measuring decent work with statistical indicators", *International Labour Review*, Vol. 142, No. 2, Geneva, 2003, p. 147-177.

Besides, other issues are not afforded the same degree of importance within the two definitions. The "decent work" definition notably focuses on the stability of employment and working time (supplementary hours and under-employment linked to part-time work), while the Commission's definition prefers to opt for criteria on flexibility and security, centered on the percentage of atypical employment contracts and on professional trajectories.

Generally speaking, the European approach clearly contrasts with the "decent work" concept. In fact, this quick comparison tends to indicate that the European notion of "quality of work" does not consider safeguarding the professional trajectories (thanks to social protection, education and income security) as an essential element of quality but primarily focuses on the implementation of flexible employment[31]. We believe that the European concept of "quality" should be rethought to take account of the need for employment transition to be both swift and secure.

Subjective Quality of Work

The method used to define the concept "quality of work" essentially consists of the establishment of an objective analytical framework to assess the features of work. But such an objective approach could not replace a subjective approach to work: indeed, does the quality of a particular job not depend primarily upon the satisfaction that the worker gains in doing it?

Even if the European definition of quality of work tries to take this subjective dimension into account, workers' personal satisfaction can only be revealed through worker-based inquiries. Such inquiries have been made and usually lead to a similar conclusion: job satisfaction is closely linked to more security in the fields of working conditions, the maintenance of the skills of the worker, the existence of a union delegation and security of employment[32]. A full analysis of the quality of work must take this conclusion into account, because it gives a better worker view of the topic.

Another point to be examined is the question of the adequacy of the worker's skills for his/her job. In fact, the analysis of the quality of the job of a specific worker necessarily presupposes that the professional skills of that worker are taken into account[33]. The probability that a job

[31] L. Davoine, C. Erhel, *op. cit.*, p. 19.

[32] L. Davoine, C. Erhel, *op. cit.*, p. 15; J.-A. Ritter, R. Anker, "Good jobs, bad jobs: Workers' evaluations in five countries", *International Labour Review*, Vol. 141, No. 4, Geneva, 2002, p. 331-358.

[33] European Commission, Communication, *Employment and social policies: a framework for investing in quality*, COM(2001) 313 final, p. 7.

would give the worker possibilities for positive changes is an essential aspect of quality, because the professional career of the worker should be analysed in general terms and not according to the worker's professional situation at one specific moment[34].

Based on the above, we are convinced that subjective quality of work must be addressed if pursuing a "quality of work" policy is to attain a positive and successful outcome. Considering quality without paying due regard to actual and concrete needs of the workers makes no sense.

Quality of Work and Economic Context

As an introductory remark, we should mention that a "quality of work" policy, which has the renewal of the European social model as a goal, remains closely linked to the economic and political context in which it is implemented. This inextricable link leads to several difficulties.

The Commission considers that the efforts aimed at increasing employment rates go hand in hand with improving the attractiveness of jobs, quality of work, increase in workforce productivity and decrease in the percentage of low-paid workers. According to the Commission, "clear positive links" are to be identified between these elements and the existing synergies should be fully exploited[35]. In other words, the Commission considers that the quality of work and the pursuit of the strategic goal of Lisbon reinforce each other[36]. However, such an assumption is to be criticised as the "positive links" between productivity and quality of work cannot be so clearly identified. We take the view that the economic approach to quality should be set aside in order to make the "quality of work" policy more effective and efficient.

---

[34] P. Ralle, "Introduction", *La qualité de l'emploi*, Centre d'études de l'emploi, Paris, La Découverte, coll. Repères, 2006, p. 7.

[35] European Commission, Communication, *Improving quality in work: a review of recent progress*, COM(2003) 728 final, p. 6.

[36] At the Lisbon summit in March 2000, the European Union "*has set itself a new strategic goal for the next decade: to become the most competitive and dynamic knowledge-based economy in the world capable of sustainable economic growth with more and better jobs and greater social cohesion*" (point 5 of the Presidency Conclusions of the Lisbon European Council of 23 and 24 March 2000). It is worth noting that these objectives have been revised downwards in the new EU2020 strategy: the purpose is no longer to make the Union "*the most competitive and dynamic knowledge-based economy in the world*" but to merely transform it into "*a sustainable market economy, i.e. an inclusive, smarter, greener economy*" (European Commission, *Consultation on the future "EU 2020" strategy*, Commission working document, COM(2009) 647 final).

a. Full Employment

In the framework of the European Employment Strategy, the Union has set itself the goal of creating more and better jobs. The objective of increasing employment rates seems however hardly achievable: unemployment rates are high, seniors have a low activity rate and young people encounter significant problems in professional insertion.

Even if they are inseparable[37], the concept of "quality of work" and "full employment" must be distinguished from one another. However, it seems that current public interventions in the field of employment tend primarily to combat unemployment, without taking account of the quality of newly created jobs[38]. One could only wonder what the future of quality of work will be in the coming years: the global financial crisis has led to an economic slowdown which has caused the disappearance of thousands of jobs throughout Europe. The risk remains that the measures adopted in order to rectify this emergency situation will not correctly take into account the improvement of the quality of the newly created jobs.

Some studies in Anglo-Saxon countries also show that job creation policies usually have significant repercussions in terms of quality, the newly created jobs being characterised by low wages and precarious working conditions. Two examples can be used to illustrate this assumption: firstly, policies aiming at redistributing working time and promoting part-time work, thanks to a decrease in the social security contributions, lead to a drastic decrease in the quality of work[39]. In fact, the original assumption of these policies is biased: part-time work which developed in the 1980s was in most cases suffered and not voluntarily executed by workers hoping to have a work-life balance[40]. This evolu-

---

37 The possibilities for a worker to find a job are an essential prerequisite for the existence of decent work. As stated by G.S. Fields: "*The first element of Decent Work is employment. It is a truism, but nonetheless true, that for a person to have a job that is decent, he or she must have a job*" (G.S. Fields, "Decent work and development policies", *International Labour Review*, Vol. 142, No. 2, Geneva, 2003, p. 241). See also the definition of decent work proposed by R. Anker (*op. cit.*) who takes this aspect into consideration.

38 Such a statement had already been made by the Director-General of the ILO in 1999 (International Labour Organisation, International Labour Conference, *Decent work*, *op. cit.*, p. 4).

39 B. Gomel, "Politiques publiques et qualité de l'emploi", *La qualité de l'emploi*, Centre d'études de l'emploi, Paris, La Découverte, coll. Repères, 2006, p. 105.

40 Because of the economic crisis in the 1970s, part-time work which had up to then developed as "prosperity" part-time work was deeply transformed. Employers made use of it in a broader way in order to rationalise labour costs, encouraged to do so by the public authorities who considered part-time work as an efficient means to ensure a better redistribution of the labour supply. This led to an increase in involuntary

tion has not always been taken into account by public authorities. Such policies also undermine careers in the ascendant and make achieving a good work-life balance even more complicated. Secondly, policies to reduce employers' costs on low wages lead to an increase in the employment rates of unqualified people, and they also slow-down wage careers and make access to a quality job more difficult[41].

At the beginning of 2008, at the 46th session of the Commission of Social Development, the European Trade Union Confederation (ETUC) accentuated the poor quality of the jobs created as a result of the global growth in preceding years. The ETUC considered that this finding was principally due to a lack of financial investment in the implementation of a real policy to promote decent work[42]. The ETUC further stated that such a policy would mainly require real investment in the quality of existing jobs before the implementation of reforms to help increase employment rates, which should in practice be translated by the suppression of precarious jobs (part-time work, fixed-term contracts, temporary work, etc.). In fact, this means reorganising working practices so that they result in improvements in the fields of education, security and work-life balance, legislation for a high level of protection at work, efficient social protection, systems safeguarding professional trajectories and a reinforcement of social dialogue[43].

b. Productivity and Economic Growth

The concept of "quality of work" seems to have traditional and inseparable links with the concept of productivity, which prevents due regard being paid to the numerous elements affecting quality, which is increasingly interpreted as aiming at promoting only the financial attractiveness of jobs.

Links between economic growth and improvement in quality of work are not yet clear: on the one hand, some people argue that the globalisation which entails an increase in the number of jobs available allows improvement in the quality of existing jobs. On the other hand, others consider that economic growth goes hand in hand with a decrease in

---

part-time employment but this evolution was never really taken into account in the regulation concerning this precarious form of employment.

41 L. Davoine, C. Erhel, M. Guergoat-Larivière, "Monitoring quality in work: European Employment Strategy indicators and beyond", *International Labour Review*, Vol. 147, No. 2-3, Geneva, 2008, p. 184.

42 European Trade Union Confederation, *UN member states must make decent work a prime commitment, say Global and European Trade Union Confederations*, Press release, 6 February 2008.

43 European Trade Union Confederation, *Quality of jobs at risk! An overview from the ETUC on the incidence and rise of precarious work in Europe*, March 2008.

quality, as globalisation entails the need to cut down the costs of the workforce, including wages[44].

However, it is unanimously admitted that an investment in human capital and workers' security ensures decent work and improves productivity for the company. It also leads to a more equitable and durable economic growth[45].

Follow-up and Current Situation

After the definition made in 2001, the notion of "quality of work" has met with some disinterest; many people consider that poor quality of work could be justified in view of the quantity of the jobs created[46], and this despite the definition of quality of work as a strategic goal of the European Employment Strategy in 2003[47].

On the occasion of the revision of the Lisbon strategy, the European Commission tried to regenerate the issue of quality of work by mentioning, in the employment policy guidelines for the years 2005-2008, the need to improve quality and productivity at work[48], a requirement which was reiterated in the guidelines for the years 2008-2010[49].

The new employment guidelines, adopted in 2010, do not explicitly make this the main purpose of national employment policies but still insist on the necessity of increasing employment rates, investing in education and learning and promoting social inclusion. These new guidelines largely refer to the Europe 2020 strategy, whose aim is primarily to cope with the consequences of the financial crisis[50].

---

44 G.S. Fields, *op. cit.*, p. 254.

45 International Labour Organisation, International Labour Conference, *Reducing the decent work deficit: a global challenge*, Report of the Director-General, 89th session, Geneva, 2001, p. 26.

46 See the so-called *"KOK's" Report, Jobs, jobs, jobs. Creating more employment in Europe, Report of the Employment Taskforce, November* 2003. This report seems to focus on the quantitative dimension of the labour market without paying any regard to its qualitative dimension.

47 European Commission, Communication, *The future of the European Employment Strategy (EES): "A strategy for full employment and better jobs for all"*, COM(2003) 6 final. The three strategic goals defined at that time were full employment, quality and productivity at work and social inclusion. Once again, the links between quality and productivity can be infuriating.

48 Council of the European Union, Decision of 12 July 2005 for the employment policies of the Member States (2005/600/CE), *O.J.E.U.* L 205, 6 August 2005, p. 21.

49 Council of the European Union, Decision of 15 July 2008 for the employment policies of the Member States (2008/618/CE), *O.J.E.U.* L 198, 26 July 2008, p. 52.

50 Council of the European Union, Decision of 21 October 2010 on guidelines for the employment policies of the Member States (2010/707/EU), *O.J.E.U.* L 308, 24 November 2010, p. 46.

Reconciling Both Concepts

In order to ensure decent work, that is to say employment of quality for everyone, the ILO pleads for the development of new economic and social systems which guarantee minimum thresholds in terms of workers' protection while at the same time allowing the system to adapt to changes within a competitive environment[51].

Hence, according to the ILO, it would seem that, some kind of flexicurity policy could lead to an improvement in the quality of work. We clearly agree with such assumption inasmuch as the concepts of flexicurity and quality of work are correctly defined.

Questionable Concepts

The European definitions of "flexicurity" and "quality of work" require some general comments. Criticism we have made of those definitions (see parts II and III) are relatively alike and indicate that the Commission's conception of the European social policy remains economic-oriented.

Indeed, the Commission still reasons on the basis that flexibility of employment, understood as more flexible jobs and a limitation on the employment protection regulation, is necessary in the current economic climate. Therefore, the Commission does not take into account the fact that this kind of flexibility is widespread and is at the origin of the massive degradation of the quality of work. We take the view that steps promoting this kind of flexibility are no longer necessary. In the current economic and social context, flexibility should be redefined and more account should be given to the need for the worker to obtain sufficient resources enabling him or her to enjoy a better work-life balance. The purpose of social policies is no longer merely to put in place some economic flexibility enabling employers to adapt their workforce to the requirements of globalisation.

The Commission calls for a new form of employment security, which is not merely focused on a specific job but more broadly based on securing workers' careers. Yet, our analysis makes it clear that this element is very limited in European social policy. Securing professional career prospects, which requires in our view a strong and efficient social protection, constitutes an essential condition not only of the quality of work but also of the implementation of a flexicurity policy and is also a premise to more flexible employment relationships. Inquiries on the subjective quality of work reveal that any worker considers his/her own

---

51 International Labour Organisation, International Labour Conference, *Decent work*, *op. cit.*, p. 4.

job security as a determining element of the quality of that job. When reviewing the notions of quality and flexicurity, it is therefore considered necessary to give more weight to the working conditions of the worker, his/her possibilities of education and professional advancement, the conditions in which real workers' involvement may be instigated, to the stability of employment and, in a broader view, to securing professional career prospects.

Finally, the links between these concepts and the economic situation are also of great significance. Because of the economic and financial crisis which began in 2008, recent social policies have as their main purpose the creation of jobs in order to fight the increase in unemployment rates. Would it still be possible to implement flexicurity measures while improving quality of work, when the public authorities focus on limiting the damage because of limited financial resources and is it possible to guarantee that newly created jobs will be quality jobs? In the same way, how can we ensure effective social protection to workers hit by the crisis?

Redefining the Concepts

In part III, we have highlighted the shortcomings of the current European definition given to the notion of "quality of work". On this basis, we take the view that "quality" should clearly be distinguished from the economic context (full employment and productivity) and that more weight should be given to securing the workers, either in a specific job (given the subjective character of "quality") or in the professional trajectory (thanks to education, lifelong learning and social protection). A global analysis of the notion would not be possible if those dimensions are not correctly taken into account.

The various components of "quality of work" can be arranged in different ways in order to permit a global analysis of the concept. Among these, one method consists of arranging the criteria of decent work in a framework including six fundamental dimensions which are: productivity at work, equity at work, dignity and social dialogue, security and social protection, work opportunities and a guarantee to work in liberty[52]. The two last dimensions could be merged into one as they both aim at assessing the existence of acceptable work opportunities and do not immediately focus on the quality of work[53].

---

52 This approach is the one adopted by R. Anker in the context of his reflection on the notion of decent work (R. Anker *et al.*, "Measuring decent work with statistical indicators", *op. cit.*).

53 A second approach consists of gathering criteria according to the four fundamental pillars of the ILO. Such an approach is adopted by Dharam Ghaï, former Director of

Considering the above-mentioned criticisms, it seems that those six (or five) fundamental dimensions incorporate all criteria on quality of work, as follows:

- productivity of work: adequate remuneration, lifelong learning opportunities, professional career (security);
- equity at work: non-discrimination and equality, diversity (dignity);
- security and social protection: health and safety at work, stability of employment, social security, working time (security);
- dignity and social dialogue: work-life balance, flexibility, social dialogue and workers' involvement (dignity and flexibility);
- opportunities to work in conditions of freedom: acceptable jobs, access to the labour market, economic context (dignity).

This approach to quality leads to the consideration that any definition of "quality of work" must be built around three connected pillars, at least from a workers' point of view. These are security, flexibility and dignity of workers. They can be examined either in relation to a specific job or in relation to a full working life.

Security	**Flexibility**	**Dignity**
in the job: Stability, health and safety, working time, appropriate remuneration	*in the job:* Work-life balance, working time and schedules	*in the job:* Trade-union freedom, social dialogue, equality and non-discrimination
of employment: Income security and social protection	*of employment:* Training, education and bottom-up careers	*of employment:* Freely choose a decent job

Job security essentially consists of stability, the health and safety of the worker, length of employment and appropriate wages. Security of employment is about the extent to which workers' salary is guaranteed and social security services are being offered.

Secondly, job flexibility gives workers the ways and means to enjoy a proper work-life balance, with notable regard to working time and hours. As for flexibility of employment, it must offer the worker lifelong learning and bottom-up career opportunities.

Finally, the dignity deserved by each worker at work must allow him/her to take part in social dialogue and to enjoy freedom of associa-

the UNRISD (D. Ghaï, "Decent work: Concept and indicators", *International Labour Review*, Vol. 142, No. 2, Geneva, p. 115).

tion, equality and non-discrimination. Dignity of employment focuses on the possibility for any worker to freely choose and find a decent job.

Considering these three pillars, it would seem that flexicurity, whose aim is to conciliate flexibility and security in the same social policy, could be in line with the promotion of quality of work. However, in order for flexicurity to be efficient and to become a real implementable social policy, the economic perception of flexicurity should be replaced by a new vision centered on workers' needs; therefore, the two components of the concept – flexibility and security – should be redefined in line with the abovementioned conception of job quality.

The concept of dignity, to which we referred above, will then permit the implementation of flexicurity measures, due to the enhancement of the role of social partners, a guarantee of a healthy, growing economy and massive investment in workers' social protection.

Conclusion: Implementation of Flexicurity and Improvement of Quality of Work

In order to implement a real policy to promote quality and decent work, all political and economic players must collaborate and coordinate their action. This is a *sine qua non* condition for the establishment of a common minimum goal and the implementation of economic and employment policies as well as the subsequent improvement in employment rates, quality of work and economic growth. The creation of jobs is indeed an essential prerequisite to any improvement in quality of work, which has beneficial effects on economic growth provided that quality is guaranteed by a set of stringent conditions.

In other words, if the primary objective of the European social model is the enjoyment of a quality job for everyone, the creation of such jobs should be at the heart of social policies. Quality should also be defined on the basis of the three abovementioned dimensions, which are the dignity, security and flexibility of workers. For the time being, the quality of a specific job is primarily linked to the socio-economic security the worker gains from it. However, more flexible forms of employment are deemed to be necessary in the long run in order to increase employment rates.

Flexicurity seems to be an ideal solution in order to increase the number of jobs available while ensuring their quality. Flexicurity and quality can go hand in hand, but we consider that the European definition given to these concepts should be reappraised in the light of a less economic approach to the labour market.

On the one hand, the European definition of quality of work overlooks some essential dimensions, such as social protection and workers' income security, and does not put sufficient emphasis on some other criteria such as the possibility of a real social dialogue, the health and safety of workers at work and lifelong learning opportunities.

On the other hand, flexicurity requires public authorities to increase the amount of financial support for income substitution and improve employment incentives; financial resources could be made available by employers in exchange for more flexible employment protection regulation[54]. However, in its 2007 Communication, the Commission remained silent on this point. Yet, implementation of flexible employment relations without massive investments in education and guidance measures for job seekers will necessarily lead to deterioration in the quality of work and an increase in social deprivation.

Our analysis clearly highlights the fact that, although they seem mutually exclusive, quality and flexicurity are compatible, provided that flexicurity be understood as the implementation of measures aimed at securing professional careers (income security and social protection) and of flexibility measures for workers, such as lifelong learning opportunities, career breaks or adequate retraining, but also the possibility for workers to enjoy public services or resort to flexible labour law in order to better conciliate their private and professional lives. We also believe that compliance with these principles of flexicurity will ensure that workers will enjoy quality employment, insofar as the third dimension, which covers respect of fundamental rights at work, is properly taken into account.

---

54 B. Gomel, *op. cit.*, p. 113.

The Social Teaching of the Catholic Church and Quality of Work

Pascal CAILLAUD

Researcher – Law and Social Change (UMR-CNRS 6297)
Maison des Sciences de l'Homme Ange Guépin – University of Nantes

Introduction

A legal and normative analysis of the concept of quality of work requires that we look at the position of Social Teaching of the Catholic Church[1] on this matter for several reasons. At first, the Social Teaching of the Catholic Church is written down. It is basically a normative discourse, which may be interesting for researchers in labour law (Lattes, 2008). As noted by Alain Supiot, the texts of this doctrine are a catalogue of labour rights individual or collective forming a "*Corpus Juris laboris*" (Supiot, 1991). Secondly, there is a strong institutional link between the Holy See and some international organisations promoting the concept of quality of work or decent work. Such is the case of the ILO, whose action has been officially recognised by the Holy See by official visits of Popes in 1969 or 1982, by the nomination of a priest as a permanent civil servant to the ILO, since 1926, by the appointment in 1967 of a permanent observer in the International Labour Conference…

As recalled in the papal encyclical *Sollicitudo Rei Socialis* by John Paul II, 30 December 1987, the Catholic Church has manifested its active interest for social issues in various ways. Whereas the preferred mode of intervention is the publication of papal encyclicals, from the encyclical *Rerum Novarum* of Leo XIII in 1891 to *Caritas in Veritate* by Benedict XVI, 29 June 2009, the pastoral constitutions of Vatican II,

[1] We must specify in advance that this chapter deals only with the Social Teaching of the Catholic Church. There will be no account of the Protestant Social Ethics of the Reformed and Lutheran Churches (Muller, 2008) or of the Social Teaching of the Russian Orthodox Church, adopted by the Holy Synod, July 19, 2000, and submitted to the Council of Bishops of the Orthodox Church, 15 August 2000.

such as the radio messages of Pius XII, the 1th June 1941, and speeches such as those by John Paul II at the International Labour Conference, 15 June 1982 are also worthy of examination. However, although not very old if compared to the long history of the Catholic Church (*Rerum Novarum* was communicated in 1891), these texts are marked by their times, and can be grouped into three periods (Hilaire, 2009).

The first period from 1891 to World War II, characterises the foundation of this teaching and is marked by the publication of *Rerum Novarum* (Leo XIII) in 1891, *Quadragesimo anno* 1931, *Mit Brennender Sorge* and *Divini Redemptoris* in 1937 by Pius XI.

A second period began with *Mater et Magistra* (1961) and *Pacem in Terris* (1963) by John XXIII and was completed in 1987 by *Sollicitudo Rei Socialis* from John Paul II. With the conciliar texts of Vatican II (*Gaudium et Spes* and *Humanae Dignitatis* in 1965) but also two encyclicals by Paul VI (*Populorum Progresso* in 1967 *Octogesima Adveniens* in 1971) and several encyclicals by John Paul II (*Redemptor Hominis* in 1979, *Dives in Misericordia* in 1980 and especially *Laborem Exercens* in 1981), this period is marked by the globalisation of the teaching, which takes heed of the problems in development and migration.

The third period began with the encyclical *Centesimus Annus* by John Paul II in 1991, while celebrating the centenary of *Rerum Novarum*, and coinciding with the fall of communism. A feature of this encyclical is to propose a "rereading of the encyclical of Leo XIII" and "bring a contemporary look at the new things around us" (RN, 2). Also this text includes more than a hundred citations of past encyclicals, still considered valid (Hilaire, 2009), and constituting an assessment and a first codification of Social Teaching. With economic globalisation and the beginning of the economic crisis, Benedict XVI kept up this trend with the encyclicals *Deus Caritas Est* in 2005 and especially *Caritas in veritate*, in 2009, dedicated to development, the economy and finance.

This sequence of texts over 120 years[2], complicates a global understanding of the social teaching. Recognising this problem, John Paul II asked the Pontifical Council for Justice and Peace to develop a *Compendium of the Social Teaching of the Church*, in order to present organically and systematically the basic points of doctrine (Pontifical Council for Justice and Peace, 2008).

---

[2] We use the following abbreviations in this chapter: Rerum Novarum (*RN*); Quadragesimo anno (*QA*); Mit Brennender Sorge (*MBS*); Divini Redemptoris (*DR*); Mater et Magistra (*MM*); Pacem in Terris (*PT*); Sollicitudo Rei Socialis (*SRS*); Gaudium et Spes (*GS*); Humanae Dignitatis (*HD*); Populorum Progresso (*PP*); Octogesima Adveniens (*OA*); Redemptor Hominis (*RH*); Dives in Misericordia (*DM*); Laborem Exercens (*LE*); Centesimus Annus (*CA*); Deus Caritas Est (*DCE*); Caritas in Veritate (*CV*).

In several Member States of the European Union, political parties (Christian Democrats) and trade unions (the French CFTC, for example) make explicit reference to Christianity in their names, and to Catholic Social teaching in their statutes. At the international level, as in the ILO which established its policy of promoting decent work in the search for "common welfare" (Article III of the Declaration of Philadelphia) or as in the EU which established its policy of "quality employment" in the context of the search for the "welfare of workers" (European Commission, 2003), the Social Teaching of the Catholic Church is based on finding the "common good". It therefore seems necessary to consider, in an institutional perspective, the research of common good by the Social Teaching of the Catholic Church before analysing the approach of the quality of work by the successive texts that form it.

I. Social Teaching of the Catholic Church and International Labour Law: the Common Good

If *Rerum Novarum* refers repeatedly to the concept of teaching (*RN*, 19), it was on the occasion of the publication of the encyclical *Quadragesimo Anno*, in 1931, that the notion of "social and economic teaching" appeared (*QA*, 19), a name repeated again by Pius XII in his radio address of 1th June 1941, commemorating the 50th anniversary of *Rerum Novarum:* "*Già il nostro Predecessore Pio XI esaltò nella prima parte della sua enciclica commemorativa la splendida messe, cui aveva maturata la Rerum novarum, germe fecondo, donde si svolse una dottrina sociale cattolica*". To mark the centenary of *Rerum Novarum*, John Paul II underlines that Leo XIII's encyclical is the source of what would come to be called the "Social Teaching" of the Church, or even "social magisterium" (*CA*, *2*).

Many political parties or national trade unions make claims for Christian Democracy in general and Social Teaching in particular. However as part of a study on policies on "quality of work," carried by major international organisations in charge of social issues, it is necessary to analyse the relationship between the Social Teaching of the Catholic Church and these organisations.

A. The Nature of the Social Teaching of the Catholic Church

The concept of "Social Teaching" does not seem so easy to define. "*It therefore belongs to the field, not of ideology, but of theology and particularly of moral theology*" (*LE*, *3* and *SRS*, *41*). Therefore, it should not be conceived as a third path between socialism and liberalism, but as a category in itself (Pontifical Council for Justice and Peace, 2008).

However, it seems that a distinction should be made between the faith and theology: Faith is the vital relationship between the believer and Christ, the source of this Faith, whilst theology is the "reflection of the intelligence on revealed truth, the effort of reason to articulate and demonstrate the consistency between the revelation and the order of nature and the experience" (Minnerath, 2010). Social Teaching needs both theology and faith and must be analysed as the authentic explanation of the Church's faith under the authority of the Magisterium (Minnerath, 2010).

Although now synthesised in the *Compendium*, the Social Teaching was not originally thought of as the organic form of a codification in the mind of the Catholic Church. It was formed over time, through the texts of the Magisterium on social issues, and should be regarded as back in the specific historical context of each text. This can be illustrated by the reference in *Centesimus Annus* to the formulation of *Rerum Novarum* regarding the right to a just wage, "*Would that these words, written at a time when what has been called "unbridled capitalism" was pressing forward, should not have to berepeated today with the same severity*"(*CA*, *8*).

Is it a normative doctrine? Does it have a prescriptive effect on its recipients? On the occasion of the *Sollicitudo Rei Socialis* encyclical on matters of development, John Paul II reminded the Church that it does not propose a system nor economic programs and policies, and has no "technical solutions" to provide (*SRS*, 41). The Social Teaching of he Catholic Church is not an ideology, but a *reflection* on the realities of the place of men in human society, and an *interpretation* of these realities in light of the Gospel (*SRS*, 41). Its purpose is not that it should apply to States or international organisations, but to guide every Christian's behaviour. Also, as a "moral theology" (*LE*, *3*), the instruction and dissemination of Social Teaching are part of "the evangelizing mission of the Church" and is intended "to guide the conduct of the person" (*SRS*, *41*). Therefore Social Teaching guides each person to "put the law of God in the earthly city" (*GS*, 43).

Everyone must try to change the rights of society, conscious that the rule of law must "take its source and legitimacy" in "moral order" (*GS*, *74*) and find its justification and its accomplishment in a search for the "common good" (*GS*, 26) (D'Onorio, 1989). Whereas moral order refers to "a transcendent, universal, absolute, of equal value for all" (*MM*, *105*), beyond the State (*GS*, *74*) and legal standards (*DH*, *7*), the common good includes "*the sum of those conditions of social life which allow social groups and their individual members relatively thorough and ready access to their own fulfillment, today takes on an increasingly universal complexion and consequently involves rights and duties with respect to the whole human race*" (*GS, 26*).

On the basis of these principles of individual commitment, the Church wishes to spread its Social Teaching.

B. Social Teaching and International Organisations

Whereas many political parties or national unions have referred to Christian Democracy ideology in general or Social Teaching in particular, our observations will refer only to organisations and groups at international level. In this chapter on the relationship between the Social Teaching of the Catholic Church and the "quality of work", it would appear that this last concept is carried by major international organisations in charge of social issues. This is the case with "Decent Work" in the International Labour Organisation (ILO) and the investment of the European Union (EU) in "job quality".

1. The End of the International Confederation of the Christian Trade Unions

At the European or world level, today there is no international organisation left aiming to confederate Christian unions and confederations claiming this doctrine.

At world level and after World War I, a conference in The Hague, in June 1919, brought together the main Christian unions in European countries (Austria, Belgium, Spain, France, Hungary, Italy, the Netherlands, Switzerland, and Czechoslovakia) which formed the International Federation of Christian Trade Unions (IFCTU). At European level, the IFCTU in 1958 created a European organisation gathering together six members from the Europe Community.

The "deconfessionnalisation" of the IFCTU began in the 1960s, in 1964, when the Congress of Liege limited the Christian references in the statutes to a simple sentence, and in 1968, the Luxembourg Congress decided to change the IFCTU into the World Confederation of Labour (WCL) to allow the non-Christian trade-union organisations of the third world to affiliate. However, the declaration of principles adopted in 1968 stipulated that the WCL is guided, "by a spiritual conception which is based on the conviction that man and the universe are created by God or by other designs that are in convergence with it".

In May 1974, the European part of the IFCTU was dissolved and its members joined the European Trade Union Confederation (ETUC).

To marginalise the World Federation of Trade Unions (WFTU), made up of unions affiliated with or sympathetic to communist parties), the WCL launched a process of increasing co-operation with the ICFTU

(International Confederation of Free Trade Unions). It started in 2006 with the merger and dissolution of the two organisations to give birth to the International Trade Union Confederation (ITUC). Their articles or statements no longer make any references to religion.

2. *The Relationship with the European People's Party*

Founded in 1965, the European Union of Christian Democrats (EUCD) joined together Christian Democratic political parties in Europe. In 1976, Congress transformed the EUCD into the European People's Party, which asked questions about Christian references within the party. It included three streams of thought. The first wanted the party to put forward the Christian Democrat conception of human society. The second wanted to promote the integration of the English and Danish conservative parties, whose countries joined the EEC in 1973. The third wished to reinforce the deconfessionnalisation, based on the legitimate right of Christians to political pluralism, as affirmed by Vatican II (De Brouwer, 1991). Finally, the exact official name of the party will be "European People's Party – Federation of Christian Democratic parties of the European Community." The preamble of its constitution begins:

> The following statute, based upon our Christian-Democratic concept of man and society and our desire to encourage in Europe a community of free individuals and responsible citizens each taking a full part in the social economic and political structures of a pluralist society, a community which is just, peaceful and united in its dealings with all the peoples of the world, is hereby enacted.

The progressive enlargement of the EPP to the European conservative parties, or non-religious parties, including those from accession countries from 1995 to 2004, did not change this view. So the last EPP statutes, adopted in Bonn in 2009, begin as follows:

> On the basis of the Christian view of mankind and the Christian Democratic concept of society, of their joint will to create a federal European Union as a Union of free peoples and citizens conscious of their own responsibilities, the Christian Democrat, Centrist and like-minded parties of the European People's Party as heirs of Europe's Founding Fathers accept these responsibilities and create an international non-profit association. This association will be a member of the Christian/Centrist Democrat International (CDI), a worldwide organisation of Christian Democrats and like-minded political parties and the International Democrat Union (IDU), a worldwide organisation of Conservative, Christian Democrat and like-minded political parties of the centre and centre right.

The organisation of the workers of the EPP, the European Union of Christian Democratic Workers (EUCDW), brings together Social Christian workers in the European countries, according to its statutes, who have embraced the principles of Catholic Social Teaching and Protestant social ethics and the goals of the EUCDW and EPP" (Article 1 of the statutes of EUCDW).

The Social Teaching of the Catholic Church is such an important reference for the EPP, evidenced by the speech of Mgr. Minnerath on 14 May 1991 at the EPP group for the centenary of *Rerum Novarum* (Minnerath, 2010) and recently, the symposium organised by parliamentary group and COMECE (Commissio Episcopatuum Communitatis Europensis), in 14 September 2010, on the encyclical *Caritas in Veritate*.

3. *The Links between the Social Teaching of the Catholic Church and the ILO*

Since it was founded in 1919, the International Labour Organisation received the support of the Christian Democratic Trade Union. Thus, in 1918, the Catholic Belgian and French federation of labour unions, asked that the peace treaty contain essential terms for a protective labour legislation. In 1919, the founding congress of the IFCTU voted a resolution that the peace treaty includes a commitment to develop international labour legislation and an International Institute of Labour, representing each country (Barbier, 1972).

After its creation, the ILO also sought and obtained various and important forms of moral support from the Holy See.

At first, Albert Thomas, a French socialist and first director of the ILO, desired the establishment of relations between the Holy See and the ILO. This resulted in 1926 in the nomination of a priest as a permanent civil servant to the ILO. From 1926 to-date, the post will always be given to a Jesuit priest from the Popular Action, which in 1961 became the CERAS – Centre for Research and Social Actions (Joblin, 2003). A concrete illustration of this presence, is a seminar in 2002 under the coordination of Father Dominique Peccoud, the then civil servant at the ILO, in cooperation with the World Council of Churches (WCC) on the issue of decent work. Devoted to the collection of views on philosophical and spiritual issues, a book has been produced containing the views of Judaism, Catholicism, Protestantism, Islam, Confucianism and Buddhism (Peccoud, 2004).

This support is also reflected in the official recognition of ILO action by the Holy See through its encyclicals or by official visits by Popes to the International Labour Conference.

In *Quadragesimo anno*, Pius XI suggested a link between the action of the ILO and the Social Teaching of the Catholic Church:

> Furthermore, after the terrible war, when the statesmen of the leading nations were attempting to restore peace on the basis of a thorough reform of

> social conditions, did not they, among the norms agreed upon to regulate in accordance with justice and equity the labour of the workers, give sanction to many points that so remarkably coincide with Leo's principles and instructions as to seem consciously taken therefrom? (QA, 22)

He added that "*Furthermore, since the various nations largely depend on one another in economic matters and need one another's help, they should strive with a united purpose and effort to promote by wisely conceived pacts and institutions a prosperous and happy international cooperation in economic life*" (*QA, 89*).

John XXIII in *Mater et Magistra*, paid tribute to the ILO:

> We must also express here Our heartfelt appreciation of the work that is being done by the International Labour Organisation – popularly known in various countries as the O.I.L. or I.L.O. or O.I.T. For many years now it has been making an effective and valued contribution to the establishment in the world of an economic and social order marked by justice and humanity, an order which recognises and safeguards the lawful rights of the workingman (MM, 103).

To mark the 50th anniversary of the organisation, Paul VI was the first Pope to go to Geneva. In his speech, he referred to the *salutary role of the ILO.* In addition to this visit, the support of Paul VI to the ILO was also apparent by the appointment in 1967 of a permanent observer, whom the Board decided to invite to the Conference each year.

In the same vein, John Paul II at the beginning of his pontificate, paid tribute to the ILO, initially by embracing its actions in his encyclical *Laborem Exercens* (*LE, 11*), then by going to the International Conference Labour, on 15 June 1982, where he affirmed that the goals of the International Labour Organisation were very similar to those that the Apostolic Church wanted to pursue in its own field and with resources appropriate to their mission (CERAS, 2009)

Beyond the concrete action of the ILO, one of the explanations to this support the Holy See holds in the reference to "common good", present both in the policy statement of the ILO, and the Social Teaching of the Catholic Church.

Article III of the Declaration of Philadelphia, on 10 May 1944 (Supiot, 2010), concerning the aims and objectives of the organisation, states that "the Conference recognises the solemn obligation of the International Labour Organisation to further among the nations of the world programmes which will achieve: full employment and the raising of standards of living; the employment of workers in the occupations in which they can have the satisfaction of giving the fullest measure of their skill and attainments and make their greatest contribution to the common well-being".

However, this reference to the common good is at the heart of the Social Teaching (Supiot, 1991). The *Compendium* considers the common good as one of its four permanent principles with the dignity of the human person, subsidiarity and solidarity. What does common good mean? It should not be reduced to "*the sum total of particular interests; rather it involves an assessment and integration of those interests on the basis of a balanced hierarchy of values; ultimately, it demands a correct understanding of the dignity and the rights of the person*" (*CA*, 47). Looking for the common good is a responsibility of each person (*Octogesima Adveniens*, 23) as the public authorities are "responsible for the common good" (*MM, 54*).

II. The Quality of Work in the Social Teaching of the Catholic Church

Quality of work in the Social Teaching of the Catholic Church has two dimensions. On the one hand, there are many texts devoted to the place of work in human societies. Beyond these considerations, the pontifical encyclicals, from 1891 to-date, also try to define, as concretely as possible, the real rights of workers.

A. Status and Boundaries of Work

In his encyclical *Laborem Exercens*, John Paul II returned to the fundamental link between work and the existence of man on earth, a link that appears in Genesis (*LE, 4*).

The work is a fundamental dimension of human existence on earth, a part of the original condition of man and precedes his fall: it is neither a punishment nor a curse. Work became tiresome because of original sin. It was only by the sweat from his face that Man will draw his nourishment from the ground (*Genesis* 3, 17.19).

The question of work is the key to all the social questions (*LE, 3*), the gradual solution of this question must be sought in an effort to make human life more human (*GS*, 38).

Work has two dimensions, objective and subjective. In its objective sense, work is understood by a technical meaning (*LE, 5*). The development of technology, whether in agriculture or industry, allows the technique to be construed and understood as a set of instruments being used by Man, as man's ally, facilitating his work. It can also however turn out to be Man's enemy, especially when the mechanisation of work supplants him and takes away personal satisfaction (*LE, 5*).

In its subjective sense, the subject of work is Man. While it's true that man is destined for work and called to work, work is "for man" and not man "for work" (*LE, 6*).

We have to compare this vision of work with the ILO constitution which has as a solemn obligation to assist the implementation of programmes to ensure "the employment of workers in the occupations in which they can have the satisfaction of giving the fullest measure of their skill and attainments and make their greatest contribution to the common well-being". It's difficult to find this meaning in the provisions of the Treaty on the Functioning of the European Union whose article 145 is "a coordinated strategy for employment and particularly for promoting a skilled, trained and adaptable workforce and labour markets responsive to economic change" The Social Teaching of the Catholic Church recognises the primacy of the subjective meaning of work in its objective dimension.

Work has a social dimension. "Work is *work with others* and *work for others*" (*AC, 31*). "Unless a social and juridical order watches over the exercise of work, unless the various occupations, being interdependent, cooperate with and mutually complete one another, and, what is still more important, unless mind, material things, and work combine and form as it were a single whole. Therefore, where the social and individual nature of work is neglected, it will be impossible to evaluate work justly and pay it according to justice" (*QA, 23*). Because of its subjective and social meaning, *work is a moral obligation, a duty for Man.* In *Laborem Exercens*, John Paul II recalls that Man has to work not just because God ordered it, but also in deference to his neighbour, his family, his nation and all of humanity to which he belongs. This obligation is born from the ambivalent situation of Man, the heir to past generations and their work, and co-architect of future generations (*LE, 16*).

Finally, *work is a right.* As recalled by the Vatican II Council, every man has the duty to work loyally and the right to work; society must help citizens by allowing them to obtain sufficient employment (*GS*, 67). However, this importance given to work has a two-fold limitation, prohibiting the activity of certain people, or calling for the protection of others regarding their particular situation.

In *Rerum Novarum*, the condemnation of *child labour* is strongly affirmed:

> in regard to children, great care should be taken not to place them in workshops and factories until their bodies and minds are sufficiently developed. For, just as very rough weather destroys the buds of spring, so does too early an experience of life's hard toil blight the young promise of a child's faculties, and render any true education impossible (RN, 33).

Similarly, *the situation of women* was apprehended. Oscillating between protection of motherhood and the necessary claims of women to have their place in the labour market, the Social Teaching of the Catholic Church wants the presence of women in this labour market to be guaranteed. Noting that women work in almost all sectors of life, *Laborem Exercens* expresses the wish that they can fulfill their missions "*in accordance with their own nature, without being discriminated against and without being excluded from jobs for which they are capable, but also without lack of respect for their family aspirations and for their specific role in contributing, together with men, to the good of society*" (*LE, 19*).

The place of disabled persons is also approached. A full member of humankind, the disabled person has rights and, as such, his participation in the life of society according to his abilities must be facilitated. Therefore "*the various bodies involved in the world of labour, both the direct and the indirect employer, should therefore by means of effective and appropriate measures foster the right of disabled people to professional training and work, so that they can be given a productive activity suited to them*" (*LE*, 22). As for all other workers, special attention should be paid to physical and psychological working conditions, to fair wages, their opportunity for promotion, etc.

By 1981, before the rise of the extreme right in Europe, the Social Teaching of the Catholic Church draws attention to the situation *of immigrant workers* and the necessary protection of their rights. It acknowledges the right of immigrants to seek better living conditions. It is necessary to develop in each country, a just legislation on the rights of immigrant workers, particularly in terms of personal life, family and social conditions (*LE, 16*). But, this legislation must not lead to disadvantages for immigrant workers in the field of labour rights in comparison to other national workers or an opportunity for financial or social exploitation. "*The value of work should be measured by the same standard and not according to the difference in nationality, religion or race*" (*LE, 23*).

Finally, the importance given to work must be reconciled with family life, another pillar of the Catholic religion. "*Work constitutes a foundation for the formation of family life, which is a natural right and something that man is called to*" (*LE, 10*). On the one hand, work makes possible the foundation of the family by ensuring its livelihood. On the other hand, the whole process of work must be organised and adapted to respect the requirements of a person and his/her life forms, and above all of family life (*LE, 19*). According to article 10 of the Charter of the Family of 22 October 1983, the organisation of work must allow the family members to live together, and should not be an obstacle to the unit, the wellbeing, the health and the stability of the family, by offering the possibility of good leisure activity.

B. Rights at Work

As Alain Supiot wrote, there is in the texts of the doctrine, a catalogue of human labour rights, a "*Corpus Juris laboris*" (*Supiot*, 1991). Three categories of traditional rights for the specialist in social law emerged from the various encyclicals: individual rights, collective rights and rights to social protection.

This categorisation, however, rests on the distinction drawn by Social Teaching, especially the encyclical *Laborem Exercens*, between *the direct employer* and *the indirect employer*, a distinction that identifies the debtor's right. The *direct employer is* the person or institution with whom the worker enters directly into a work contract in accordance with definite conditions. We must understand many different factors for *the indirect* employer, unlike the direct employer, that exercise a determining influence on the shaping of both the work contract and, consequently, of just or unjust relationships in the field of human labour (*LE, 16*). "*The indirect employer substantially determines one or other facet of the labour relationship, thus conditioning the conduct of the direct employer when the latter determines in concrete terms the actual work contract and labour relations*" (*LE, 17*). The State must be considered as an indirect employer, whose role is to have a just labour policy, by the determination of a legal framework inside which economic relationships are included, presupposing certain equality between the parties (*CA, 15*).

1. Individual Rights

The remuneration of the worker is the first issue raised by the Social Teaching of the Catholic Church. The payment of a just wage is an obligation for the employer, as presented in the encyclical *Rerum Novarum.* The encyclical even allows an exception to the principle of the freedom of contract in order to safeguard this objective.

> Let the working man and the employer make free agreements, and in particular let them agree freely as to the wages; nevertheless, there underlies a dictate of natural justice more imperious and ancient than any bargain between man and man, namely, that wages ought not to be insufficient to support a frugal and well-behaved wage-earner. If through necessity or fear of a worse evil the workman accepts harder conditions because an employer or contractor will afford him no better, he is made the victim of force and injustice (*RN, 34*).

The importance of fair wages is reaffirmed by *Laborem Exercens*; the key question of social ethics and remuneration for work remains the most important way to achieve justice in the relations between workers and employers (*LE, 19*).

The question of time devoted to work and the rest-time of workers is also central in the founding texts of the Doctrine. In *Rerum Novarum*, the right is affirmed to rest, within the meaning of "a rest hallowed by religion" (*RN, 33*). This right is extended by *Laborem Exercens* to regular weekly rest, comprising Sunday at least, but also a longer period of rest, called annual leave, or any leave taken several times during the year in shorter periods (*LE*, 19). Although the issue of the remuneration of this leave is not explicitly raised by the encyclical, it appears normal, because this issue is covered under the services and welfare expenditure. With the weekly rest and paid leave, the recognition of non-working holidays is also affirmed, so that "in the respect of religious freedom and the common good of all" (*Compendium, 286*), national laws recognise Sunday and the liturgy.

Finally, the protection of the health and the mental or physical safety of employees is a concern of the papal encyclicals. If the right to social security is asserted to compensate for any injury to employees because of their activity (see below), the prevention of this injury is also invoked, especially against the new forms of management. Thus, Social Teaching affirms the right to have workplaces and working methods which do not adversely affect the physical health of workers and do not adversely affect their moral integrity (*LE, 19*).

If these requirements – fair pay, right to rest, protection of physical and mental health – appear as minimum guarantees for the worker, it should also be noted that the Social Teaching of the Catholic Church, in *Mater et Magistra*, considers the elevation of skills and qualifications as a priority towards the development of scientific progress and the modernisation of production systems. In this perspective, it is therefore necessary to empower workers to educate themselves and study. Written in 1961, *Mater et Magistra* fits perfectly into the context of promoting lifelong education for employees, as advocated at the time by UNESCO (Faure, 1971). This concern can be found in most texts from the Magisterium, to *Centesimus Annus*, which defend at the same time the recycling of professionals in order to facilitate the transition of workers from crisis sectors to other sectors in development, but also the development of policies at the expense of the State and Society as a whole to give workers knowledge and skills always to better their work and render it more skilled and productive (*CA, 15*).

2. Collective Rights

Referring to the abolition of their professional corporations in the 18th century, as a source for workers' protection, Leo XIII in 1889 recognised the right to form associations and corporations (*RN, 20*) whether composed of workers only, or mixed, involving both workers and employers. Whereas most texts of the Social Teaching of the Catholic Church confirm the interest in trade unions and professional groups, *Gaudium et Spes* construed this as a fundamental right of the individual (*GS, 68*) The encyclical *Laborem Exercens* confirmed the importance of trade unions in modern industrialised societies (*LE, 20*). As an "essential element of social life", trade unions must help to defend the existential interests of workers. While condemning the class struggle (*LE, 20*) and the organic link between unions and political parties (*EA, 20*), the Social Teaching recognises the status of trade unions as a "*mouthpiece for the struggle for social justice*" (*LE, 20*).

Other collective rights of the workers (Dorssemont, 2011) arise from this recognition of the trade union role.

The right to strike, is recognised as just and legitimate method by the Social Teaching of the Catholic Church, and is directed as a sort of ultimatum addressed primarily to employers but also to any "competent body" (*LE, 20*) Its exercise should not result in personal criminal sanctions for the worker who has taken advantage of it (*LE, 19*). This right may however be limited when it comes to essential services to the socioeconomic life: it must be always be recognised, and be included, if necessary, in appropriate legislation.

Also of relevance is *the participation of workers in the life of the company*. A truly human community must provide workers with an active role in its operation, not only by consultation to gather their opinion but also by giving them the right to take part in its functioning one (*MM, 92*). Although never explicitly mentioned, the bodies for worker representation in the organisation of the company have indeed to promote the participation of everybody in business management, either directly or through freely chosen representatives (*GS, 68*).

Finally, there is *collective bargaining*, explicitly recognised from the pontificate of John XXIII as a means of cooperation between capital and labour (*MM, 97*). Little evoked in the various texts of the Social Teaching, the bargaining capacity of unions and the freedom of association, however, are strongly defended by the recent "*Caritas in Veritate*" encyclical, *vis-à-vis* the limitations introduced by governments for reasons of economic utility.

3. The Right to Social Protection

It is probably on the issue of social protection that the Social Teaching of the Catholic Church was recently most insistent, especially during the pontificate of John Paul II. Whereas *Mater et Magistra* evoked the necessity of providing insurance and social security, it focused on this issue in particular relation to the agricultural policy in order to avoid excessive disparity in protection between agricultural workers and those in industry or trade (*MM, 135*).

Written shortly after the start of the economic crisis, *Laborem Exercens* goes further by considering as necessary the introduction of various social benefits whose goal is to provide health care to workers and their families. Thus, they need access to cheap or even free medical assistance to defray expenses for health care, especially in case of accident (*LE, 19*). The right to retirement and old-age insurance is also affirmed and seems considered as part of the indices, together with the remuneration of the work itself and a just definition of the relationship between the worker and the employer (*LE, 19*). In the same way, the situation of unemployment, "a real social disaster" requires the indirect employers, national or international agents responsible for the whole orientation of labour policy, to establish benefits for the unemployed to ensure them of financial assistance for themselves and their families (*LE, 18*).

Conclusions

Although considered a "*Corpus Juris laboris*" (*Supiot*, 1991), the Social Teaching of the Catholic Church is constantly evolving and is the object of regular consolidation as shown in the analysis of its historical evolution. The moral and religious nature of the precepts did not prevent the Social Teaching of the Catholic Church from expanding its influence on major international organisations in charge of the question of quality of work, such as the ILO and EU. The place it allocates to work in a general sense, in human society, the description of individual, collective and social rights of workers, can be considered close to the requirements of the ILO on decent work.

Like the ILO in promoting decent work, it does not impose coercive rules, but encourages States, through their citizens, to work to develop the worker protection. Just as the ILO, the common good is the main objective. Also in accordance with the ILO, with its universal vocation, the Social Teaching of the Catholic Church is addressed to all countries and legal systems on the planet.

This is how it differs from European policy of "work quality". This policy is intended for the 27 Member States of the European Union whose economic and legal systems are fairly similar. Also, we can find in the list of the rights proclaimed by the Social Teaching of the Catholic Church, which we have analysed, the majority of European dimensions on the quality of work and employment: such as the intrinsic job quality, skills, life-long learning, career development, gender equality, health and safety at work, inclusion and access to the labour market, work organisation and work-life balance, social dialogue and worker involvement, diversity and non-discrimination (European commission, 2001).

But, the European issues of flexibility and productivity (overall work performance) are not regarded as major subjects in the texts of the Social Teaching of the Catholic Church, even in the most recent. This is probably because the most important difference between the European approach to work quality and the Social Teaching of the Catholic Church is in the relationship between Man and work: when *Laborem exercens* proclaims that "*work is 'for man' and not man 'for work'* (*LE*, *6*), Article 145 of TCE promotes "*a skilled, trained and adaptable work-force and labour markets responsive to economic change*".

Part II

Some Essential Aspects of Collective and Individual Rights at Work

The Concept of Employee and Quality of Employment

Silvia BORELLI

Researcher, Labour Law, University of Ferrara

I. Quality of Work and Employment Status

"Quality in work – *better jobs* – means not only looking at, or taking account of, the existence of paid employment but also looking at the characteristics of that employment. It is a relative and a multi-dimensional concept. In its broadest definition, it involves taking into account: the objective characteristics related to employment, both the wider work environment and the specific characteristics of the job; worker characteristics – the characteristics the employee brings to the job; the match between worker characteristics and job requirements; and the subjective evaluation (job satisfaction) of these characteristics by the individual worker"[1].

Like the decent work agenda promoted by the ILO[2], the focus of European policy is not only on the creation of jobs, but also on the creation of jobs of acceptable quality. Therefore, it is important to consider the type of work contract[3].

---

1 European Commission, *Employment and social policies: a framework for investing in quality*, COM(2001) 313 final.

2 See ILO, *Toolkit for Mainstreaming Employment and Decent Work*, 2007.

3 EU quality in work dimension "Flexibility and security" takes into account the specific indicator "diversity and reasons for contractual and working arrangements". "Employment status" is one of the European Foundation Job and Employment Quality indicators, while "Employment security" is one of the four key aspects of quality of work considered by EF (*Quality of work and employment in Europe*, 2007). A heading of the core ILO statistical indicators on decent work concerns "stability and security of work". "Non-standard forms of employment" is also one of the six sub-indices defined by the ETUI to describe different aspects of job quality (Leschke, Watt, Finn, 2008: 8).

Labour Law was created and developed to protect those who work under an open-ended and full-time employment contract. The standard employment contract is nowadays eroding, while part-time and temporary contracts are becoming more widespread. Non-standard workers are usually employed in low skilled and low-income jobs (with a low level of job satisfaction), have less career opportunities and no job security. They also tend to work in more hazardous jobs. Moreover, these relationships result in disadvantages in social security benefits, related to the value of benefits received (because the maximum duration of payments is shorter, the amount of payment is lower or the waiting period to qualify for a treatment is longer) or even related to the eligibility for benefits[4]. Again, trade unions have great difficulty in organising and defending non-standard workers due to their instability and the competition with standard workers[5]. Other negative economic effects have been identified, such as the loss of work-based skills, a reduction in private consumption, caused by increasing uncertainty about future income, a rise in private debt payment defaults or an increasing burden for unemployment assistance and other welfare schemes.

Transitions towards job stability[6] are difficult and have become even more so, given the recent crisis, which has caused a massive expulsion of non-standard workers from the labour market[7]. The rise of such atypical (sometimes precarious) forms of work has generated a segmen-

---

4 For example, in some cases part-time employees working less than a specific number of hours per week are not insured against main risks, or temporary workers on contracts below a certain duration are not eligible for selected benefits (*Flexicurity: indicators on the coverage of certain social protection benefits for persons in flexible employment in the EU, final report*, Alphametrics Ltd., 2007).

5 European Foundation for the Improvement of Living and Working Conditions, *Trade Union strategies to recruit new groups of workers*, 2010, p. 13.

6 Job stability is measured in terms of continuity or discontinuity of employment over a given period of time, whereas job security depends on the aspects of the current job as well as the possibility of alternative jobs. "Transition between non-employment and within employment and within employment by pay level and type of contract" is considered in the context of the EU intrinsic job quality dimension. The Transition Labour Market Theory "emphasizes the need to ease secured transitions between work, education and training, unemployment and inactivity, non-paid activity and family care. The point is to shift from labour market and social policies based on 'insider-outsider' logic to policies encompassing the whole lifecycle by securing professional trajectories, or to shift from security 'in' employment to security 'of' employment" (Pena-Casas, 2009, p. 56. See also: Levêque, 2010; Schmid G., 2010; Dickens, 2004).

7 See *Benchmarking Working Europe 2011*, Etui, p. 30. Dahl S.A., Nesheim T. and Olsen K. (2009) have spoken about "cumulative employment disadvantage": since the mobility from low quality jobs is low, disadvantages from early life continue into a working career.

tation of the labour market between well-protected workers with permanent contracts and less-protected workers with atypical contracts[8].

Moreover, the diffusion of atypical jobs produces an occupational segregation on the basis of gender, race, nationality and age. In fact, non-standard employment is heavily concentrated on women, young people, immigrants, i.e. on the more vulnerable part of the labour force[9].

From the job quality perspective, it should also be considered whether non-standard forms of work are exercised involuntarily. In some cases, new types of contract can be regarded as a gateway for disadvantaged groups towards occupation (for example, young labour market entrants), facilitate reintegration into the labour market or be a solution for work-life balance (especially, part-time contracts)[10]. In many cases, however, these forms of work are accepted only because a permanent or a full-time job could not be found. The European Foundation for the Improvement of Living and Working Conditions has therefore distinguished workers trapped in atypical forms of work from workers that want an atypical employment contract[11].

Moreover, flexibility is more frequently used to satisfy employers' production needs than workers time use preferences[12]. During the recent global recession, for example, short time working schemes (i.e. a temporary reduction in working time mainly aiming to maintain an existing employer/employee relationship) have been effective in reducing the vulnerability of employment and providing assistance to firms in economic difficulty[13].

8 A recent example of legislation aimed to correct the segmentation of the labour market, reduce fixed-term work, improve job stability and internal flexibility is the Ley 35/2010 adopted by the Spanish Parliament (Rodrìguez-Pinero y Bravo-Ferrer, 2010).

9 See *More and better jobs? Labour market developments in the Euro area since 1999*, Companion report to the ELNEP economic forecast and policy recommendations, 2008.

10 Involuntary non-standard workers should also include those who combine part-time work with care or household activities in the absence of sufficient affordable services for children and other dependent persons. Positive and negative aspects of part-time for the employer, the individual and the government are highlighted by the European Foundation for the Improvement of Living and Working Conditions in the *European Company Survey 2009. Part-time work in Europe* (see, in particular, table 1, p. 6).

The requirement to develop part-time work "on a voluntary basis" is stated in Clause 1 of the Framework Agreement on part-time work.

11 European Foundation for the Improvement of Living and Working Conditions, *Flexible forms of work: 'very atypical' contractual arrangements*, 2010.

12 For example, zero-hour and on-call workers are more likely to work during "unsocial hours"; temporary workers have less control over their working time.

13 Such schemes cover "benefits compensating for the loss of wage or salary due to formal short-time working arrangements, and/or intermittent work schedules, irre-

Finally, non-standard contracts could be (ab)used for the purpose of denying employees their rights. The ETUI report "*Benchmarking in Europe 2009*" underlines that "country differences in terms of temporary employment can be explained, at least in part, by regulations in force for regular contracts and the relative differences in employment protection legislation between regular and temporary contracts. Employers in countries where the regulation of permanent jobs is relatively lax will have fewer incentives to make use of temporary contracts. Stricter rules applicable to permanent contracts, on the other hand, may tend to increase the incidence of temporary work and to limit the extent to which temporary contracts will be converted into permanent ones". The creation of a dual labour market whereby firms aim at circumventing overly rigid dismissal rules by opting for temporary contracts is also considered in the context of "Flexible and reliable contractual arrangements", one of the four components of Flexicurity policy[14].

It should be clarified that most dimensions of job quality have been affected by the economic crisis. As a consequence, the concept of quality of work is going to be revised[15]. Attention has now shifted to sustaining employment levels and to creating more efficient indices[16], focused on economic growth and job productivity[17]. Guidelines for

---

spective of their cause, and where the employer/employee relationship continues". Looking forward, these schemes are likely to lose their effectiveness if a weak labour demand persists. The risk is that a "too late withdrawal of measures may carry substantial costs in terms of locking-in labour to declining activities, thereby preventing the necessary reallocation of resources, damaging future growth prospects, distorting competition and interfering with the functioning of the internal market" (A. Arpaia, N. Curci, E. Meyermans, J. Peschner and F. Pierini, 2010; *ERM REPORT 2010. Extending flexicurity – The potential of short-time working schemes*, European Foundation for the Improvement of Living and Working Conditions, 2010).

14 Manca, Governatori, Mascherini, 2010; Dickens, 2004: 601.

15 *An Agenda for new skills and jobs: A European contribution towards full employment*, COM(2010) 682 final, p. 15; *Ad Hoc Group report on the 2010 thematic review. Part 2. 'Quality in work'*, Report endorsed by Employment Committee (EMCO) on 24 November 2010.

16 "The security of employment can be the most important criterion of quality in a period of economic crisis while other criteria may seem more important in the more clement times". In the current revised EES and in the Social Policy Agenda for 2005-2010, quality of work and employment "is no longer presented as a crucial element to foster well-being of European citizens and workers or the European Social Model but increasingly interpreted in terms of job productivity and financial attractiveness for job creations" (R. Pena-Casas, 2009: 45).

17 The Europe 2020 strategy is entirely based on "growth", that should be smart, sustainable and inclusive. The Communication of European Commission (*Europe 2020. A strategy for smart, sustainable and inclusive growth*, COM(2010) 2020 final, p. 12) mentions "quality jobs" (and not job quality) only once, as an outcome of smart growth a strategy that "requires improving the quality of our education,

employment policies state that "Member States should introduce a combination of flexible and reliable contractual arrangements, active labour market policies, effective lifelong learning, policies to promote labour mobility, and adequate social security systems to secure labour market transitions accompanied by clear rights and responsibilities for the unemployed to actively seek work". But, Member States should also "tackle labour market segmentation with measures addressing precarious employment, underemployment and undeclared work" and address "the quality of jobs and employment conditions"[18]. Evidently, there is a contradiction between the two points: on the one hand, Member States should raise job quality and fight segmentation opposing precarious employment; on the other hand, they should promote flexible and reliable contractual arrangements and ensure the effective functioning of labour markets through investing in successful transitions. A possible solution can be found in the Annex 3 of *Annual Growth Survey*[19] where the Commission invites Member States to focus "on the reduction of segmentation in the labour market which could be facilitated by altering employment protection legislation, by for instance extending the use of open-ended contractual arrangements with a gradual increase of protection rights to diminish the existing divisions between those holding atypical and permanent contracts"[20].

The European Commission proposal widely differs from the one presented by the European Parliament, which calls "for the creation of flexible and secure contractual arrangements ensuring equal treatment", but "is firmly convinced that employment contracts of an indefinite duration must continue to be the main form of employment and considers that, in the context of modern work organisation, provision should be made for contracts that are flexible in terms of working arrangements and secure with regard to job protection and rights"[21].

---

strengthening our research performance, promoting innovation and knowledge transfer throughout the Union, making full use of information and communication technologies and ensuring that innovative ideas can be turned into new products and services", and that this "must be combined with entrepreneurship, finance, and a focus on user needs and market opportunities" (see Pochet, 2010; Marlier, Natali, 2010; Sepùlveda Gòmez, 2011: 298).

18 Council Decision of 21 October 2010 on guidelines for the employment policies of the Member States, guideline No. 7.

19 COM(2011) 11 final, p. 12.

20 See also Communication from the Commission, *An Agenda for new skills and jobs: A European contribution towards full employment*, COM(2010) 682 final, p. 5.

21 European Parliament Resolution of 6 July 2010 on atypical contracts, secured professional paths, and new forms of social dialogue, par. 35.

II. The Concept of Employee in European Law: Between *casuistique* and *systematique*

European Labour Law is shaped like a "mosaic law" (Rodotà, 2005, p. 19). Therefore, in this context, an "alphabet of concepts" is still absent (Kahn-Freund, 1967, p. 635). When the European legislator decides to regulate on a specific subject, he can develop European definitions or he can refer to the concepts of each Member State. The choice is strictly related to the purposes of the European law. If it is intended to establish a uniform level of protection throughout Member States, the concept of employee should have a European meaning. In fact, "if the definition of this term were a matter within the competence of national law, it would therefore be possible for each Member State to modify the meaning of [...] [this concept] and to eliminate at will the protection afforded by the Treaty to certain categories of person", so that European Law would be deprived of all effect and his objectives would be frustrated (ECJ, 19 March 1964, case 75/63, *Unger*). Whereas, if European law is intended to coordinate national laws (ECJ, 24 April 1980, case 110/79, *Coonan*) or to achieve partial harmonisation (ECJ, 11 July 1985, case 105/84, *Danmols Inventar*), each Member State is free to define an employee in the context of its own national legislation.

As a consequence, "there is no single definition of worker/employed or self-employed person in European law; it varies according to the area in which the definition is to be applied" (ECJ, 14 October 2010, case C-345/09, *van Delft*, par. 88; ECJ, 16 July 2009, case C-208/07, *von Chamier-Glisczinski*, par. 68; ECJ, 12 May 1998, case C-85/96, *Martinez Sala*, par. 31-36)[22]. Supiot[23] has called it a "*casuistique* approach",

---

22 In particular, the European Court of Justice has stated that "the concept of worker used in the context of Article 39 EC [45 TFUE] and Regulation No 1612/68 does not necessarily coincide with the definition applied in relation to Article 42 EC [48 TFUE] and Regulation No 1408/71" (ECJ, 16 July 2009, case C-208/07, *von Chamier-Glisczinski*, par. 68). For the purposes of European social security law, the definition of worker and the concept of a person insured under the social security legislation of one or more Member States overlap. In fact, "the concept of 'worker' employed by Regulation No 1408/71 includes all persons who are insured, if only against one risk, under compulsorily or optional insurance with a general or specific social security scheme mentioned in Article 1(a) of Regulation No 1408/71, irrespective of whether there is an employment relationship" (ECJ, 11 November 2004, case C-372/02, *Adanez-Vega*, par. 46), or "whether or not he pursues a professional or trade activity" (ECJ, 4 May 1999, C-262/96, *Sürül*, par. 85). The concept of the socially insured will not be taken into account in this chapter.

23 *Les notions de contrat de travail et de relation de travail en Europe, Rapport pour la Commission des Communautés Européennes*, Brussels, 1992.

while Freedland and Kontouris[24] have referred to a "regulated self-designed contracts approach".

This *casuistique* approach is, however, problematic. European integration is a continuous process, designed to provide national legal systems with common principles and values (Art. 3 Tue). It is therefore difficult to distinguish the cases in which the EU intends to establish a uniform level of protection from those in which only partial harmonisation (or coordination) is meant to be achieved. Moreover, even in the latter cases, the term "employee" defined by reference to the national laws of the Member States, has to be interpreted, so far as possible, in the light of the words and the purpose of the directive concerned in order to achieve the result sought by European law (ECJ, 4 July 2006, case C-212/04, *Adeneler*, par. 108).

Moreover, the *casuistique* approach allows Member States to decide the meaning of the term "employee". Member States are then able to exclude certain categories of persons from the protection guaranteed by European Law, thereby risking the creation of unfair competition, to place an obstacle to social progress, social cohesion, social justice and protection, as well as to prevent the achievement of European Union fundamental objectives (Art. 3 Tue).

Again, a clarification of the situation of dependent employment would also enhance "legal certainty and transparency for both employers and workers with regard to the scope, coverage and enforcement of labour law"[25].

An attempt to develop a consistent system of concepts (a "*systematique* approach" for Supiot; "standardized contract typology approach" for Freedland and Kontouris) is nowadays performed by the European legislator and the European Court of Justice. The former has mentioned the definition of a worker within the meaning of Art. 45 TFUE, whereas it is No. 87 of Directive 123/2006 on services in the internal market. The latter has used the same definition to interpret legislation on equality between men and women (ECJ, 14 December 1995, case C-317/93, *Nolte*) and for the purposes of applying Directive 2003/88 on the organisation of working time (ECJ, 14 October 2010, case C-428/09, *Union syndicale "Solidaires Isère"*, par. 27) and Directive 92/85 on the health and safety at work of pregnant workers and workers who have recently given birth or are breastfeeding (ECJ, 20 September 2007, case C-116/06, *Kiiski*, par. 25).

---

24 *Toward a Comparative Theory of the Contractual Construction of Personal Work Relations in Europe*, in *Industrial Law Journal*, 2008, p. 62.

25 European Parliament resolution of 6 July 2010 on atypical contracts, secured professional paths, and new forms of social dialogue, par. 32.

In *Allonby*, the European Court of Justice has stated that "the term 'worker' within the meaning of Article 141(1) EC is not expressly defined in the EC Treaty". It is therefore necessary, in order to determine its meaning, to apply "the generally recognised principles of interpretation, having regard to its context and to the objectives of the Treaty" (par. 64)[26]. In this decision, the European Judges hold that the term 'worker' "cannot be defined by reference to the legislation of the Member States but has a Community meaning" and that it "cannot be interpreted restrictively" (par. 66) because "article 141(1) EC constitutes a specific expression of the principle of equality for men and women, which forms part of the fundamental principles protected by the Community legal order" (par. 65). Therefore, whenever a European law implements a European fundamental principle, the concept may not be interpreted differently according to the law in Member States. On the contrary, it has an autonomous European meaning, developed through the interpretation of the provisions concerning workers' freedom of movement.

In *Union syndicale Solidaires Isère*, the European Court of Justice holds that, since the Directive 2003/88 made no reference to either Article 3(a) of Directive 89/391 or the definition of a 'worker' as derived from national legislation and/or practices, the concept of a worker may not be interpreted differently according to each national law but it has a European meaning. Then, the Court quotes the definition laid down in *Lawrie-Blum*, a case on workers' freedom of movement. The same argument is used in *Kiiski*: the concept of a worker for the purposes of Directive 92/85 may not be interpreted differently according to each national law and it must have a European meaning, that has developed according to Art. 45 TFUE.

Any time that the European Court of Justice has found it necessary to refer to a European concept of worker, despite the absence of definitions in the relevant European law, the definition recalled is that stated in *Lawrie-Blum*. As a consequence, the concept of employee within the meaning of Article 45 TFUE can be considered a general concept of EU Law.

---

26 In the opinion of the European Court of Justice, "the authors of the Treaty did not intend that the term 'worker', within the meaning of Article 141(1) EC, should include independent providers of services who are not in a relationship of subordination with the person who receives the services". In fact, "for the purpose of that article, 'pay' means the ordinary basic or minimum wage or salary and any other consideration, whether in cash or in kind, which the worker receives directly or indirectly, in respect of his employment, from his employer" (ECJ, 13 January 2004, case C-256/01, *Allonby*, par. 68).

III. The Concept of Employee within the Meaning of Art. 45 TFUE

The European Court of Justice has consistently held that the concept of employee within the meaning of Art. 45 TFUE has a specific European meaning and "must not be interpreted narrowly" (ECJ, 16 July 2009, case C-208/07, *von Chamier-Glisczinski*, par. 69). In more recent decisions, it refers to an "independent" or an "autonomous" meaning in EU law, underlining that the term "worker" cannot be left to national definitions.

"The essential feature of an employment relationship, according to that case-law, is that for a certain period of time a person performs services for and under the direction of another person in return for which he receives remuneration" (ECJ, 3 July 1986, case 66/85, *Lawrie-Blum*, par. 17; ECJ, 11 September 2008, case C-228/07, *Petersen*, par. 45; ECJ, 16 July 2009, case C-208/07, *von Chamier-Glisczinski*, par. 69; ECJ, 4 June 2007, cases C-22/08 and 23/08, *Vatsouras*, par. 26; ECJ, 7 September 2004, case C-456/02, *Trojani*, par. 15; ECJ, 23 March 2003, case C-138/02, *Collins*, par. 26; ECJ, 17 July 2007, case C-94/07, *Raccanelli*, par. 33; ECJ, 17 March 2005, case C-109/04, *Kranemann*, par. 12; ECJ, 8 June 1999, case C-337/97, *Meeusen*, par. 13; ECJ, 6 November 2003, case C-413/01, *Ninni-Orasche*, par. 24)[27].

Any employment relationship is based on the following three essential elements: subordination, the payment of remuneration in return for services rendered and the pursuit of "activities which are real and genuine, to the exclusion of activities on such a small scale as to be regarded as purely marginal and ancillary" (ECJ, 14 October 2010, case C-345/09, *van Delft e a.*, par. 89; ECJ, 23 March 1982, case 53/81, *Levin*, par. 17).

The European Court of Justice does not consider the nature of employment relationships under national law (ECJ, 20 September 2007, case C-116/06, *Kiiski*, par. 26)[28]. In order to understand whether an individual is a worker for the purposes of European law, it is necessary to ascertain that the individual has pursued, pursues or will pursue a real

27 Coursier, 2003: 305; Esteve, 2004: 63; Giubboni, 2009; Nogler, 2010: 83.

28 Both public law status (civil servants and public sector employees with a work relationship under public law) and private law contracts (also in the public sector) are covered. Furthermore, persons with a contract for occasional employment, part-time workers, trainees, fixed-term workers, professional and/or amateur sportsmen and sportswomen, persons who perform working activities of a rehabilitative nature would also fall within the definition of a worker, if their activity is effective and genuine (European Commission, *Reaffirming the free movement of workers: rights and major developments*, COM(2010) 373 final, p. 5).

and genuine activity for remuneration (ECJ, 7 September 2004, case C-456/02, *Trojani*, par. 24).

Again, "neither the origin of the funds from which the remuneration is paid nor the limited amount of that remuneration, nor indeed the fact that the person in question seeks to supplement that remuneration by other means of subsistence such as financial assistance drawn from the public funds of the State in which he resides, can have any consequence in regard to whether or not the person is a 'worker' for the purposes of European Union law" (ECJ, 4 February 2010, case C-14/09, *Genc*, par. 20; ECJ, 4 June 2007, cases C-22/08 and 23/08, *Vatsouras*, par. 27 and 28). It is therefore necessary to ascertain whether, in return for the activities performed, the person concerned receives any form of remuneration and "if the services performed are capable of being regarded as forming part of the normal labour market" (ECJ, 7 September 2004, case C-456/02, *Trojani*, par. 24).

The European Court of Justice states that the services have to be performed "for and under the direction of another person", without specifying that "another person" is the employer. As a consequence, the fact that the contractual employer could be different from the user has no consequence in regard to whether or not the person is a worker for the purposes of European Law.

In many cases, the European Court of Justice has clarified whether the activities performed are marginal and ancillary or real and genuine. That corresponds to the claims of Member States to avoid freedom of movement for inactive persons. Nowadays, these concerns are less important, since Directive 2004/38 recognises the right for each European citizen to move and reside in any Member State.

To decide whether the activity is real and genuine, "all circumstances of the case relating to the nature of the activities concerned and the employment relationship should be taken into consideration"[29]. In any case, the low number of hours of work performed or short duration of employment cannot prevent an EU citizen from being considered a worker (ECJ, 4 February 2010, case C-14/09, *Genc*, par. 22). In fact, for the overall assessment of employment relationships it is necessary to take into account all factors which characterise an employment relationship (ECJ, 4 June 2007, cases C-22/08 and 23/08, *Vatsouras*, par. 29 and 30), such as the right to paid leave, the continued payment of wages in the event of sickness, the relevant collective agreement, and the total length of an employment relationship with the same undertaking (ECJ, 4 February 2010, case C-14/09, *Genc*, par. 27).

[29] Communication from the Commission, *Reaffirming the free movement of workers: rights and major developments*, COM(2010) 373 final, p. 5.

At present, it becomes more and more important to verify the existence of subordination. The distinction between employees and self-employed workers is fundamental when we are dealing with the borderline between workers' freedom of movement and freedom of establishment (or freedom to provide services). In fact, "any activity which a person performs outside a relationship of subordination must be classified as an activity pursued in a self-employed capacity for the purposes of Articles 43 and 49 of the Treaty" (Whereas No. 87 Dir. 2006/123). As stated by the Advocate General in the opinion on case C-161/07, "in such a situation, the question of who constitutes a worker is no longer a matter of [...] [national] law and must be subject to [...] [European] scrutiny. It can be answered only by reference to the [...] [European] definition of a worker, as developed by the Court of Justice through interpreting the provisions on freedom of movement for workers" (par. 44)[30].

Moreover, since the concept of a worker within the meaning of Art. 45 TFUE is nowadays used to interpret other Directives, the distinction between employees and self-employed workers is essential to limit their scope.

The European Court of Justice has had few occasions to specify the nature and the level of supervision necessary to establish the existence of a relationship of employment subordination (Advocate General, opinion, 2 September 2010, case C-232/09, *Danosa*, par. 69). In order to assess the existence of a relationship of employment subordination, it is necessary to take into account all the factors and circumstances characterising the relationship between the contracting parties (ECJ, 11 November 2010, case C-232/09, *Danosa*, par. 46). In the context of this assessment, particular weight should be placed on the nature of the duties entrusted to the worker, on the context in which those duties were performed, on the scope of power and the extent to which he or she was supervised within the company and on the circumstances under which the person could be dismissed (ECJ, 11 November 2010, case C-232/09, *Danosa*, p. 47).

In Danosa, the European Court of Justice stated that "a member of a capital company's Board of Directors, who provides services to that company and is an integral part of it, must be regarded as having the status of worker for the purposes of Directive 92/85, if that activity is carried out, for some time, under the direction or supervision of another body of that company and if, in return for those activities, the Board Member receives remuneration" (par. 56). In its final decision, the Court has not recalled either the power of dismissal or the power to give

[30] Cavalier e Upex, 2006: 587; Nogler, 2009; Roccella, 2008.

instructions on a day-to-day basis, mentioned in the opinion of the Advocate General[31]. Therefore, the constituent elements of a relationship of subordination are two-fold: the worker has to be an integral part of the company (integration)[32] and he/she has to perform the working activity under the direction or control of another person (control)[33].

In other cases, the European Court of Justice has referred to the economic risk entailed in the activity or to the liability arising from the contractual relationship and the liability for any damages caused to third parties (ECJ, 25 July 1991, case C-202/90, par. 13 and 14). The fact of being liable for damages caused to third parties and bearing the economic risk of the business are, however, the result of performing tasks independently, under his/her own responsibility (ECJ, 25 July 1991, case C-202/90, par. 11 and 12).

In Directive 2009/52/CE, concerning sanctions and measures against employers of illegal immigrants from a third-country, "[employment]… means the exercise of activities covering whatever form of labour or work regulated under national law or in accordance with established practice for *or* under the direction and/or supervision of an employer" (Art. 2 par. 1.c; Whereas No. 7; emphasis is added)[34]. The two constituent criteria for a relationship of subordination (integration and control) are, in this case, alternative.

As specified in the Whereas No. 6, the definition included in Directive 2009/52/CE "should be used only for the purposes of this Directive". The wider meaning of subordination is functional for the specific purposes of this Directive. In particular, it helps to prohibit "the em-

---

31 In his opinion, the Advocate General stated that "a woman member of a capital company's Board of Directors, such as the applicant, must be regarded as a worker if the following three conditions are met: (i) by virtue of the conditions in accordance with which she was appointed, she formed an integral part of the company; (ii) she performed her duties under the control of bodies such as the shareholders' meeting or the supervisory board, which she did not control or over which she was unable to exercise a decisive influence; and (iii) she could be removed from her post by one or other of those bodies on the sole ground that they had lost confidence in her" (par. 99).

32 The element of integration in the company distinguishes the worker's situation from that of an agent "who receives a mandate from a company to perform a specific task, but remains a third party in relation to that company" (Advocate General, 2 September 2010, case C-232/09, *Danosa*, par. 78).

33 The same criteria are stressed by some French judges: "le travail au sein d'un service organisé peut consituer un indice du lien de subordination lorsque l'employeur determine unilateralment les conditions de travail" (Cass. Soc. 13 novembre 1996, in *Bull. civ.*, No. 386, in *Semaine juridique édition Entreprises*, 1997, II, 91).

34 The same definition can be found in Art. 2 b) of Dir. 2009/50 on the conditions of entry and residence of third-country nationals for the purposes of highly qualified employment.

ployment of illegally staying third-country nationals in order to fight illegal immigration" (Art. 1). Therefore, the concept of an "employee" must have a specific European meaning because of the general principle of specificity in Criminal law and to avoid unfair competition between Member States. It is peculiar that the European legislator has decided to widen the scope of the definition of subordination to fight illegal immigration and not to guarantee better working conditions.

IV. Criteria for the Interpretation of the European Concept of "Employee"

As the European Court of Justice has consistently held, it is for the National Courts to undertake an assessment of the actual circumstances necessary to determine whether there is an employment relationship or a self-employment relationship in the cases pending before it (ECJ, 11 November 2010, case C-232/09, *Danosa*, par. 56). Nevertheless, the European Court of Justice "provides the national courts with the criteria for the interpretation of European Union law which they require in order to dispose of dispute which they are called upon to resolve", replying "in rather abstract and general terms to a question on the interpretation" referred to it (ECJ, 4 February 2010, case C-14/09, *Genc*, par. 30 and 31).

First, the concept of employee "must be defined in accordance with objective criteria characterizing the employment relationship in view of the rights and duties of persons concerned" (ECJ, 6 November 2003, case C-413/01, *Ninni-Orasche*, par. 24; ECJ, 3 July 1986, case 66/85, *Lawrie-Blum*, par. 17). Therefore, the formal classification of an individual as a self-employed worker under national law does not exclude the possibility that the same individual could be classified as an employee for the purposes of EU Law "if that person's independence is merely notional, thereby disguising an employment relationship" within the meaning of that law (ECJ, 11 November 2010, case C-232/09, *Danosa*, par. 41; ECJ, 13 January 2004, case C-256/01, *Allonby*, par. 71).

This means that, whenever the three constituent elements of an employment relationship are deemed to exist (namely subordination, the payment of remuneration, the pursuit of real and genuine activities), neither the way in which national law or the parties themselves classify the relationship between them nor the fact that there is no contractual relationship between the parties concerned can rule out the application of EU law (ECJ, 11 November 2010, case C-232/09, *Danosa*, par. 42). Thus, the recognition of the status of "employee" does not "depend on how the parties concerned describe the working relationship or on whether a contract of employment has been entered into" (Advocate General, 2 September 2010, case C-232/09, *Danosa*, par. 66).

The same principle has been affirmed by ILO in Recommendation No. 198/2006: "for the purposes of the national policy of protection for workers in an employment relationship, the determination of the existence of [...] [an employment] relationship should be guided primarily by the facts relating to the performance of work and the remuneration of the worker, notwithstanding how the relationship is characterised in any contrary arrangement, contractual or otherwise, that may have been agreed between the parties" (par. 9)[35].

Moreover, the European judges have asserted that the National Court must "make an overall assessment of all the circumstances of the case brought before it, having regard both to the nature of the activities concerned and the relationship of the parties involved" (ECJ, 11 November 2010, case C-232/09, *Danosa*, par. 29).

Obviously, "factors relating to the conduct of the person concerned before and after the period of employment are not relevant in establishing the status of a worker" (ECJ, 6 November 2003, case C-413/01, *Ninni-Orasche*, par. 28). On the contrary, it is necessary to consider "the extent of any limitation on [worker's] freedom to choose the timetable", "the place and content of their work" (ECJ, 13 January 2004, case C-256/01, *Allonby*, par. 72), the degree of supervision to which the worker was subject, the power of dismissal, and in general all the indicators of a relationship of subordination (see above)[36].

The fact that no obligation is imposed on the workers to accept an assignment is of no consequence in this context (ECJ, 13 January 2004, case C-256/01, *Allonby*, par. 72). This statement is relevant to get over the *mutuality of obligation* criterion, used by the English Court to deny employee status to casual workers and temporary agency workers (McCann, 2007). In these cases, the judges found that there was no mutuality of obligation (and no contract of employment) since the employees were not under any obligation to work for the employers/agencies (nor to accept an assignment when offered) and, correspondingly, the

35 The Italian Constitutional Court has affirmed the same principle (called "principio dell'irrilevanza del *nomen iuris*") in two important sentences (C. cost. 121/1993 and 115/1994; see also Cass. 19271/2009; D'Antona, 1995).

36 In the opinion on 'New trends in self-employed work: the specific case of economically dependent self-employed work', the European Economic and Social Committee has stated that "an employee is someone who works under the direction and supervision of another person, who is then classed as an employer, a situation that is itself determined on the basis of several factors, i.e.: obligation to provide one's own labour, working for a single employer over a specific length of time, employees not being responsible for their company's financial risks and work being conducted on another's account" (par. 4.1.3).

employers/agencies were not under any obligation to provide them with work[37].

In the Resolution of 24 October 2006 on the application of Dir. 96/71, the European Parliament exhorted the European Commission to adopt a Communication to establish "transparent and coherent criteria to determine employee status and self-employed status in relation to Labour law" (par. 9)[38]. This would help to solve the problem with regard to "false" self-employed persons.

The same problem has been underlined by the ILO in Employment Relationship Recommendation 198/2006, asking Member States to "combat disguised employment relationships in the context of, for example, other relationships that may include the use of other forms of contractual arrangements that hide the true legal status, noting that a disguised employment relationship occurs when the employer treats an individual as other than an employee in a manner that hides his or her true legal status as an employee, and that situations can arise where contractual arrangements have the effect of depriving workers of the protection they are due" (par. 4.b). In particular, the Member States are requested to define "specific indicators of the existence of an employment relationship" (par. 13)[39].

For the purpose of facilitating the determination of the existence of an employment relationship, ILO Recommendation invites Members to consider the possibility of "providing for a legal presumption that an employment relationship exists where one or more relevant indicators is present" (par. 11.b). However, a presumption of salaried status in the host State can constitute an unlawful restriction on freedom to provide services within the meaning of article 56 TFUE[40]. In fact, persons

37 Muschett v. HM Prison Service [2010]EWCA Civ 25; Wynn and Leighton, 2006; Brown, 2008.

38 In Belgium, for example, in December 2006, the government laid down "criteria aimed at better circumscribing the status of a self-employed worker and distinguishing it from that of employee". The law also envisages the establishment of a commission on the regulation of employment relationships, which will determine the status of a worker in the event of doubt (European Employment Observatory Review, *Self-employment in Europe 2010*).

39 On criteria to identify subordination listed by ILO Recommendations, see Davidov, 2002.

40 Article 56 TFUE "requires not only the elimination of all discrimination against service providers from other Member States, but also the abolition of any restriction on the freedom to provide services, even any restriction applies without distinction to national providers of services and to those of other Member States, which is liable to prohibit, impede or render less advantageous the activities of service providers from other Member States who lawfully provide similar services in their Member State of origin" (ECJ, 15 June 2005, case C-255/04, *Commission/France*, par. 37).

recognised as service providers established in their Member State of origin who go to another country to pursue their activities on a temporary, self-employed basis, are at a disadvantage because of the presumption of salaried status in the host country[41]. In order to avoid their contract being classified as an employment contract, "they must prove that they do not work as employees but, on the contrary, are self-employed" (ECJ, 15 June 2005, case C-255/04, *Commission/France*, par. 38).

The presumption of salaried status can also hinder the freedom of establishment of the economic operators. Indeed, a provision requiring a citizen of one Member State to rebut the presumption of salaried status by providing proof of his/her self-employed status, makes access to a self-employed activity subject to an additional condition compared to those applicable to other economic operators, and prevents that economic activity from being pursued during the certification procedure (ECJ, 22 December 2008, case C-161/07, *Commission/France*, par. 42).

In both cases, the European Court of Justice has held that the objective to fight concealed employment can be reached through measures less restrictive, for example "putting in place of regular administrative checks possibly coupled with obligations concerning the communication of information on the part of the economic operators potentially affected" (ECJ, 22 December 2008, case C-161/07, *Commission/Austria*, par. 39). Again, "the establishment of a system of *ex post facto* control, together with deterrent penalties to prevent and identify individual instances of use of bogus amateur or unpaid status, would suffice to combat concealed employment effectively" (ECJ, 15 June 2005, case C-255/04, *Commission/France*, par. 53).

Nevertheless, a presumption of salaried status in the host State cannot, *a priori*, be regarded as an unlawful restriction to EU law. Since we are dealing with the boundaries between freedom of movement for workers and freedom of establishment (or freedom to provide service), we should refer to the concept of subordination as developed by the Court of Justice through interpretation of the provisions on freedom of movement for workers. Only, "if the applicable national definition of worker proves to be too wide and encompasses beneficiaries of freedom of establishment [or freedom to provide service], it will be the source of

[41] The disadvantages linked to the status of employment contract could be the obligation to pay contributions as an affiliate of a social security scheme for employed persons, the scheme for paid annual leave (ECJ, 15 June 2005, case C-255/04, *Commission/France*, par. 38), or the application of the transitional rules that limit the freedom of movement for workers from new Member States (ECJ, 22 December 2008, case C-161/07, *Commission/Austria*).

an unjustified restriction" (Advocate General, 18 September 2008, case C-161/07, *Commission/Austria*, par. 46)[42].

As stated above, the distinction between employee and self-employed relies on the existence of a relationship of subordination. In fact, "an activity which can be carried out in the course of employment can, in principle, also be done independently" (Advocate General, 18 September 2008, case C-161/07, *Commission/Austria*, par. 48), but self-employed persons "work outside a relationship of subordination and bear the responsibility for the activity" (Advocate General, 18 September 2008, case C-161/07, *Commission/Austria*, par. 45). Again, it becomes more and more necessary to establish European indicators on the employment relationship.

As regards social security for migrant workers, it should also be considered that, the certificate (E101) that establishes a presumption that posted workers are properly affiliated to the social security system of the Member State in which the undertaking which posted those workers is established, "is binding on the competent institution of the Member State to which those workers are posted" (ECJ, 26 January 2006, case C-2/05, *Kiere*, par. 24). However, the competent institution of the Member State which issued that certificate has "to reconsider the grounds for its issue and, if necessary, withdraw the certificate if the competent institution of the Member State to which the workers are posted expresses doubts as to the correctness of the facts on which the certificate is based and, consequently, of the information contained therein" (ECJ, 26 January 2006, case C-2/05, *Kiere*, par. 27). In this case, the presumption of employment or self-employment relationship in the home State is justified by the requirement to guarantee the principle that workers have to be covered but by only one social security system.

V. Conclusion

The European legislator and the European Court of Justice have performed an attempt to develop a European concept of worker, recalling the definition within the meaning of Article 45 TFUE to interpret other provisions concerning European Labour Law. Moreover, the European Court of Justice has provided the national courts with the general criteria for the interpretation of the concept of worker in the European Union law. Nowadays, it becomes more and more important to verify the existence of subordination, one of the essential elements which any

42 A presumption of salaried status is set down by Art. 69 Law 276/2003 in "lavoro a progetto". The Italian judges are still discussing whether it is a presumption *iuris et de iure* (i.e. no evidence of self-employment relationship is allowed) or a presumption *iuris tantum* (i.e. evidence of a self-employment relationship is allowed).

employment relationship is based on. Indeed, the distinction between employees and self-employed workers is fundamental to draw the borderline between workers' freedom of movement and freedom of establishment or freedom to provide services. The distinction between employees and self-employed workers is also essential to limit the scope of numerous Labour Law Directives. To solve these problems, it would be extremely effective to establish indicators on the employment relationship for European Law, as ILO has already done for its regulations. Since 2006 the European Parliament has exhorted the European Commission to adopt a Communication to establish "transparent and coherent criteria to determine employee status and self-employed status in relation to Labour law". We are waiting for an answer.

Job Quality in Atypical Forms of Employment

Reality or Utopia?

Silvia BORELLI

Researcher, Labour Law, University of Ferrara

I. The General Form of Employment Relationship: the Contract of an Indefinite Duration

The preamble to the agreement on fixed-term work, as well as Whereas No. 15 of the Directive 2008/104, states that contracts of an indefinite duration "are, and will continue to be, the general form of employment relationship between employers and workers", since they "contribute to the quality of life of the workers concerned and improve performance" (Whereas No. 6 of the Agreement on fixed-term work). Therefore, "the benefit of stable employment is viewed as a major element in the protection of workers, whereas it is only in certain circumstances that fixed-term employment contracts are liable to respond to the needs of both employers and workers" (ECJ, 4 July 2006, case C-212/04, *Adeneler*, par. 62; ECJ, 23 April 2004, cases 378/07, 379/07, 380/07, *Angelidaki*, par. 105)[1]. The maintenance of full-time open-ended contract as a general form of the employment relationship should avoid the risk of segmentation of the labour market between secure contractual arrangements under standard contracts and precarious situations in non-standard (atypical) forms of employment[2].

1 "Fixed-term employment contracts are a feature of employment in certain sectors or in respect of certain occupations and activities" (ECJ, 23 April 2004, cases 378/07, 379/07, 380/07, *Angelidaki*, par. 104; ECJ, 4 July 2006, case C-212/04, *Adeneler*, par. 61; ECJ, 15 April 2008, case C-268/06, *Impact*, par. 86; Sciarra, 2007).

2 B. Burgoon, F. Dekker, 2010: 126. The segmentation of the labour market frequently goes together with the segregation of some groups, since atypical jobs are most prevalent amongst the young, the old, immigrants, disabled people and women (Hugh Frazer and Eric Marlier, 2010: 32).

At the moment, European law follows two different strategies (Giubboni, 2011). On one hand, it deals with the concepts of employee, part-time worker, fixed-term worker and temporary agency worker (*systematique* approach)[3]. On the other hand, it prohibits discrimination, a specific declaration of one of the fundamental principles of European Union law, namely the general principle of equality (ECJ, 10 June 2010, cases C-395/08 and C-396/08, *Bruno e Pettini*, par. 58)[4]. This latter strategy can be assessed as the *casuistique* approach since it aims to guarantee, case by case, atypical workers the same rights and duties as permanent full-time employees, without any reference to the type of employment contract.

II. Atypical Form of Work: Definition

The European Court of Justice has consistently affirmed that the short duration of employment relationship or the limited number of working hours do not prevent a person from being regarded as a worker according to the meaning of Article 45 TFUE (ECJ, 4 February 2010, case C-14/09, *Genc*, par. 25). Again, it has been declared Directive 2003/88 "draws no distinction between workers employed under [...] [fixed-term] contract and those employed under a contract of indefinite duration", and so it covers both casual and seasonal contracts (ECJ, 14 October 2010, case C-428/09, *Union syndicale "Solidaires Isère"*, par. 31). The same argument can be found in the text on EU equality law (ECJ, 17 June 1998, case C-243/95, *Hill and Stapleton*). Recently, the Court of justice has held that "part-time work constitutes a particular mode of performing the employment contract, characterised by the simple fact that the normal hours of work are reduced" (ECJ, 10 June 2010, cases C-395/08 and C-396/08, *Bruno e Pettini*, par. 72)[5].

Furthermore, Directive 2008/94 on the protection of employees in the event of the insolvency of their employer (Art. 2) and the Directive

---

3 As Collins (2010: 42) states, "as long as employers can use their freedom of contract to construct any type of contract for the performance of work that achieves the flexibility and efficiency they seek, rather than being confined to a limited range of types of contract, any coherence and transparency in the legal test for determining the proper scope of employment law will prove elusive".

4 "Les principes d'égalité de traitement et de non-discrimination font partie de l'ordre juridique de l'Union. Ces principes ont été consacrés notamment aux articles 20 et 21 de la charte des droits fondamentaux de l'Union européenne" (ECJ, 11 November 2010, *order*, case C-20/10, *Vino*, par. 52).

5 See also Commission staff working paper – *Report on the implementation of the European social partners' – Framework Agreement on Telework* (SEC(2008)2178): "since telework only affects the organisation of work and does not create a special employment status, all rights enshrined in the law and in contractual arrangements should be granted to teleworkers on a comparable basis".

2001/23 on the transfer of undertaking (Art. 2 par. 2) specify that, even if they are without prejudice to national law as regards the definition of the terms "employee" and "employer", Member States cannot exclude from their scope part-time employees within the meaning of Directive 97/81/EC, employees with a fixed-term contract within the meaning of Directive 1999/70/EC and employees with a temporary employment relationship within the meaning of Directive 91/383/EEC.

Finally, European Parliament "recommends that workers on atypical contracts be covered by existing EU directives that cover worker categories within the EU, including the Working Time Directive (1993/104/EC), the directive on temporary agency work (2008/104/EC), the directive on part-time work (1997/81/EC) and the Council Directive concerning the framework agreement on fixed-term work (1999/70/EC)" (European Parliament resolution of 6 July 2010 on atypical contracts, secured professional paths, and new forms of social dialogue, par. 10). In this regard, the broad definitions of part-time worker, fixed-term worker and temporary agency worker as set out in the Directives have to be taken into account. Moreover, it should be noted that, if EU law aims to apply the principle of non-discrimination to atypical workers in order to prevent an employer using such an employment relationship to deny those workers rights which are recognised for permanent full-time workers (ECJ, 13 September 2007, C-307/05, *Del Cerro Alonso*, par. 37), its scope has to be interpreted extensively.

In particular, for the purpose of Directive 97/81, the term "part-time worker" refers to "an employee whose normal hours of work, calculated on a weekly basis or on average over a period of employment of up to one year, are less than the normal hours of work of a comparable full-time worker" (clause 3). Member States can, for objective reasons, exclude wholly or partly from the terms of the agreement part-time workers who work on a casual basis (clause 2).

The European Court of Justice has stated that a contract of employment "under which hours of work and the organisation of working time are dependent upon the quantity of available work and are determined only on a case-by-case basis by agreement between the parties", comes within the scope of the Framework Agreement annexed to Directive 97/81 (ECJ, 12 October 2004, case C-313/02, *Wippel*, par. 30 and 40).

Directive 1999/70 defines a "fixed-term worker" as "a person having an employment contract or relationship entered into directly between an employer and a worker where the end of the employment contract or relationship is determined by objective conditions such as reaching a specific date, completing a specific task, or the occurrence of a specific event" (clause 3; see also Art. 1.1 Directive 91/383/CE)[6]. The definition of "fixed-term workers" for the purposes of the framework agreement "encompasses all workers without drawing a distinction according to whether their employer is in the public or private sector" (ECJ, 7 September 2006, case C-53/04, *Marrosu and Sardino*, par. 41; ECJ, 4 July 2006, case C-212/04, *Adeneler*, par. 56). Member States may decide that the agreement on fixed-term workers does not apply to initial vocational training relationships and apprenticeship schemes, as well as to employment contracts and relationships which have been concluded within the framework of a specific public or publicly-supported training, integration and vocational retraining programme (clause 2). Specific fixed-term contracts aimed at training, integration and vocational retraining should be expressly declared in national law and strictly interpreted[7].

Instead, Directive 2008/104 "applies to workers with a contract of employment or employment relationship with a temporary work agency who are assigned to user undertakings to work temporarily under their supervision and direction" (Art. 1.c); see also Art. 1.2 Directive 91/383/CE). Member States can "provide that this Directive does not apply to employment contracts or relationships concluded under a specific public or publicly supported vocational training, integration or retraining programme" (Art. 1). It is also specified that temporary work agencies must be recognised as employers (Art. 2).

These broad definitions should prevent the creation of new types of contract from provoking the ultra-segmentation of the labour market. Recently, the European Foundation for the Improvement of Living and Working Conditions has made a distinction between atypical and very atypical employment relationships (such as very short fixed-term workers or temporary agency workers – i.e. less than 6 months, very short part-time workers – i.e. less than 20 hours a week, non-contract workers,

---

6 Even if "the use of fixed-term employment contracts founded on objective reasons is a way to prevent abuse" (ECJ, 4 July 2006, case C-212/04, *Adeneler*, par. 67; par. 7 of the general considerations in the Framework Agreement), "the Framework Agreement does not compel the Member States to adopt a measure requiring every first or single use of a fixed-term employment contract to be justified by such objective reasons" (ECJ, 23 April 2004, cases 378/07, 379/07, 380/07, *Angelidaki*, par. 90). However, recently, the Court of Justice has recognised that "the use of fixed-term contracts as opposed to contracts of indefinite duration is exceptional" (ECJ, 10 March 2011, case C-109/09, *Deutsche Lufthansa*, par. 30).

7 This is not the case, for example, of the Italian Contratto di inserimento (Art. 54 d. lgs. 276/2003). The European Court of justice has not yet clarified whether the "socially useful worker" or "the public service worker" should be included in the scope of the Framework Agreement (ECJ, 1 October 2010, *order*, case C-3/10, *Affatato*, par. 30).

on-call workers, zero-hour workers)[8]. Affirming that all these new typologies of contract of employment are in the scope of Directives on atypical workers is a way for "grouping atypical contracts together for the purpose of simplification" and for extending "the protection of workers in atypical forms of employment"[9].

A. Principles of Non-discrimination and Atypical Workers

In EU law, the purpose of protecting atypical workers is achieved mainly by principles of non-discrimination (Zappalà, 2009). These principles impose that "in respect of employment conditions"[10], part-time workers and fixed-term workers shall not be treated in a less favourable manner than, respectively, comparable full-time workers or comparable permanent workers solely because they work part-time or they have a fixed-term contract (Clause 4 of Framework agreement on part-time worker; Clause 4 of Framework agreement on fixed-term worker)[11]. The Directive 2008/104, on one hand limits the scope of the principle to "the basic working and employment conditions" (Art. 1.1.f), on the other hand it simplifies the comparison, affirming that the working conditions of temporary agency workers "shall be, for the duration of their assignment at a user undertaking, at least those that would apply if they had been recruited directly by that undertaking to occupy the same job" (Art. 5.1)[12].

This is relevant since sometimes it is not easy to identify a comparable permanent full-time employee. In the UK, for example, the Fixed-term employees Regulation (FTER)2002 (prevention of less favourable treatment) requires that he/she is employed by the same employer, is

---

8 Very atypical contractual arrangements are mostly spread in some specific sectors, as construction, hotel and restaurant, agriculture and fishing (European Foundation for the Improvement of Living and Working Conditions, *Flexible forms of work: 'very atypical' contractual arrangements*, 2010).

9 European Parliament resolution of 6 July 2010 on atypical contracts, secured professional paths, and new forms of social dialogue, par. 6.

10 Both Framework Agreements do not regulate social security matters. However, the term "employment conditions" "covers pensions which depend on an employment relationship between worker and employer, excluding statutory social security pensions, which are determined less by that relationship than by considerations of social policy" (ECJ, 10 June 2010, cases C-395/08 and C-396/08, *Bruno e Pettini*, par. 42).

11 See also Commission staff working paper – *Report on the implementation of the European social partners' – Framework Agreement on Telework* (SEC(2008)2178): "teleworkers should be treated in the same way as workers who are permanently present on the firm's premises".

12 Thus, the application of the principle of equal treatment, within the context of Directive 2008/104, does not require identification of a worker recruited by the user undertaking, engaged in the same or similar work/occupation, due regard being given to seniority and qualification/skills.

engaged in the same or broad similar work, works or is based at the same establishment (or another establishment of the same employer) and is at work[13].

Principles of non-discrimination only concern the different treatment between atypical employees and comparable full-time permanent employees. Therefore, they do not affect different treatment between atypical employees with different employment contracts (ECJ, 1 October 2010, *order*, case C-3/10, *Affatato*, par. 56).

The ECJ has affirmed that clause 4 of the Framework Agreement on fixed-term work "prohibits, in a general manner and in unequivocal terms, any difference in treatment of fixed-term workers in respect of employment conditions which is not objectively justified", and so its subject-matter appears to be sufficiently precise to be relied upon by an individual and to be applied by the national court (ECJ, 22 December 2010, cases C-444/09 and C-456/09, *Gavieiro Gavieiro*, par. 75; ECJ, 15 April 2008, case C-268/06, *Impact*, par. 60). Since the formulation of Clause 4 of the Framework Agreement on part-time worker is identical, it can also be recognised as a provision having direct effect.

Again, it must be recalled that, as stated in *Kücükdeveci*, it is for the national court, hearing proceedings between individuals, to ensure that the principle of non-discrimination on grounds of age, "a general principle of European Union law in that it constitutes a specific application of the general principle of equal treatment", is complied with, disapplying any contrary provision in national legislation (ECJ, 19 January 2010, case C-555/07, *Kücükdeveci*, par. 56). This statement has two main consequences: firstly, the general principles of non-discrimination can be applied to subjects that do not come within the scope of Directives (but are within the responsibility of the European Union); then they can be applied to proceedings between individuals, getting round the fact that "a directive cannot of itself impose obligations on an individual and cannot therefore be relied on as such against an individual" (ECJ, 19 January 2010, case C-555/07, *Kücükdeveci*, par. 46)[14].

---

13 See *Biggart v. University of Ulster* [00778/05, 19 February 2007]; A. Koukiadaki, *Case Law Developments in the Area of Fixed-Term Work*, in *Industrial Law Journal* 2009, p. 89. As regard Part-time worker Regulations 2000, the House of Lords (*Matthews and others v. Kent and Medway Towns Fire Authority and others* [2006]UKHL 8) has affirmed that "the question whether a full time worker is employed under the same type of contract as a part-time worker is to be approached broadly, having regard to the purpose" of the Framework Agreement, and that "the underlying purpose [of PTWR] seems to be to ensure that it is not left to the employer to decide whether or not to treat persons falling within the same category differently".

14 See Fontanelli, 2010: 1145.

Principles of non-discrimination have two different purposes: ensuring equal treatment of atypical employees and persons employed on the basis of a standard contract, and avoiding disadvantages for atypical workers. In the first context, they assure atypical workers at least the same working and employment conditions for permanent full-time workers[15]. Thus, they establish a minimum standard *per relationem* (i.e. referring to working conditions in a standard employment relationship).

Therefore, in the event that employment protection legislation is reformed "to reduce over-protection of workers with permanent contracts", as suggested by European Commission[16], this will not diminish the existing divisions between those holding atypical and permanent contracts, nor "provide protection to those left outside or at the margins of the job market". On the contrary, any reduction of employment protection for permanent employees will provoke a worsening of atypical workers' condition of employment, and will contradict the notion that employment stability is "a major element in the protection of workers" (ECJ, 4 July 2006, case C-212/04, *Adeneler*, par. 62).

Ensuring equal treatment, principles of non-discrimination do not allow Member States, social parties and employer to set a minimum period for a contract of employment or a minimum number of working hours in order for employees to qualify for a right (i.e. continuity of employment) (ECJ, 26 June 2001, case C-173/99, *Bectu*, and ECJ, 9 February 1999, case C-167/97, *Seymour-Smith and Perez*)[17]. It is possible to give access to particular conditions of employment subject to a period of service, time worked or earnings qualification, only where justified by objective reasons and appropriate (Clause 4.4 of the Framework Agreement on part-time work; Clause 4.4 of the Framework Agreement on fixed-term work)[18]. Each qualifying condition must be strictly interpreted[19].

---

15 See ILO Recommendation No. 165: "the terms and conditions of employment, including social security coverage, of part-time workers and temporary workers should be, to the extent possible, equivalent to those of full-time and permanent workers respectively". On part-time work see also Convention No. 175 and Recommendation No. 182.

16 Communication from the Commission, *Annual Growth Survey: advancing the EU's comprehensive response to the crisis*, COM(2011) 11 final, p. 7.

17 This rule is expressly mentioned in Art. 1.3 of Directive 2008/94 and Art. 2.2.a) of Directive 2001/23.

18 Qualifications relating to access by part-time workers to particular conditions of employment should be reviewed periodically (Clause 4.4 of the Framework Agreement on part-time work).

19 ILO Convention No. 102 on social security authorises a qualifying period, which is an obligation to have worked or contributed for a minimum period (Servais, 2008).

Again, "where appropriate, the principle of *pro rata temporis* shall apply" (Clause 4.2 of the Framework agreement on part-time work; Clause 4.2 of the Framework Agreement on fixed-term work; see ILO Recommendation No. 165). The European Court of justice has clarified that the principle of *pro rata temporis* can only be applied "to divisible performance, such as that deriving from financial employment conditions linked, for example, to remuneration and pensions" (ECJ, 10 June 2010, cases C-395/08 and C-396/08, *Bruno e Pettini*, par. 34; on the calculation of the amount of pension, see: ECJ, 23 October 2003, cases C-04/05 and C-05/05 *Schönheit and Becker*, par. 90 and 91, and ECJ, 16 July 2009, case C-537/07, *Gómez-Limón Sánchez-Camacho*, par. 59)[20].

Principles of non-discrimination preclude national legislation from excluding atypical workers from its scope (ECJ, 22 April 2010, case C-486/08, *Zentralbetriebsrat der Landeskrankenhäuser Tirols*, par. 47). Moreover, principles of non-discrimination preclude national legislation from excluding a specific category of atypical workers from the calculation of staff numbers within the meaning of its provision (ECJ, 18 January 2007, case C-385/05, *Confédération générale du travail e.a.*, par. 38). Such legislation, in fact, can have the consequence of exempting certain employers from the obligations laid down in EU Directives[21] and of depriving employees of the rights granted under these directives, and so it is liable to render the Directives ineffective (ECJ, 18 January 2007, case C-385/05, *Confédération générale du travail e.a.*, par. 38 and 41).

In most cases, however, some adjustments of the rights concerned are needed to effectively remove differences in treatment between persons employed under a standard contract and persons employed under an atypical contract. In fact, the majority of workers' rights and protection have been built around standard employment relationships. Atypical workers can therefore suffer disadvantages due to the limited period of the employment contract or the number of working hours, or "due to the contractual arrangement, that is involving three parties and a triangular

---

[20] On the contrary, "the principle of *pro rata temporis* is not applicable for the purpose of determining the date required to acquire pensions rights, since that depends solely on the worker's length of service. The length of service is, in fact, the actual duration of the employment relationship and not the amount of time worked during that period. In accordance with the principle of non-discrimination as between full-time and part-time workers, therefore, the length of the period of service taken into account for the purpose of determining the date on which a worker becomes entitled to a pension should be calculated for a part-time worker as if he had held a full-time post, periods not worked being taken into account in their entirety" (ECJ, 10 June 2010, cases C-395/08 and C-396/08, *Bruno e Pettini*, par. 66).

[21] This happens when the Directive allows Member States to limit the obligations imposed on undertakings which have a specific number of employees (see, for example, Art. 7.5 of Directive 2001/23).

contractual relationship between the temporary agency (the employer), the company where the work is performed (workplace) and the worker"[22].

The European Court of justice has consistently stated that prohibitions on discrimination established in Directives on equal treatment between men and women also regard national provisions that "discriminate indirectly against women where, although worded in neutral terms, they work to the disadvantage of a much higher percentage of women than men, unless that difference in treatment is justified by objective factors unrelated to any discrimination on grounds of sex" (ECJ, 7 October 2004, case C-312/02, *Sweden/Commission*, par. 43)[23]. In the judgments on discrimination against atypical workers, the same declaration has not yet been made. Nevertheless, the Court of justice has recognised that the prohibition on discrimination laid down in Directive 97/81 and Directive 1999/70 is "simply a specific expression of one of the fundamental principles of European Union law, namely the general principle of equality" and that Clause 4 of the two Framework Agreements "must be interpreted as articulating a principle of European Union social law which cannot be interpreted restrictively" (ECJ, 10 June 2010, cases C-395/08 and C-396/08, *Bruno e Pettini*, par. 32 and 58; ECJ, 22 December 2010, cases C-444/09 and C-456/09, *Gavieiro Gavieiro*, par. 49; ECJ, 13 September 2007, case C-307/05, *Del Cerro Alonso*, par. 27 and 38). Therefore, it is likely that the Court of justice will interpret Clause 4 of the Framework Agreement on part-time work, Clause 4 of the Framework agreement on fixed-term work and Art. 5 of Directive 2008/104 as a prohibition on direct and indirect discrimination. This will help, for example, in the event of successive fixed-term contracts with the same employer, to ensure that the total period of these contracts shall be taken into account for the purpose of calculating the qualifying period for entitlement to a right (see Clause No. 3.1.b) of the Framework Agreement on parental leave, revised by Directive 2010/18/UE) or the seniority for pay increases (see, for example, Italian Cass. S.U. 20074/10 on the recognition of working period under a contratto di formazione e lavoro). In this case, the interpretation of Clause No. 4 of the Framework Agreement on fixed-term work as a prohibition against direct and indirect discrimination is essential to pursue its aim, i.e. "to prevent the

---

[22] European Foundation for the Improvement of Living and Working Conditions, *Flexible forms of work: 'very atypical' contractual arrangements*, 2010. In the *Agenda for new skills and jobs: A European contribution towards full employment* (COM(2010) 682 final, p. 6), the Commission proposes to make the level of unemployment benefits commensurate with "the individual work history" and to review "the pension system to ensure adequate and sustainable pensions for those with gaps in pensions-saving contributions", due to short-term contracts.

[23] EU law forbids also indirect discriminations on the ground of nationality, race, ethnic origin and all other factors considered by Directive 2000/78.

status of employees from being insecure" (ECJ, 10 March 2011, case C-109/09, *Deutsche Lufthansa*, par. 31)[24]. In general, the suggested interpretation of EU directives on atypical workers increases their effectiveness, as required by the Commission's *Agenda for new skills and jobs* (COM(2010) 682 final).

Both Clause 4 of the Framework Agreement on part-time work and Clause 4 of the Framework Agreement on fixed-term work permit a difference in treatment to be justified "by the existence of precise and concrete factors, characterising the employment condition to which it relates, in the specific context in which it occurs and on the basis of objective and transparent criteria in order to ensure that that unequal treatment in fact responds to a genuine need, is appropriate for achieving the objective pursued and is necessary for that purpose" (ECJ, 22 December 2010, cases C-444/09 and C-456/09, *Gavieiro Gavieiro*, par. 55; ECJ, 486/08, par. 44; ECJ, 13 September 2007, case C-307/05, *Del Cerro Alonso*, par. 58)[25]. A more complex system of justification is established in Art. 5 of Directive 2008/104.

III. *Au-delà du salariat…*

The European Employment Observatory has recently examined the quality of self-employment jobs (*Self-employment in Europe 2010*, European Commission. Directorate-General for Employment, Social Affairs and Equal Opportunities, 2010). Its analysis emphasises three main aspects: first of all, the working conditions of the self-employed are usually worse than those of employees, since they have fewer opportunities for training, their work is more stressful and more dangerous, they do not have the same social protection, their income is lower and their working hours are longer and more flexible. Another issue concerns dependent self-employment, where a person may effectively work for just one employer or perform the work concerned personally and directly. Finally, the report covers false self-employment, cases of workers who are formally self-employed but who work under the same conditions as employees.

In its resolution of 6 July 2010 on atypical contracts, secured professional paths, and new forms of social dialogue, the European Parliament "emphasises the importance of self-employment" and supports "the

---

24 K. Schulze Buschoff, P. Protsch, 2008: 51.

25 "Those factors may result, in particular, from the specific nature of the tasks for the performance of which [employment] contracts have been concluded and from the inherent characteristics of those tasks or, as the case may be, from pursuit of a legitimate social-policy objective of a Member State" (ECJ, 22 December 2010, cases C-444/09 and C-456/09, *Gavieiro Gavieiro*, par. 55).

special position of independent freelance workers as a vital force in economic recovery, as a 'way in' or an alternative to the labour market" (par. 4 and 5). At the same time, the European Parliament "considers that all employees, regardless of their employment status, should be guaranteed a set of core rights" (par. 6 and 37).

The latter approach reflects the notion of determining the scope of labour law in view of the policy objectives of the regulation. The principle of equality between men and women, enshrined in Article 23 of the Charter of Fundamental Rights of the European Union, for example, "must be ensured in all areas including employment, work and pay" (ECJ, 11 November 2010, case C-232/09, *Danosa*, par. 71)[26]. A similar broad scope can be given to the principle of non-discrimination enshrined in Article 21 of the Charter of Fundamental Rights and implemented by Directive 2000/43 and Directive 2000/78.

The same approach (determining personal scope of labour law in view of the policy objectives in the regulation) can be found in EU law on the right to move and reside freely within the territory of the Member States. This right is now a primary and individual right conferred on every citizen of the Union[27]. In any case, the distinction between employee and self-employed, and between persons being whether engaged in economic activity or not is still important, since the limitations and conditions laid down in the Treaty and the measures adopted to give it effect are different (ECJ, 23 March 2003, case C-138/02, *Collins*, par. 32; opinion of Advocate general, 4 June 2009, cases C-22/08 and 23/08, *Vatsouras*, par. 55)[28].

---

[26] In Danosa, the ECJ stated that, whichever directive applies (Directive 92/85 or Directive 86/613 – now Directive 2010/41 – or Directive 76/207 – now Directive 2006/54), "it is important to ensure, for the person concerned, the protection granted under EU law to pregnant women in cases where the legal relationship linking her to another person has been severed on account of her pregnancy" (ECJ, 11 November 2010, case C-232/09, *Danosa*, par. 70). In fact, the objective pursued by the rules of EU law governing equality between men and women, and in particular the protection of women before and after they give birth, cannot be achieved if the protection against dismissal granted to pregnant women under EU law depends "on the formal categorisation of their employment relationship under national law or on the choice made at the time of their appointment between one type of contract and another" (ECJ, 11 November 2010, case C-232/09, *Danosa*, par. 69).

[27] "Union citizenship should be the fundamental status of nationals of the Member States when they exercise their right of free movement and residence. It is therefore necessary to codify and review the existing Community instruments dealing separately with workers, self-employed persons, as well as students and other inactive persons in order to simplify and strengthen the right of free movement and residence of all Union citizens" (Whereas No. 3 Dir. 2004/38).

[28] Bercusson, 2009: 376.

This approach also affects also the interpretation of the concept of the worker within the meaning of Article 45 TFEU; this concept must not be strictly interpreted because it determines the scope of a fundamental right (ECJ, 16 July 2009, case C-208/07, *von Chamier-Glisczinski*, par. 69).

In general, the scope of a regulation that implements a fundamental right should be determined in view of its objectives and must not be interpreted strictly. In such cases, the protection cannot depend on the type of contract of employment but must be guaranteed to all persons and against all offences[29]. The duty to respect a fundamental right does not depend on the existence of a contractual relationship but on the proximity (contatto sociale) between persons.

Another important issue regarding the extension of the scope of labour law concerns "economically dependent self-employed work". This concept covers situations which fall between the concepts of subordinate employment and independent self-employment. Although formally "self-employed", this category of persons remains economically dependent on a single principal or client/employer for its source of income[30].

This category has been legally recognised by only a minority of European countries. The main objective of the existing national legislation is to afford particular categories of workers better protection, without classing them as employees[31]. However, the scope and the content of this category differ from one country to another. The criteria for distinguishing economic dependency are also really different[32]. Moreover,

---

29 *Transformation of labour and future of labour law in Europe. Final report* (1999), A. Supiot (ed.), Report for the European Commission. Collins (2006: 139; 2007: 2) has spoken of inter-textuality/inter-legality. In his opinion, "the values found in expressions of rights in constitutional documents need to be translated into concept and principles that fit into structures and coherent principles of private law. The two parts of the law, private law and public law, need to be normatively compatible, whilst not expressing and articulating those principles and rights in the same way".

30 Green Paper, *Modernising labour law to meet the challenges of the 21st century*, p. 11 COM(2006) 708 final; Perulli, 2002; Perulli, 2010: 621; Razzolini, 2010.

31 "Economic dependency is the basis for specific rights not recognised for other types of self-employed workers, but less extensive than the rights accorded to employees. The coverage accorded to economically dependent self-employed workers varies considerably from one country to another" (Opinion of the European Economic and Social Committee on *New trends in self-employed work: the specific case of economically dependent self-employed work*, 2011/C 18/08).

32 In some countries, an economically dependent self-employed worker is someone who performs the work concerned personally and directly. Other criteria relate to the proportion of income from a single client, the duration of the relationship between worker and client, the existence of continuous and coordinated contractual relationship. Moreover, a worker can be qualified as economically dependent if the way he/she

there is a great diversity in national regulations on economically dependent self-employed workers.

As affirmed by the European Economic and Social Committee, "any recognition of economically dependent self-employed work might lead to people hitherto defined as employees being transferred to the category of economically dependent self-employed work"; therefore, "the recognition of economically dependent self-employed work cannot be entirely separated from issues of 'bogus self-employment', a reality which can be testified to in a number of EU countries" (par. 1). Combating bogus self-employment with an adequate system of checks, enforcement and sanctions is necessary to avoid distortions of competition and differences in the minimum social standard applied across Member States[33].

Therefore, "economically dependent self-employed work can only exist as a status if it is clearly distinguished from waged work" (par. 5.1.2 of Opinion of the European Economic and Social Committee on 'New trends in self-employed work: the specific case of economically dependent self-employed work'). In this regard, the European Economic and Social Committee suggests an identification of the aspects common to the definitions of employed persons in the different EU Member States and a clear definition of the criterion for legal subordination. In fact, self-employed workers are "all persons pursuing a gainful activity for their own account" (i.e. not in a relationship of dependence) (Art. 2.a) Directive 2010/41)[34]. Thus, "before any attempt is made to gain a better insight into self-employed but economically dependent work, a clear, accurate definition of employees needs to be established" (par. 1.5). In this regard, "a set of common European criteria which would provide guidelines for determining the nature of the employment status, independently of the legitimate wish of the parties", would be really effective (Joint conclusions and recommendations from the European social

organises production is determined by the client's activity (Opinion of the European Economic and Social Committee on *New trends in self-employed work: the specific case of economically dependent self-employed work'* par. 4.1.4).

33 European Parliament resolution of 9 March 2010 on the Report on Competition Policy 2008 (2009/2173(INI). Bogus self-employed workers allow employers to circumvent taxes and social insurance contributions. Furthermore, these workers are more flexible and cheaper than employees (see the recent survey of Research Institute for Labour and Social Affairs in the Czech Republic on the EWCO website).

34 In the UK persons are considered self-employed if: they run their own business and takes responsibility for its success or failure; they have several customers at the same time; they can decide how, when and where to work; they are free to hire other people to do the work for them or help them at their own expense; they provide the main items of equipment to do the work (EERO, *Self-employment in Europe* 2010, European Commission. Directorate-General for Employment, Social Affairs and Equal Opportunities, 2010).

partners in the construction industry on self-employment and bogus self-employment).

Sometimes, the concept of "economically dependent self-employed work" has been used to limit the scope of EU law. For example, in its *Proposal for a Directive amending Directive 2002/15/EC on the organisation of the working time of persons performing mobile road transport activities*, the European Commission suggested that "the notion of mobile worker covered by the directive also included the so-called 'false' self-employed drivers, i.e. those drivers who are not tied to an employer by an employment contract but who do not have the freedom to have relations with several customers" (COM(2008) 650). This proposal was rejected by the European Parliament which demanded the full inclusion of self-employed drivers within the scope of the Directive[35]. Nowadays, the Directive is applied to mobile workers (Art. 3.d) as well as to self-employed drivers, i.e. anyone "who is entitled to work for himself and who is not tied to an employer by an employment contract or by any other type of working hierarchical relationship, who is free to organise the relevant working activities, whose income depends directly on the profits made and who has the freedom to, individually or through a cooperation between self-employed drivers, have commercial relations with several customers" (Art. 3.e).

For the purposes of the Directive, those drivers who do not satisfy the criteria laid down by Art. 3.e) shall be subjected to the same obligations and benefit from the same rights as those provided for mobile workers. Therefore, if one of the elements of the self-employed relationship (absence of hierarchical relationship, freedom to organise his/her own activities, freedom to have commercial relationships with several customers, dependency for income on the profits made) is absent, the relationship should be qualified as mobile work, even if there is no contract of employment.

IV. Conclusion

In this chapter, it has been shown the different strategies followed by European Law to maintain full-time open-ended contract as a general form of the employment relationship. On one hand, it deals with the concepts of employee, part-time worker, fixed-term worker and temporary agency worker. The broad definitions of these atypical contracts

---

35 According to MEPs, it is in the general interest that the rules on working time, driving times and rest periods for both mobile workers and self-employed drivers should be properly applied in order to improve the health and safety protection of persons performing mobile road transport activities, to improve road safety and to align conditions of competition.

should prevent the creation of new types of contract from provoking the ultra-segmentation of the labour market. On the other hand, it prohibits discrimination, a specific declaration of one of the fundamental principles of European Union law, namely the general principle of equality. Principles of non-discrimination have two different purposes: ensuring equal treatment of atypical employees and persons employed on the basis of a standard contract; adapting the rights concerned to effectively remove differences in treatment between persons employed under a standard contract and persons employed under an atypical contract. The Court of justice has not yet recognised this second function to the principles of non-discrimination regarding atypical workers. Since these principles are "a specific expression of one of the fundamental principles of European Union law", the general principle of equality, it is likely that the Court of justice will interpret them as a prohibition on direct and indirect discrimination.

The chapter also considers the quality of self-employment jobs. Again, two approach are developed: one reflects the notion of determining the scope of labour law in view of the policy objectives of the regulation; the other regards the extension of the scope of labour law concerns "economically dependent self-employed work". The first approach underlines that the scope of a regulation that implements a fundamental right should be determined in view of its objectives. In such cases, the protection cannot depend on the type of contract of employment but must be guaranteed to all persons and against all offences. The second approach concerns the extension of the scope of labour law to these formally "self-employed", that are economically dependent on a single principal or client/employer for its source of income. As stated, any recognition of economically dependent self-employed work must avoid any transferring of people hitherto defined as employees to the category of economically dependent self-employed work. Therefore, "economically dependent self-employed work" can only exist as a status if it is clearly distinguished from waged work. To that purpose, a set of common European criteria to determine employee status and self-employed status in relation to Labour law would be really effective.

The Freedom of Association and the Effective Right to Collective Bargaining in EU Labour Law, as a Lever for Better and Decent Jobs

Filip DORSSEMONT

Professor of Labour Law at the Law Faculty of the Université catholique de Louvain

I. Introduction

The freedom of association and the effective recognition of the right to collective bargaining have been enshrined in the ILO Declaration on fundamental principles and rights at work. They are quintessential to the promotion of *decent work*. The Freedom of Association Committee has consistently held that the right to strike is an intrinsic corollary to the right to organise protected by Convention No 87. There can be no doubt that the right to strike which is an essential means through which workers and their organisations may promote and defend their economic and social interests is covered by the Declaration[1]. Illicit restrictions to the right to strike undermine the effective recognition of the right to collective bargaining.

As early as 2001, the European Commission had issued a Communication related to the issue of Quality in Work [COM(2001) 313 final][2]. The European Commission has committed itself to contribute to the promotion of *decent work*, albeit it has insisted on the restrictions which flow from its competences. In this respect, it has explicitly referred to

1 See International Labour Office, *Freedom of association in practice: lessons learned. Global report under the follow up to the ILO Declaration on Fundamental Principles and Rights at Work 2008*, International Labour Conference, 97th Session 2008 Report I (B), Geneva, 14-16.

2 Communication of the Commission to the Council, the European Parliament, the Economic and Social Committee and the Committee of the Regions, *Employment and social policies: a framework for investing in quality*.

the fact that issues of freedom of association and collective bargaining are excluded from or only partially covered by the Union's legislative competences and policies [COM(2006) 249 final]. The present paper seeks to examine how the Commission's understanding of concepts of both decent work and Quality in Work take sufficient recognition of the freedom of association and effective recognition of the freedom of collective bargaining into account as a lever to promote better and decent jobs. Furthermore, it examines to what extent the European Court of Justice recognises and respects both freedoms.

The first Communication of the Commission [COM(2001) 313 final] on the issue of Quality in Work, does not pay any reference to these fundamental rights. Instead the Commission focused its attention on "social dialogue" and "worker involvement". Both issues were issues covered under "The work and wider labour market context". The Communication construes this as one of two dimensions to apprehend the main elements of Quality in Work. The semantics of the Commission's Communication seem to provide evidence of its reluctance to recognise fundamental rights. The approach is much more functional. The impetus is being placed on the functions involved in the exercise of those rights. Thus, Social Dialogue and Worker Involvement refer to two distinct functions in a system of industrial relations[3]. In a classical approach they can be linked to two distinct players, *id est* trade unions and workers' representatives. From a legal perspective, these functions can be *directly* linked to two distinct fundamental rights, *id est* the freedom of collective bargaining and the right to information and consultation. Indirectly, they presuppose that a legal system recognises the right for workers to organise.

In sum, the Commission's Communication does not contain any *explicit* reference to the two fundamental workers' rights in the ILO Declaration on fundamental principles and rights at work. The reference to "social dialogue", does warrant the necessity to promote the freedom of collective bargaining. On the other hand, the reference to the issue of worker involvement, goes *beyond* the ILO Declaration. This leads to the hypothesis that the European Union seeks to promote a right to information and consultation, to which the ILO Declaration does not seem to pay any tribute at all.

The *prima facie* analysis of the Commission's communications on Quality in Work as well as that on Decent Work needs to be comple-

[3] A later communication of the Commission has elucidated the concepts of social dialogue and worker involvement and corroborates this interpretation: Communication of the Commission to the Council, the European Parliament, the Economic and Social Committee and the Committee of the Regions, *Improving quality in work: a review of recent progress* [COM(2003) 728 final].

mented by an examination of the recognition by the Court of Justice of the freedom of association, freedom of collective bargaining and the right to information and consultation as general principles of EU law. This chapter examines to what extent the weak recognition of the right to organise (alias the freedom of association) and the right to collective bargaining as general principles of EC law and of EC labour law (staff cases) undermines the credibility of the Union's alleged commitment to promote decent work.

It also examines to what extent the Commission's commitment to worker involvement as an indicator of Quality in work could undermine the position of trade unions at enterprise level in a way that is at odds with ILO standards.

In recent times, a *tsunami* of three judgements (Laval, Viking, and *Rüffert*) has imposed severe restrictions on the right of trade unions to have recourse to collective action and on the Member States' duty of to promote collective bargaining. In a recent examination, the ILO's Committee of Independent Experts seems to question the conformity of the *Laval* and *Viking* judgements with core ILO conventions. Furthermore, some scholars have construed the case law of the Court in *Rüffert* to be at odds with ILO Convention 94 (Labour Clauses [Public Contracts] Convention). *In sum*, despite the much more unambiguous recognition of a right to take collective action in *Laval* and *Viking*, both cases raise the question of whether the way in which the Court "balances" the right to take collective action against so called fundamental *economic* freedoms does not severely weaken the impact of such a recognition as a means to promote decent work.

Last but not least, the question arises as to whether the recent "constitutionalisation" of the Charter of Nice and the proposed accession to the European Convention on Human Rights will create a momentum for a future *Rechtsfortbildung* by the Court of Justice, strengthening the freedom of association and the freedom of collective bargaining.

II. The Freedom of Association, the Right to Collective Bargaining and the Right to Information and Consultation in the ECJ Case Law

Until recently, the European Court of Justice had a *poor* record in upholding fundamental trade union rights. Ever since, *Laval* and *Viking*, it has a *bad* record.

References by the Court to the freedom of association (right to organise) as a general principle of EC Law have been extremely rare. The Court of Justice has been primarily concerned with recognition of the freedom of association as a principle of "Labour Law", *id est* in its jurisprudence related to staff cases[4]. In the *Bosman case*, the Court *did* recognise the freedom of association, enshrined in Article 11 of the European Convention on Human Rights, as being one of the fundamental rights which are protected as general principles of EC Law[5]. Though the case undoubtedly refers to a labour dispute, the freedom of association was not invoked by the employee involved, nor could the associations concerned considered to be "employers' associations", in the classical interpretation of the term. *In sum*, the case has no bearing on the issue of the right to organise in a context of industrial relations, *id est* the right to trade union association. On the other hand, the AG Jacobs in *Albany* did consider the more *specific right to form and join trade unions* to be a *general* principle of EC law[6]. The AG did base that reasoning on the principles laid down in the *Bosman* and the *Maurissen* judgements. Since, the latter is a staff case; it is hazardous to state that the Court was in fact developing "general" principles of EC Law.

The only immediate tribute to the freedom of association *in the context of industrial relations* was made in the *Werhof* case[7]. The Court did construe that the freedom of association entailed a negative right of employers *not* to organise. Furthermore, it ruled that such a right was at stake, in so far as employers were being forced to apply employment conditions enshrined in a collective agreement signed by employers' organisations to which they were not affiliated. The judgement needs to be criticised in so far as the Court pretends that *Gustafsson*[8] would warrant a supposition that an obligation to apply a collective agreement to which he is not a party would affect an employer's negative freedom to organise[9]. In fact, a closer reading of *Gustafsson* reveals quite the opposite. The reasoning by the Court could in fact turn out to be dramatic in view of the obligation of a foreign service provider to apply collective agreements which were made generally applicable.

---

4 See *inter alia:* ECJ, 8 October 1974, *Union syndicale, Massa and Kortner*, C-175/73, ECJ, 18 January 1990, *Henri Maurissen and Union syndicale*, C-193/87 and C-194/87.

5 ECJ, 15 December 1995, *Union royale belge des sociétés de football association ASBL contre Jean-Marc Bosman*, C-415/93, § 79.

6 Joined opinion of Mr Advocate General Jacobs delivered on 28 January 1999, *Albany International BV v Stichting Bedrijfspensioenfonds Textielindustrie*. Reference for a preliminary ruling: Kantongerecht Arnhem – Netherlands, Case C-67/96, § 139.

7 ECJ, 9 March 2006, Hans *Werhof v Freeway Traffic Systems GmbH & Co. KG*. C-499/04.

8 European Court of Human Rights, 28 March 1996, *Gustafsson v Sweden*, No. 15573/89.

9 ECJ, 9 March 2006, *Hans Werhof v Freeway Traffic Systems GmbH & Co. KG.*, C-499/04, § 33.

The record of the Court of Justice with regard to the freedom of collective bargaining was even more troublesome. In *Albany* the Court did not take the freedom of collective bargaining into consideration in order to address the question of whether competition rules could restrict the validity of collective agreements declared universally applicable[10]. Advocate General Jacobs did deny that the freedom of collective bargaining could be deduced from the recognition of the freedom of association as a general principle of EC law. He stated that: "it cannot be said that there is sufficient convergence of national legal orders and international legal instruments on the recognition of a specific fundamental right to bargain collectively[11]."

Instead, he argued that the collective bargaining process, like any other negotiation between economic actors, is (…) "sufficiently protected by the general principle of freedom of contract. In our view, such an approach is questionable. It neglects the quintessential difference between individual and collective autonomy[12]."

In *Ueapme*, the Court of first instance did interpret the Maastricht Agreement on Social Policy as precluding an enforceable right to take part in the negotiations which could amount to an agreement concluded at Community level[13]. The Court construed the bargaining process as being based on the "*mutual*" willingness to initiate the process provided for in Article 4 of the Agreement". *In sum*, the Court highlighted the voluntary nature of the bargaining process based upon mutual recognition of the social partners. The voluntary nature of the bargaining process is consistent with the case law of the European Court on Human Rights as well as with the approach to freedom of collective bargaining under the European Social Charter. Unfortunately, the Court did *not* refer to this conceptual framework.

In a recent case, *Commision v Germany*, (ECJ, 15 July 2010, C-271/08) the Court could not avoid the question of whether the right to bargain collectively did constitute a general principle of EU Law. The Commission had started an infringement procedure against the German Republic since local authorities and local authority undertakings had awarded service contracts in respect of occupational old-age pensions

---

10 See ECJ, 21 September 1999, *Albany International BV v. Stichting Bedrijfspensioenfonds Textielindustrie*, C-67/96.

11 Joined opinion of Advocate General Jacobs delivered on 28 January 1999, *Albany International BV v Stichting Bedrijfspensioenfonds Textielindustrie*. Reference for a preliminary ruling: Kantongerecht Arnhem – Netherlands. Case C-67/96, § 160.

12 Joined opinion of Advocate General Jacobs delivered on 28 January 1999, *Albany International BV v Stichting Bedrijfspensioenfonds Textielindustrie*. Reference for a preliminary ruling: Kantongerecht Arnhem – Netherlands. Case C-67/96, § 161.

13 ECJ, 17 June 1998, *Ueapme v. Council of the European Union*, T-135/963.

directly, without a call for tenders at European Union level. The Commission argued that this constituted a violation of Council Directive 92/50/EEC of 18 June 1992 relating to the coordination of procedures for the award of public service contracts (OJ 1992 L 209) and Directive 2004/18/EC of the European Parliament and of the Council of 31 March 2004 on the coordination of procedures for the award of public works contracts, public supply contracts and public service contracts (OJ 2004 L 134, p. 114).

Germany replied that these decisions were based upon collective agreements which, because of their nature and subject matter, fell outside the field of application of Directives 92/50 and 2004/18 in view of the so-called *Albany immunity* which shields collective agreements from competition rules. The Court did not accept this argument and was thus forced to consider whether the application of these directives had to be balanced against the right to bargain collectively. It did accept that the right to bargain collectively had to be recognised as a general principle of EU law. The Court in this respect referred to the fact that this right had been enshrined in Article 6 of the European Social Charter and in the provisions of instruments drawn up by the Member States at Community level or in the context of the European Union, such as Article 12 of the Community Charter of the Fundamental Social Rights of Workers (9 December 1989) and Article 28 of the Charter of Fundamental Rights of the European Union ("the Charter"). The Court explicitly indicated that the latter constituted an instrument to which Article 6 TEU accorded the same legal value as the Treaties.

Unfortunately, just as was the case in *Viking* and *Laval*, this only prompted the Court to suggest a need to balance the fundamental economic freedoms underlying these directives against the "general principle" concerned.

In the infamous *Viking* and *Laval* case, the Court did recognise a right to have recourse to collective action as a general principle of EC law[14]. The Court construed the right to have recourse to collective action partially by reference to ILO instruments related to the freedom of association and partially by reference to the European Social Charter[15].

Though the ECJ case law on information and consultation procedures is prolific, it has rarely made any reference to the right to infor-

---

14 ECJ, 11 December 2007, C-483/05 (*Viking*) and 18 December 2007, C-341/05 (*Laval*).

15 For a previous analysis: F. Dorssemont, "The right to take collective action v. fundamental economic freedoms in the aftermath of *Laval* and *Viking*", in M. De Vos, *European Union Internal Market and Labour Law: Friends or foes*, Antwerpen, Oxford, Intersentia, 2009, 45-104.

mation and consultation as a *general principle* of EU law. The Court appears to be extremely reluctant to make reference to fundamental rights, in so far as the text of the various EC Directives related to worker involvement in a case of restructuring can be held to be sufficiently clear in order to solve interpretational problems. In Mono Car Styling, the Court had to assess whether the right to information and consultation in a case of collective redundancy needed to be construed as a right held by individual workers or whether it had to be construed as a "collective right". Though such a question would warrant an analysis of the international and European instruments' recognition of such a right, the Court, as opposed to the Advocate General, decided to stick to a literal and systematic interpretation of the isolated text of the EC Directive 98/59[16].

III. Worker Involvement and Trade Unions

A major difference between the ILO approach to decent work and to that of "Quality in Work" is the explicit reference to worker involvement, in the wording of information and consultation procedures. The ILO Declaration refers to "collective bargaining". The concept of collective bargaining is much more precise than the concept of social dialogue to which the Commission tends to refer. Collective bargaining amounts to consensual legal instruments, *id est* collective agreements. In its traditional approach, collective bargaining is a prerogative of trade unions.

The notion of Worker Involvement has been introduced in Community Law by the *Societas Europaea* Directive 2001/86. Article 2 h) defines involvement of employees as: "any mechanism, including information, consultation and participation, through which employees' representatives may exercise an influence on decisions to be taken within the company".

Hence, worker involvement needs to be distinguished from collective bargaining for two distinct reasons. Firstly, it is not construed as a trade union prerogative. It is being granted to employees' representatives. The notion of employees' representatives tends to be defined by reference to national law and/or practice. Secondly, worker involvement amounts to unilateral decisions adopted within the company. It does not amount to collective agreements. Furthermore, many EC Directives explicitly indicate that information and consultation procedures do not affect the exercise of the *managerial prerogative*.

---

16 ECJ, 16 July 2009, C-12/08 (*Mono Car Styling*), § 38: "In that regard, it is clear, first of all, from the text and scheme of Directive 98/59 that the right to information and consultation which it lays down is intended for workers' representatives and not for workers individually."

Though both phenomena need to be distinguished, the exercise of worker involvement through employee representatives entails the risk of undermining the position of trade unions within the undertaking. For this reason, many ILO instruments related to worker involvement and/or elected worker representatives contain an interesting caveat. They indicate that these procedures and the recognition of elected representatives cannot be used to undermine the position of trade unions[17]. Hence, it is regrettable that the EC directives promoting worker involvement do not contain any such caveat. This objection is relevant, in so far as the European Union has never *promoted* collective bargaining at company level and in fact has not yet adopted an optional framework in order to promote collective bargaining at transnational company level in a way that would safeguard the position of trade unions.

IV. *Viking, Laval* and *Rüffert* versus ILO Conventions No. 87, 94 and 98

The *Laval* and *Viking* cases of the ECJ have been referred to above as recognising a right to take collective action as a general principle of EU labour law. In so far as this recognition is not restricted to one kind

---

[17] Article 5 of the ILO Convention No. 135 Workers' Representatives Convention, 1971: "Where there exist in the same undertaking both trade union representatives and elected representatives, appropriate measures shall be taken, wherever necessary, to ensure that the existence of elected representatives is not used to undermine the position of the trade unions concerned or their representatives and to encourage co-operation on all relevant matters between the elected representatives and the trade unions concerned and their representatives".

Article 3 of the ILO Convention No. 154 Collective Bargaining Convention 1981: "1. Where national law or practice recognises the existence of workers' representatives as defined in Article 3, subparagraph (b), of the Workers' Representatives Convention, 1971, national law or practice may determine the extent to which the term *collective bargaining* shall also extend, for the purpose of this Convention, to negotiations with these representatives. 2. Where, in pursuance of paragraph 1 of this Article, the term *collective bargaining* also includes negotiations with the workers' representatives referred to in that paragraph, appropriate measures shall be taken, wherever necessary, to ensure that the existence of these representatives is not used to undermine the position of the workers' organisations concerned."

See also: R94 Co-operation at the Level of the Undertaking Recommendation, 1952: "1. Appropriate steps should be taken to promote consultation and co-operation between employers and workers at the level of the undertaking on matters of mutual concern not within the scope of collective bargaining machinery, or not normally dealt with by other machinery concerned with the determination of terms and conditions of employment". R143 Workers' Representatives Recommendation, 1971: 2 b) elected representatives, namely representatives who are freely elected by the workers of the undertaking in accordance with provisions of national laws or regulations or of collective agreements and whose functions do not include activities which are recognised as the exclusive prerogative of trade unions in the country concerned.

of collective action, *id est* strike action, the recognition can be said to have a "liberal" nature. In fact, the collective actions concerned were not strike actions, but were a circular calling for a boycott (*Viking*) and a blockade of a construction site (*Laval*).

In *Laval* a dispute arouse between the Swedish trade unions and a Latvian service provider who was awarded a public works contract following a tender bid for the renovation and extension of school premises in the town of Vaxholm. The Swedish trade unions organised a blockade of the construction site when the Latvian service provider refused to conclude a tie in an agreement with a Swedish union to pay the wages which were generally (though not universally) applicable in the Swedish construction sector. Instead, the Latvian service provider applied the wage scales which were enshrined in a collective agreement previously concluded with a Latvian trade union. The Court adopted an even more severe stance. It ruled that the freedom to provide services and Article 3 of the Directive 96/71 on the Posting of Workers precluded a trade union, in a Member State deprived of statutory minimum wages as well of a system of universally applicable collective agreements from attempting, by means of collective action in the form of a blockade ("blockad") to force a provider of services established in another Member State to enter into negotiations with it on the rates of pay for posted workers. Nor could the trade union force the service provider to sign a collective agreement, the terms of which provided, at least for some matters, more favourable conditions than those resulting from the relevant legislative provisions, while other terms related to matters not referred to in Article 3 in the Posting of Workers Directive." *In sum*, and contrary to *Viking*, the Court denied that the collective action concerned had a legitimate goal, thus depriving the referring judge of any margin for appreciation.

In so far as the industrial disputes in *Laval* and *Viking* are interwoven with aspects of collective bargaining, it goes without saying that the restrictions imposed on the right to have recourse to collective action undermine a trade union's capacity to engage in collective bargaining.

In the *Rüffert* case, the ECJ had to rule on the conformity of the *Landesvergabegesetz* in Lower Saxony with the freedom to provide services and the Posting of Workers Directive. A statute related to public contracts provided that:

"1. Contracts to which this Convention applies shall include clauses ensuring to the workers concerned wages (including allowances), hours of work and other conditions of labour which are not less favourable than those established for work of the same character in the trade or industry concerned in the district where the work is carried on:

(a) by collective agreement or other recognised machinery of negotiation between organisations of employers and workers representative respectively of substantial proportions of the employers and workers in the trade or industry concerned; or

(b) by arbitration award; or

(c) by national laws or regulations.

2. Where the conditions of labour referred to in the preceding paragraph are not regulated in a manner referred to therein in the district where the work is carried on, the clauses to be included in contracts shall ensure to the workers concerned wages (including allowances), hours of work and other conditions of labour which are not less favourable than:

(a) those established by collective agreement or other recognised machinery of negotiation, by arbitration, or by national laws or regulations, for work of the same character in the trade or industry concerned in the nearest appropriate district; or

(b) the general level observed in the trade or industry in which the contractor is engaged by employers whose general circumstances are similar.

3. The terms of the clauses to be included in contracts and any variations thereof shall be determined by the competent authority, in the manner considered most appropriate to the national conditions, after consultation with the organisations of employers and workers concerned, where such exist.

4. Appropriate measures shall be taken by the competent authority, by advertising specifications or otherwise, to ensure that persons tendering for contracts are aware of the terms of the clauses (Art. 2 ILO Convention no. 94 concerning labour clauses in public contracts).

The ILO Convention No. 94 can be seen as a means for governments to promote collective bargaining. The ECJ ruling in *Rüffert* severely restricts that capacity.

The Committee of Experts on the Application of Conventions and Recommendations dedicated a general survey to the application of ILO Convention No. 94 at the 97th Session of the International Labour Conference. At the time, the *Rüffert case* was still pending. Hence, the Committee was unable to dwell on the impact of the case law on those States who had ratified the Convention.

In the latest report of the ILO Committee of Experts, drafted for the 99th session of the International Labour Conference, the Committee had to examine the impact of the case law in *Viking* and *Laval* on the freedom of trade union association in the United Kingdom. following critical observations from the British trade union BALPA supported by the ITF. The ILO Committee refused to accept the defence of the British Government which disclaimed any responsibility whatsoever for the attitude adopted by the judiciary, "because any adverse impact of Viking and Laval would be a consequence of European Union law to which the United Kingdom is obliged to give effect, rather than of any unilateral action by the United Kingdom itself". The Committee stated that it was in no position to judge the correctness of the ECJ holdings as such, but that it did have to "examine whether the impact of these decisions at national level was such as to deny workers' freedom of association rights under Convention No. 87"[18].

The ILO Committee of Experts considers that "it has never included the need to assess the proportionality of interests bearing in mind a notion of freedom of establishment or freedom to provide services"[19]. The Committee considered that the "doctrine that is being articulated in these ECJ judgements is likely to have a significant restrictive effect on the exercise of the right to strike in practice in a manner contrary to the Convention".

In sum, the ECJ case law in *Viking* and *Laval* sheds serious doubts on the credibility of the Commission's findings on the proclaimed objectives of the European Union to promote decent and better jobs.

Last but not least, both cases are problematic in view of the obligations the European Union imposes *in foro externo* to non-communitarian service providers tendering within the framework of the Community's external assistance. Thus, Article 10 of Regulation 2110/2005 on access to Community external assistance *in foro externo* obliges "tenderers who have been awarded contracts to respect internationally agreed core labour standards, e.g. the ILO core labour standards, conventions on freedom of association and collective bargaining, elimination of forced and compulsory labour, elimination of discrimination in respect of employment and occupation, and the abolition of child labour".

V. Epilogue: Constitutionalising Workers' Rights and the Prospects of their Accession to the European Convention on Human Rights

Due to ratification of the Lisbon Treaty, the consolidated Treaty on European Union now provides that "The Union *shall* accede to the

18 Report III (1A) Report of the Committee of Experts on the Application of Conventions and Recommendations, International Labour Conference 99th Session 2010, 209.

19 Report III (1A) Report of the Committee of Experts on the Application of Conventions and Recommendations, International Labour Conference 99th Session 2010, 209.

European Convention for the Protection of Human Rights and Fundamental Freedoms" (Article 6 § 2 TEU).

The accession to the European Convention on Human Rights constitutes a greater step forward in a constitutional recognition of fundamental rights within the European Union. In our view, it goes beyond recognition of fundamental rights as mere general principles of the Union's law. In fact, Article 6 § 3 TEU, *as such*, already recognise such an impact on the fundamental rights, as guaranteed by the European Convention on Human Rights.

Due to this accession, the status of the fundamental rights enshrined in the European Convention on Human Rights will differ fundamentally from those enshrined in the Charter of Fundamental Rights. In fact, at their best, the rights enshrined in the Charter have the same *legal value* as conflicting fundamental freedoms enshrined in the EU Treaties. Furthermore, the Charter itself has upgraded some of the fundamental freedoms which have the potential to conflict with fundamental (workers') rights. Thus, Article 15 of the Charter has proclaimed the freedom of establishment and freedom to provide services as proper "fundamental freedoms". In *Viking* and *Laval*, both freedoms were considered as qualified restrictions to the fundamental right to strike and the fundamental freedom of collective bargaining. Last but not least, Article 16 of the Charter has consecrated the freedom to conduct a business. The only international Court to interpret the Charter will be the ECJ. For the ECJ, it will be one among other "constitutional" principles to be taken into account.

In sum, in my view, the prospect that the Treaty's reference to the Charter of Fundamental rights might provoke a *shift* in the way the Court deals or even has to deal with potential conflicts between the right to strike and so-called fundamental (economic) freedoms is extremely weak.

The prospects stemming from Accession to the European Convention on Human Rights to change the economic constitution of the European Union or at least adding a flavour of economic governance are more promising. An accession to the European Convention on Human Rights might add some dimension to the flat simple juxtaposition of fundamental freedoms and fundamental rights integrated into one Charter. It puts genuine fundamental (workers') rights at the heart of the matter. Since the European Convention on Human Rights is corroborated by judicial supervision, it will force all European institutions, including the ECJ, to abide by the judgements delivered in Strasbourg. As opposed to Luxembourg, Strasbourg will not dwell on the question of whether human rights can restrict fundamental economic freedoms. It will assess whether and to what extent these fundamental economic freedoms can actually restrict genuine fundamental rights. It will force the European institutions to justify restrictions to citizens' rights, instead of forcing citizens to justify the exercise of their human rights.

The accession to the European Convention on Human Rights is by no means a certainty. Though Article 6 TEU provides that the Union *shall* accede, Article 218, § 8 of the Treaty on the functioning of the European Union provides that such a decision needs to be taken unanimously by the Council. This requirement for unanimity does not, as such, provide an argument for Member States to question the obligatory nature of their constitutional duty under the Treaty on the functioning of the European Union to decide in favour of the accession. Article 238 § 8 TFEU does indicate that ratification of the Lisbon Treaty as such is not sufficient to guarantee that the decision of the Council will become effective. The article provides that the decision will become effective solely "after it has been approved by the Member States in accordance with their respective constitutional requirements".

The question arises as to whether the accession of the European Union to the EConvHR creates a momentum to rebalance the conflict between fundamental freedoms and genuine fundamental rights, such as the right to take collective action and the freedom of collective bargaining. In the landmark judgements of *Demir and Baykara*[20] as well as in *Enerji*[21], the Court had to assess the conformity of a provision under Turkish law which deprived civil servants the right to have recourse to any kind of collective action and to form trade unions. The judgements do not deal with restrictions based upon conflicting rights and freedoms. These recent judgements do not provide sufficient guidance to predict anything whatsoever.

In two judgements from the Strasbourg Court (*Unison* and *Federation of Offshore Workers' Trade Unions*)[22] which preceded both landmark judgements, the Court did adopt a broad interpretation of the conflicting private and public interests which could justify restrictions to the right to take collective action. Hence, at first sight, the prospects seem bad. As mentioned above, the Court in *Demir and Baykara* did indicate, however, that the Court was under an obligation to interpret Article 11 of the EconvHR in the light of "international law other than the Convention, the interpretation of such elements by competent organs, and the practice of European States reflecting their common values."

---

20 European Court of Human Rights, 12 November 2008, *Demir and Baykara v. Turkey*, No. 34503/97.

21 European Court on Human Rights, 21 April 2009, *Enerji Yapi-Yol Sen*, No. 68959/01.

22 European Court of Human Rights, 10 January 2002, *Unison v. UK*, No. 53574/99 and European Court of Human Rights, 27 June 2002, *Federation of Offshore Workers' Trade Unions and Others v. Norway*, No. 38190/97.

Since both judgements were ruled in discordance with the ILO's supervisory bodies as well as with the jurisprudence of the European Committee on Social Rights, the persuasive authority of these "precedents" is poor. In this respect, it is worthwhile to recall that the European Committee on Social Rights has refused to take into account mere business interests as a justified restriction for the right to take collective action. Thus, it has refuted that a "proportionality test" was compatible with the exhaustive nature of the restrictions under Article 31 ESC[23].

Irrespective of the accession of the European Union to the EConvHR, the European Court on Human Rights will be a competent forum to challenge national legislation and case law which have been influenced by the ECJ case law in *Laval* and *Viking*. In so far as domestic courts will refer to these cases to restrict the right to have recourse to collective action, this case law can be challenged. Thus, the Court will have the opportunity to scrutinise the ECJ in an indirect way. Unfortunately, the Court is known for being extremely cautious in assessing whether the action by contracting parties to the EConvHR based upon EC Law is contrary to that convention[24].

---

23 See in this respect: ECSR, XVI-1, Conclusion with regard to Belgium. See for the situation on Belgium: F. Dorssemont, "La (non)conformité du droit belge relative à l'action collective par rapport à la Charte sociale européenne", X. *Actualités du dialogue social et du droit de grève*, Waterloo, Kluwer, 2009, 167-202.

24 In this respect, see *inter alia* S. Douglas-Scott, "A tale of two courts: Luxembourg, Strasbourg and the growing European Human rights acquis", in *Common Market Law Review*, 2006, pp. 629-630, 639-638 and "Relations between international courts and community Courts: Mutual deference or subordination?", *Common Market Law Review* 2005, pp. 581-585. The leading case is European Court on Human Rights, 30 June 2005, Bosphorus Hava Yolları Turizm ve Ticaret Anonim Şirketi v. Ireland, §§ 155-156: "In the Court's view, State action taken in compliance with such legal obligations is justified as long as the relevant organisation is considered to protect fundamental rights, as regards both the substantive guarantees offered and the mechanisms controlling their observance, in a manner which can be considered at least equivalent to that for which the Convention provides (see *M. & Co.*, […] p. 145, an approach with which the parties and the European Commission agreed). By "equivalent" the Court means "comparable"; any requirement that the organisation's protection be "identical" could run counter to the interest of international cooperation pursued […]. However, any such finding of equivalence could not be final and would be susceptible to review in the light of any relevant change in fundamental rights protection. If such equivalent protection is considered to be provided by the organisation, the presumption will be that a State has not departed from the requirements of the Convention when it does no more than implement legal obligations arising from its membership of the organisation. However, any such presumption can be rebutted if, in the circumstances of a particular case, it is considered that the protection of Convention rights was manifestly deficient. In such cases, the interest of international cooperation would be outweighed by the Convention's role as a "constitutional instrument of European public order" in the field of human rights (see *Loizidou v. Turkey* (preliminary objections), judgment of 23 March 1995, Series A No. 310, pp. 27-28, § 75)."

PART III

RELATIONS EMPLOYMENT/SOCIAL SECURITY

Suitable Employment and Job of Quality

Elise DERMINE

Assistant in Social Security Law,
Catholic University of Louvain, CRIDES

Introduction

If the issue of quality of employment is usually approached from a "labour law" angle, Social Security also has a role to play in the promotion of quality of employment or, at least, in the fight against the growth of insecure jobs.

Since the late 1990s, Social Security should no longer be limited to ensuring the financial autonomy of individuals outside the labour market (*decommodification* logic)[1], it must also play a role as a springboard into the labour market (*commodification* logic).

The concept of suitable employment in unemployment insurance is central to this tension. The objective of this concept is to use human resources as efficiently as possible (quantity of jobs – *commodification*), while protecting the unemployed against the obligation to perform a job that does not conform to the notion of human dignity and does not allow them to plan for their future[2] (quality of employment – *decommodification*).

Unemployment insurance systems as an impetus to fulfilling the concept of suitable employment play a role as a bulwark against the growth of insecure employment. The criteria selected to define a suitable job play a part in the construction of the definition of a job of quality.

---

1 G. Esping-Andersen, *The three worlds of welfare capitalism*, 1990, Princeton University Press.

2 For this definition of the job of quality, see: Service de lutte contre la pauvreté, la précarité et l'exclusion sociale, *Rapport 2008-2009* Partie 1, Une contribution au débat et à l'action politiques, III. Les critères de l'emploi convenable, une protection contre l'emploi précaire?, p. 97.

Logics of activation have been developing within the systems of unemployment insurance since the 1990s. Activation is pursuing a worthy goal: to increase the chances of reintegrating the unemployed into the labour market. It does however run the risk of disqualifying jobs considered as suitable, in favour of a greater activity ratio. This risk is increased tenfold in times of global jobs crisis, during which the "quantity of employment" angle naturally tends to overshadow the "quality of employment"[3] angle.

Objective and Description of the Contribution

The first part is devoted to developing an analytical framework incorporating the different dimensions that shape a job of quality.

In the second part, is confronted, to this theoretical framework, the international framing (ILO, Council of Europe and EU) of the concept of suitable employment[4], to assess whether it includes the necessary safeguards to ensure that a suitable job plays a part as a springboard into jobs of quality. The criteria for suitable employment will be checked to examine whether they achieve each dimension of a job of quality.

I. The Quality of Employment

After having clarified the notion of *quality of employment* (A), we will point the different dimensions of a *job of quality* (B).

A. A Plural Concept

The general term *quality of employment* actually encompasses two separate concepts in its structure: the *job of quality*[5] and the *quality of work*[6]. To define a *job of quality*, you must regard its quality:

---

3 Conscious of this risk, ILO pleads for a recovery centered on decent work: ILO, Report of the Director-General, "*Tackling the global jobs crisis. Recovery through decent work policies*", International Labour Conference, 98th session 2009, Report I(A).

4 For an analysis of the translation of the concept of suitable employment in the French legislation, see, in this book: P. CAILLAUD, "'*Valid offer' or 'reasonable offer' of employment: the French concept of suitable employment?*".

5 Concept developed by the European Foundation for the Improvement of Living and Working Conditions ("*Quality of work and employment in Europe: issues and challenges*", *Foundation paper*, No. 1, February 2002).

6 During a seminar on the quality of employment, E. LOZANO (DG Employment, Social Affairs and Equal Opportunity at the European Commission) explained that the various descriptions retained by the European Commission or by the ILO, namely "quality of jobs, quality of/in work, decent work and quality of employment" are actually distinct concepts with a more or less comprehensive content (E. Lozano, Comments on the conceptual paper of the task force: "towards international quality

- *In se*, that is to say its intrinsic characteristics;
- And *in concreto*, that is to say its adequacy with the personal characteristics of the worker.

As for the *quality of work*, this relates to the overall functioning of the labour market and its links with the social protection system.

This term comprises a vertical approach. It does not address the quality of a job for a worker at a given period but for all the worker's career, i.e. to the different jobs held and to any periods without work. Particular attention is therefore paid to securing career paths. To assess the quality of work in its vertical dimension specific criteria must be used, such as the possibility of training during a career, the opportunity to benefit from social protection between jobs or the possibility of finding a new job. Through this last criterion, we observe that the quantity of jobs plays a part in its vertical approach to the construction of the quality of work.

Moreover, the concept of quality of work also follows a horizontal path. At a given time, its objective is not to look at the characteristics of a particular job but over all jobs existing at this time. The criterion of the quantity of jobs is also important in the construction of the horizontal approach of quality of work. In this holistic approach, the quantity of employment is one of the criteria for evaluating the quality of work in both its vertical and horizontal approaches. The wolf is in sheep's clothing – any improvement in this criterion is likely to involve a deterioration in other aspects of quality of work, and particularly in times of crisis.

The quality of work and the job of quality are at a "crossroads of views"[7]. Apart from the perspective of workers, the views of employers and society are also legitimate. The views can either converge or diverge. As noted by L. Davoine, productivity and quality of work are important criteria for employers and workers. Other aspects should be taken into account by society, such as the under-utilisation of manpower and expertise, human and social costs, inequalities, discrimination and distribution of jobs of quality. Regarding job characteristics, employers have an interest, according to a classic model, in minimising wages to stay competitive whilst workers strive for higher wages[8]. On the discur-

---

of employment framework", *invited paper by European Commission*, 30 March 2007, Joint UNECE/EUROSTAT/ILO Seminar, 18-20 April 2006, Geneva, http://www.unece.org/stats/documents/2007.04.labour.htm).

7 L. Davoine, *La qualité de l'emploi: une perspective européenne*, Thèse, Université Paris 1 Panthéon-Sorbonne, 29 November 2007, p. 21.

8 L. Davoine, *op. cit.*, 2007, p. 21 et s.

sive level, the quality in work concept[9], as defined in the Commission Communication of 2001[10], covers the concept of both a job of quality and that of quality of work. However, despite the willingness of the European Employment Strategy to also include the characteristics of a job of quality, one can only note the absence of criteria to evaluate systematically the inherent quality of jobs[11], it is more fundamentally a matter of evaluating the functioning of the labour market[12] in particular through macro-economic indicators (such as the employment rate, unemployment rate, education, labour productivity, etc.).

The concept of decent work developed by the ILO[13] goes further towards a comprehensive approach to the quality of work. However, it covers an area broader than the European Union concept of quality of work since it focuses not only on the functioning of the labour market but also on that of social security[14]. At the European Union level, the Open Method of Coordination Social Protection and Social Inclusion has been established to assess the functioning of social security through

---

9 About the notion of quality in work developed at the European level, see, in this book: J. Deumer, *Reconciling the European notions of "quality in work" and "flexicurity"*.

10 Communication from the Commission to the Council, the European Parliament, the Economic and Social Committee and the Committee of the Regions, "Employment and social policies: a framework for investing in quality", COM(2001) 313, Brussels, 20 June 2001: "*It is proposed (...) that the main elements of quality in work can be grouped under two broad dimensions:*

Job characteristics*: objective and intrinsic characteristics, including: job satisfaction, remuneration, non-pay rewards, working time, skills and training and prospects for career advancement, job content, match between jobs characteristics and worker characteristics;*

The work and wider labour market context*: gender equality, health and safety, flexibility and security, access to jobs, work-life balance, social dialogue and worker involvement, diversity and non-discrimination*".

11 The "intrinsic quality of jobs" constitutes in fact one of the ten criteria for evaluation of the quality of work. It is evaluated through only two indicators: an index of wage rises and an index of mobility per type of contract (permanent – temporary).

12 Peña-Casas, 2007; J. Leschke et A. Watt, avec M. Finn, "*Putting a number on job quality? Constructing a European Job Quality Index*", *WP 2008.03, ETUI-REHS Research department*, p. 6; L. Davoine, *op. cit.*, 2007, p. 355 et s.

13 ILO, International Labour Conference, "A decent work", Report of the Director-General, 87th session, Geneva, 1999, p. 3; ILO, International Labour Office, General Report, 7th CIST, ICLS/17/2003/1, Geneva, November 2003; R. ANKER *et al.*, "*La mesure du travail décent: un système d'indicateurs statistiques de l'OIT*", *Revue internationale du travail*, Vol. 142, No. 2, Geneva, 2003, pp. 160-193.

14 J. Deumer, *Reconciling the European notions of "quality in work" and "flexicurity"* (in this book).

a variety of indicators[15]. The quantity of employment is therefore a measure of both the quality of work (UE) and decent work (ILO)[16].

This study is dedicated to the concept of suitable job. By means of the criteria used to define this notion, it can be determined whether a job, given its inherent characteristics, must be accepted at a given time, by an unemployed person with regard to his/her personal characteristics.

The objective of this chapter is to check whether the criteria for suitable employment conceived at international level guarantee that the worker's return to the workforce is only for a job of quality. It is therefore important to compare the concept of a suitable job with the elements used to define a job of quality. The criteria that define the quality of work on the global job market are irrelevant when assessing the criteria for a suitable job. In Chapter 2, therefore, there will be a focus on the development of a table representing the different dimensions of the job of quality.

B. Dimensions of the Job of Quality

The quality of jobs is a diverse political concept that must be rigorously examined; it concerns a political objective for the constant improvement in jobs. This is thus not a matter of setting a rigid normative framework for the job of quality; there is no need to set minimal standards that a job should meet to be considered as a job of quality. Authors who are examining the definition of a job of quality tend rather to identify dimensions to be taken into account when assessing the quality of a job. Progress in any one of these fields contributes to improving the quality of jobs.

---

15 Communication from the Commission to the Council, the European Parliament, the European Economic and Social Committee of the Regions, "working together, working better: a new framework for the open coordination of social protection and inclusion policies in the European Union", Brussels, 22 December 2005, COM(2005) 706 final; Communication from the Commission to the European Parliament, the Council, the European Economic and Social Committee and the Committee of the Regions, "*A renewed commitment to social Europe: Reinforcing the Open Method of Coordination for Social Protection and Social Inclusion*", Brussels, July 2008, COM(2008) 418 final.

16 Thus, "employment opportunities" constitutes one of the eleven criteria to evaluate decent work. According to this criterion, each person must have an opportunity of finding employment if he/she so wishes, because decent work does not have any meaning without the possibility for the potential worker to enter the labour market. In the same way, "inclusion and access to the labour market" constitutes one of the ten quality standards which were fixed by the Council of Europe after the Summit of Laeken in December 2001.

J. Deumer[17] articulates the criteria of quality jobs and quality of work around three poles: security, flexibility and dignity – and has produced the following table:

Table 1

Security	Flexibility	Dignity
In the job: Stability, health and safety, duration of the work, adequate remuneration	*In the job:* Reconciliation between private and professional life, duration of the work	*In the job:* Trade-union freedom, social dialogue, participation, equality and non-discrimination
Of Work: Income security and social protection	*Of Work:* Training opportunities and ascending career	*Of Work:* Free choice of a suitable job

Source: J. Deumer

The European Foundation for the Improvement of Living and Working Conditions, an agency of the European Union with a tripartite composition, uses four dimensions to define the quality of employment and work[18]:

- *Career and employment security* (employment status, income, social protection, workers' rights);
- *Health and well-being* (health problems, risk exposure, work organisation);
- *Reconciliation of working and non-working life* (working/non-working time, social infrastructures);
- *Skills Development* (qualifications, training, learning organisation, career development).

From these two approaches, we propose to retain the following table of the job of quality:

[17] J. Deumer, "*Flexicurité et qualité de l'emploi: le cas du travail à temps partiel*", *Courrier hebdomadaire du CRISP*, 2010, 29/30, No. 2074-2075.

[18] European Foundation for the Improvement of Living and Working Conditions, "*Quality of work and employment in Europe: Issues and challenges*", *Foundation paper No. 1*, February 2002.

Table 2

Objective	Job of quality – Dignity	
Means	Security	Flexibility
Criteria related to the job (Quality of the job *in se*)	*Career and employment security* *Health and well-being*	*Reconciliation between working and non-working life* *Training opportunities and improved career prospects*
	Trade-union freedom and social dialogue *Equality and not discrimination*	
Criteria related to the personal characteristics of the unemployed (Quality of the job *in concreto*)	*Adequacy with the personal characteristics of the worker*	

Source: E. Dermine

We do not consider dignity as one of the three poles in the definition of the job of quality, unlike J. Deumer. In our view, a dignified job is a job of quality, i.e. a job that allows you to live but also to "blossom"[19]. The dignified job and the job of quality are two concept "packages" and the exercise here is to give them shape.

The job of quality is defined by two poles: security and flexibility, around which we articulate the synthetic dimensions selected by The European Foundation. In order to best approximate the job of quality, we identified two cross-cutting tools that are useful for the achievement of each criterion and which therefore participate in improving the quality of jobs. They are:

1. The trade union freedom and the social dialogue that permit the defense of the workers' interests and generate progress in all dimensions of a job of quality, in terms of both security and flexibility.
2. The principles of equality and non-discrimination which must be respected in all areas that affect the quality of the job.

Finally, to assess the quality of a job in concrete terms, it seems absolutely necessary to consider the adequacy of that job, in terms of both its security dimension and its flexibility dimension, allied with the personal characteristics of the worker. This does not regard the subjective dimension of the quality of a job, i.e. taking into consideration the

19 On this definition of the job of quality, see: *Service de lutte contre la pauvreté, la précarité et l'exclusion sociale, Rapport 2008-2009* Partie 1, Une contribution au débat et à l'action politiques, III. Les critères de l'emploi convenable, une protection contre l'emploi précaire?, p. 97.

wishes of heterogeneous workers[20], but. to verify whether the job corresponds to the specific characteristics of the worker: for age, education level, beliefs, etc.[21]

The quality of the job is defined according to the point of view of the worker, rather than that of the employer or company. This contribution indeed fits into a logic for the protection of the workers' rights as well as for the quality of jobs available to them.

II. Suitable Employment, a Bulwark against the Growth of Insecure Jobs?

In all forms of unemployment insurance, the risk covered is involuntary unemployment. Voluntary inactivity is not compensated under unemployment insurance. The concept of suitable employment can make the distinction between voluntary unemployment and involuntary unemployment. It is thus *a tool for control* of the availability to work.

As explained above, the concept of suitable employment also plays a role in protecting the unemployed, in that they cannot be obliged to accept a job that would not be suitable. This concept involves minimum standards below which a job must not be accepted. Because of this protective function the concept of suitable employment has an impact on job quality. It also represents the symbolic boundary drawn by the legislator between bad jobs and the jobs of which he accepts the development in his country. Unlike the concept of job quality which is a political objective, suitable employment is a legal concept whose content is defined by the law in its broadest sense and by jurisprudence. In this part, we will precise how the notion of suitable employment is

---

20 On this subject, see: Hamermesh (1999), *The changing distribution of job satisfaction*, National Bureau of Economic Research; see also: L. Davoine, *op. cit.*, 2007, p. 87 et s. (Chapitre II de la Partie I: La satisfaction au travail: un critère de la qualité de l'emploi?); Vecerník J. (2003), "Skating on Thin Ice: A Comparison of Work Values and Job Satisfaction in CEE and EU Countries", *International Journal of Comparative Sociology*, Vol. 44, No. 5, pp. 444-471; Kalleberg A. and Vaisey S. (2005), "Pathways to good job: work quality among the machinist", *British Journal of Industrial Relations*, Vol. 43, No. 3, pp. 431-454; Clark, A. (2005), "*What makes a good job? Evidence from OECD countries*", in S. Bazen, C. Lucifora and W. Salverda (eds.), *Job Quality and Employment Behaviour in Europe* (pp. 11-30), Palgrave.

21 The European Commission also makes the distinction between:

- *the match between worker characteristics and job requirements*;
- *and the subjective evaluation (job satisfaction) of these characteristics by the individual worker.*

(Communication from the Commission to the Council, the European Parliament, the Economic and Social Committee and the Committee of the Regions, "*Employment and social policies: a framework for investing in quality*", COM(2001) 313, Brussels, 20 June 2001, p. 7).

apprehended by International organizations (ILO, Council of Europe, European Union). In our task to compare the criteria for suitable employment with the theoretical framework, we will then check, for each international level, whether there are minimal standards for each dimension and tool, identified as components of the quality of a job.

A. The Concept of Suitable employment According to ILO

1. The Texts and Their Effectiveness

The main ILO standards applied to unemployment benefits are Convention 102 of 1952 concerning social security, in its Part IV on "unemployment benefit", Convention 168 and Recommendation 176 of 1988 on the promotion of employment and protection against unemployment. Article 20 of Convention 102 specifies that unemployment is covered as it is due to the inability to find a suitable employment. The concept of suitable employment is specified in other provisions:

- Article 21, 2 of Convention 168:

2. 2. In assessing the suitability of employment, account shall be taken, in particular, under prescribed conditions and to an appropriate extent, of the age of unemployed persons, their length of service in their former occupation, their acquired experience, the length of their period of unemployment, the labour market situation, the impact of the employment in question on their personal and family situation and whether the employment is vacant as a direct result of a stoppage of work due to an on-going labour dispute.

- Articles 14 and 25 of the Recommendation 176:

14.

(1) The concept of suitable employment should, under prescribed conditions, not apply to:

(a) employment involving a change of occupation which does not take account of the abilities, qualifications, skills, work experience or the retraining potential of the person concerned;

(b) employment involving a change of residence to a place in which suitable accommodation is not available;

(c) employment in which the conditions and remuneration are appreciably less favourable than those which are generally granted, at the relevant time, in the occupation and district in which the employment is offered;

(d) employment vacant as a direct result of a stoppage due to an ongoing labour dispute;

(e) employment such that, for a reason other than those covered in clauses (a) to (d), and with due regard to all attendant circumstances, including the family responsibilities of the person concerned, the refusal of the employment is not unreasonable.

(2) In assessing the criteria specified in clauses (a) to (c) and (e) above, account should be taken in general of the age of the unemployed persons, of their length of service in their former occupation, of their acquired experience, of the duration of their unemployment, of the state of the labour market and of the repercussions of the employment on their personal and family situations.

The implementation of these agreements is monitored regularly by The Committee of Experts On The Application of Conventions and Recommendations (CEACR). States submit regular reports on the application in law and in practice of the conventions they have ratified[22]. They must also submit reports on their legislation and practice in regard to non-ratified conventions and on the difficulties which prevent or delay ratification[23]. Regarding recommendations, States also specify the extent to which they have applied or plan to implement them[24].

Following an examination of these reports and observations from the workers' organisations and employers, the CEACR makes observations or requests for explanations. In addition, The Conference Committee on the Application of Standards, in its general report, draws the attention of the Conference to the most serious cases of difficulty encountered with the States regarding the application of ratified standards[25].

2. *Comparison with the Theoretical Framework*

a. The Criteria Related to the Unemployed Person

It is noted that the criteria used by the ILO are essentially related to the unemployed person; to assess the suitability of employment, it is necessary to take account of the age of the unemployed person, the seniority acquired in a former profession, abilities, qualifications, aptitudes and professional experience. In this connection CEACR recalled on several occasions that the professional and social status of the unem-

---

22 Article 22 of the ILO Constitution.

23 Article 19 (5) e) of the ILO Constitution.

24 Article 19 (6) d) of the ILO Constitution.

25 In addition to this regular control mechanism, there is a procedure for complaint (Articles 26 to 34 of the ILO Constitution) and a procedure for representation (Articles 24 and 25 of the ILO Constitution) on the application of ratified conventions.

ployed person must at least be protected during the initial period of unemployment lasting 26 weeks in accordance with Convention 168[26].

A job matching the personal characteristics of the unemployed is the essence of the concept of suitable employment as defined in ILO Conventions and interpreted by its supervisory bodies. If this line of approach is to help protect the interests of the unemployed, however, it also involves an essentially economic approach to the most efficient allocation of human resources and this is in the interest of the society as a whole.

Thus, following the Committee of Experts, according the definition of the contingency contained in Article 10, paragraph 1, the aim of the Convention consists precisely in offering unemployed persons protection from the obligation to take up any unsuitable job, "*so as to ensure for the benefit of the workers and society that the most effective utilization is made of human resources potential*"[27]. In the pursuit of this economic objective, the Convention requires, at least during the initial period of unemployment, that account be taken of the professional and social status of the unemployed.

In 1997, Norway adopted a reform of unemployment insurance, which resulted, *inter alia*, in a removal of any references to the personal characteristics of the unemployed when assessing the suitability of a proposed job. In its comments, the CEACR has condemned the Norwegian attitude on the economic objective of matching the labour supply and demand:

> (...) such labour market policy would inevitably lead to a lowering of the skills level of the national workforce and the substantial reduction of the employment opportunities for unskilled workers at the low end, pushing them into long-term unemployment and exclusion. Thus, favouring the supply-side over the demand-side approach in regulating the labour market, orienting the employment market service to providing workers suitable for jobs rather than jobs suitable for workers, would in the long run lead to labour market imbalances and inefficiencies and to situations of underutilization of the human resources potentia[28].

---

26 ILO CEACR, *Individual Direct Request to Norway concerning Employment Promotion and Protection against Unemployment Convention*, 1988 (No. 168), 1998, 69th session; ILO CEACR, *Individual Direct Request to Sweden concerning Employment Promotion and Protection against Unemployment Convention*, 1988 (No. 168), 2007, 78th session, http://www.ilo.org/ilolex/english/index.htm.

27 ILO CEACR, *Individual Direct Request to Norway concerning Employment Promotion and Protection against Unemployment Convention*, 1988 (No. 168), 1999, 70th session, http://www.ilo.org/ilolex/english/index.htm.

28 ILO CEACR, *Individual Direct Request to Norway concerning Employment Promotion and Protection against Unemployment Convention*, 1988 (No. 168), 2000, point 1, §4, http://www.ilo.org/ilolex/english/index.htm.

b. The Criteria Related to Employment

Work on job-related criteria (Quality of employment *in se*) is on the other hand very limited.

One element which comes to the fore relates to the job security: "*The concept of suitable employment should, under prescribed conditions, not apply to employment in which the conditions and remuneration are appreciably less favorable than those which are generally granted, at the relevant time, in the occupation and district in which the employment is offered*"[29][30]. The provision refers to the practice which does not guarantee a minimum wage needed to provide a certain measure of security. In Recommendation 176, as regards reconciliation between professional and family life, it is expected that is not a suitable employment "*an employment involving a change of residence to a place in which suitable accommodation is not available*"[31].

In order to rationalise the allocation of human resources, it is logical that efforts are focused on taking into account the personal characteristics of the unemployed rather than the intrinsic characteristics of jobs. The concept of suitable employment should enable any worker to be

---

[29] Article 14 c) of Recommendation No. 176.

[30] *Individual Observation concerning Convention No. 44, Unemployment Provision,* 1934, to United Kingdom, 1996, http://www.ilo.org/ilolex/english/index.htm (the United Kingdom has not ratified Convention No. 168): "*As regards more particularly the question of whether the level of remuneration constitutes good cause for refusing unemployment benefit, the Government indicates that, following the introduction in 1988 of extensive in-work benefits available to people in full-time work, such as family credit, housing benefit, council tax benefit and disability working allowance, legislation provided that the level of remuneration would not normally be adduced as good cause for refusing a job. As the UK policy concentrated on incentives to help people back into work, the so-called "going rate" for a job in a particular locality has become largely an irrelevance; it was impossible for someone to be able to rely solely on the level of pay in a job as the reason for refusing to take it, without taking into account his position as regards the in-work benefits (...). The Committee notes this information. Secondly, with regard to the Government's assertion that the actual level of remuneration has become largely an irrelevance in judging the suitability of employment because of the in-work benefits involved, the Committee observes that all of the benefits mentioned by the Government (family credit, housing benefit, council tax benefit and disability working allowance) are income-tested and cannot be considered, in view of their nature and objectives, either as an element of the wage or as a condition of employment within the meaning of Article 10, paragraph 1(b), of the Convention. Furthermore, such benefits are available to all full-time employees who meet the conditions and not just those persons who have commenced employment after a period on unemployment benefits. In these circumstances, the Committee cannot but again express the hope that the Government will not fail to take the necessary measures to ensure the full application of the above-mentioned provisions of the Convention*".

[31] Article 14 b) of Recommendation No. 176.

allocated a job that best meets his/her qualifications in order to maintain the quality of the workforce. There is, on the other hand, no systematic will to improve the quality of jobs *in se*, by enacting minimum standards below which a job could not be offered to jobseekers.

c. A Third Criterion: the State of the Labour Market?

Job-related criteria and criteria related to the unemployed are presented in Table 2 to assess the quality of a job. To assess the suitability of employment, the ILO has established a third angle of evaluation: the state of the labour market. Under Article 21, 2 of Convention 168 and Article 14 (2) of Recommendation 176, the state of the labour market is a criterion for assessing the suitability of employment. It is also in the light of the economic objective that we understand that the ILO has adopted the state of the labour market as a criterion to evaluate suitable employment. When there are fewer jobs available, workers must be more flexible; the demand has to adapt to the supply of labour

As represented in Table 2, the state of the labour market is certainly not a criterion to be used for as regards job quality. This assertion is tantamount to granting an independent value to the quality of jobs in the margins of the quantity of jobs, since the quantity of jobs is regarded as a prerequisite condition for the quality of employment.

So that the concept of suitable employment ensures its role as a bulwark against the growth of insecure employment, the requirements of suitable employment are not expected to vary, depending on the state of the labour market. In practice, the CEACR does not admit, however, that the state of the labour market justifies that no consideration be given to the personal characteristics of the unemployed, at least during the initial period of unemployment.

As explained above, in 1997, Norway removed all references to the personal characteristics of the unemployed to assess the suitability of the proposed job. It justified this measure by the state of the Norwegian labour market: "*during periods of low unemployment when the demand for labour is strong and the employment market service has more jobs to place people into, it may be necessary for it to fill jobs that are not very suitable to the unemployed people to whom they are offered*"[32]. This justification has not been endorsed by the CEACR which reaffirmed that the professional characteristics of the unemployed, were in any event, to be taken into account during the first period of unemployment.

[32] ILO CEACR, Individual Direct Request to Norway concerning Employment Promotion and Protection against Unemployment Convention, 1988 (No. 168), 2000, http://www.ilo.org/ilolex/english/index.htm.

d. Application of Table 2

Objective	Job of quality – Dignity	
Means	Security	Flexibility
Criteria related to the job (Quality of the job *in se*)	*Career and employment security*: + *Health and well-being*: -	*Reconciliation between working and non-working life*: +/- *Training opportunities and improved career prospects*: -
	Trade-union freedom and social dialogue: + *Equality and not discrimination*: -	
Criteria related to the personal characteristics of the unemployed (Quality of the job *in concreto*)	*Adequacy with the personal characteristics of the worker*: +	

Source: E. Dermine

B. The Concept of Suitable Employment within the Council of Europe

1. The Texts and their Effectiveness[33]

The European Code of Social Security is an instrument laying down minimum standards for social security and encouraging contracting parties to exceed these standards. It has been proposed for signature by the States on 16 April 1964 and took effect on 17 March 1968, a year after the deposit of the third instrument of ratification. It aims to reinforce Convention 102 while increasing the threshold for minimum requirement. In the section devoted to unemployment benefits[34], it refers to the concept of suitable employment, but without defining it.

The application of the Code is monitored through regular reports from States submitted to a committee of experts, the Committee of Experts on Social Security (CS-SS). This Committee puts forward its findings to the Committee of Ministers of the Council of Europe. The latter Committee studies these conclusions and decides by a two-thirds majority if the social security systems meet minimum standards set by

---

33 J. Nickless, *European Code of Social Security*, Editions of the Council of Europe, November 2002; A. Gómez heredero, *Social security – Protection at the international level and developments in Europe*, Editions of the Council of Europe, Paris, December 2008.

34 Part IV of the Code, which deals with unemployment benefits, has been accepted by 16 countries: Cyprus, Denmark, Estonia, Spain, France, Ireland, Norway, the United Kingdom, Slovenia and the Czech Republic; though Germany, Belgium, Luxemburg, the Netherlands, Portugal and Sweden accepted the higher standards of the Protocol.

the Code. If it judges that this is not the case, it adopts a resolution requesting the defaulting party to remedy any deficiency and to meet its international obligations.

A mechanism of institutionalised cooperation has been established between the Council of Europe and the ILO: the national reports are considered by the ILO's CEACR before being reviewed by the CS-SS of the Council of Europe, which ensures a harmonious interpretation of the texts, including the concept of suitable employment. Shortly after the implementation of the Code and the accompanying Protocol, the Committee of Ministers decided to revise it to improve standards and introduce greater flexibility[35]. The draft of the Revised European Code of Social Security was approved and ready for signature on 6 November 1990. It has not yet entered into force[36]; hence we will not compare it with the theoretical framework adopted[37].

2. *Comparison to the Theoretical Framework*

a. The Criteria Related to the Personal Characteristics of the Unemployed

In the absence of any definition of suitable employment in the Code and Protocol, the bodies monitoring the application code and protocol give substance to the notion. In its resolutions, the Committee of Ministers only verifies whether the State takes into consideration the social and professional status of the unemployed to assess whether it has respected the concept of suitable employment contained in the wording of Article 20 of the Code. It is noted besides that the revised Code exclusively refers to criteria related to the unemployed person to appreciate the suitable character of a job.

This understanding of the concept of suitable employment highlights the economic objective that the Council of Europe assigns, like the ILO, to suitable employment to preserve the quality of workmanship and use of human resources as efficiently as possible[38].

---

35 A. Gómez heredero, *Social security – Protection at the international level and developments in Europe*, Editions of the Council of Europe, Paris, December 2008, p. 30.

36 It must be ratified by two States to come into effect.

37 Contrary to the Code and the Protocol, the revised Code, in its article 19.2, includes criteria which must be taken into account when considering the suitable nature of a job. The text of this article is almost word for word identical to Article 19, paragraph 2 of ILO Convention No. 168.

38 Resolution ResCSS(2000)28 on the application of the European Code of Social Security and the Protocol thereto by Norway (Period from 1 July 1998 to 30 June 1999), Council of Europe, Committee of Ministers, 733rd meeting of the Ministers' Deputies, 7 December 2000.

In its national reports, Germany justifies the removal of the protection for a specified period for the profession or qualifications of the unemployed by the fact that such protection would lose "more and more importance in a world of open and mobile working, where workers face the need to adapt their professional interests and adjust their aspirations for employment needs of the labor market". The Committee of Ministers condemned the measure under Article 20 of the Code, reaffirming that the notion of suitable employment should improve the functioning of the labour market while preserving the acquired professional qualifications, at least during the initial period of unemployment[39].

Whilst the ILO justifies the consideration of the personal characteristics of the unemployed only from the economic objective, the Committee of Ministers of the Council of Europe adds a *social objective*:

> the concept of suitable employment fulfils, besides the economic goal of preserving the quality of the workforce, the no less important social goal of preserving workers against compulsion occurring when they are forced to perform work below their level of education and skills. The term "suitable" guarantees, in fact, that any employment offered by the employment services will be considered in respect of its quality, having regard to the qualifications and skills of the individual jobseeker. Similarly, unemployed persons themselves will be treated with due regard for their professional and social status and not as ordinary labourers, physically and mentally fit for any job[40].

The Committee of Ministers stresses the fact that suitable employment is not just a tool for balancing the supply and demand of labour for the good of society as a whole; it emphasised the social dimension of suitable employment that helps protect the unemployed from the obligation to accept jobs that do not correspond to training or professional status[41].

Thus, in a communication to Denmark which indicated it had waived the consideration of personal characteristics of the unemployed to

---

39 Resolution ResCSS(2004)5 on the application of the European Code of Social Security and the Protocol thereto by Germany (Period from 1 July 2002 to 30 June 2003), Council of Europe, Committee of Ministers, 894rd meeting of the Ministers' Deputies, 9 September 2004.

40 Resolution ResCSS(2003)11 on the application of the European Code of Social Security and the Protocol thereto by Norway (Period from 1 July 2000 to 30 June 2001), Council of Europe, Committee of Ministers, 833rd meeting of the Ministers' Deputies, 26 March 2003.

41 Resolution ResCSS(2009)17 on the application of the European Code of Social Security and the Protocol thereto by Sweden (Period from 1 July 2007 to 30 June 2008), Council of Europe, Committee of Ministers, 972rd meeting of the Ministers' Deputies, 10 June 2009.

motivate them to enter the labour market, the Committee of Ministers indicated:

> such "motivation" of unemployed persons to subordinate their will and professional aspirations to the dictate of the labour market goes against the very objectives of social security enshrined in the Code. However desirable it may be for the labour market authorities and for society as a whole to move more people into employment, unemployed persons should be treated with due respect for their professional, social and family status and not as ordinary labourers, physically and mentally fit for any job[42].

Also in this protectionist approach towards workers' rights, the Committee of Ministers affirms the relationship between suitable employment and the principle of freedom of choice in employment, which is also based on the model of social security contained in the Code. On this basis, it considered difficult to reconcile the fundamental freedom of the individual to choose his employment without any form of economic constraint, with the presence in the Norwegian legislation of constraining elements of working under the threat of the suppression of unemployment benefits in the event of a refusal to accept a unsuitable job, or to participate in a suitable programme for integration into the labour market or to obtain income derived from free-lance work instead of suitable employment[43].

One can feel through this discourse the influence of the approach in terms of rights and freedoms of the European Social Charter[44].

National reports on the Code reflect the growing importance of reintegration in the labour market in different States, in comparison with the compensation by means of unemployment insurance. For example, Germany stated that placement of the unemployed takes precedence over the payment of unemployment benefits to replace wages[45]. Since

---

[42] Resolution ResCSS(2006)3 on the application of the European Code of Social Security and the Protocol thereto by Denmark (Period from 1 July 2004 to 30 June 2005), Council of Europe, Committee of Ministers, 972rd meeting of the Ministers' Deputies, 6 September 2006.

[43] Resolution ResCSS(2003)27 on the application of the European Code of Social Security and the Protocol thereto by Norway (Period from 1 July 2001 to 30 June 2002), Council of Europe, Committee of Ministers, 866rd meeting of the Ministers' Deputies, 17 December 2003.

[44] The European Committee of Social Rights control reforms concerning work availability wit regard to the article 12 of the European Social Charter (see: Conclusions XVII-1 (Denmark) of the European Committee of Social Rights concerning the application of the article 12.3 of the European Social Charter).

[45] Resolution ResCSS(2005)7 on the application of the European Code of Social Security and the Protocol thereto by Germany (Period from 1 July 2003 to 30 June 2004), Council of Europe, Committee of Ministers, 938rd meeting of the Ministers' Deputies, 21 September 2005: "*the government states that the placement and inte-*

2002, in Denmark, the unemployed must be available for a "reasonable" job from the first day of unemployment, the term "reasonable job" meaning that this may not necessarily be in the field of the former professional activity of the unemployed. According to Denmark, this modification to the rules of availability aims at "motivating" the unemployed "*into having the necessary will and readiness to match, at any time, the requirements of the labour market*"[46].

While recognising that international and European standards call for coordination between unemployment insurance and employment policy[47], the Committee of Ministers reiterated however that, according to these standards, placement may only be made in suitable jobs, i.e. jobs taking into account the profession and acquired skills of the unemployed, at least for a given period[48]. It is not a question of eclipsing the

---

gration efforts of the employment agencies are first and foremost aimed at reintegrating unemployed persons into working life in line with their professional qualifications and personal interests. However, if such integration turns out to be impossible, the community of insured persons (who finance the unemployment insurance scheme in Germany by means of their contributions) may expect that an unemployed person also accept other jobs that are offered on the labour market. Any other policy leads to a situation in which unemployment would take precedence over (possible and acceptable) employment and would thus contradict the legally enshrined precedence of placement into employment over the receipt of wage replacement benefits (section 4 of Book III of the Social Code). Accordingly, German employment services have made increased efforts over the last few years to promote the willingness required on the part of unemployed persons to participate and make adjustments in the context of their reintegration into working life, and they have also taken measures to enforce this aim".

46 Resolution ResCSS(2006)3 on the application of the European Code of Social Security and the Protocol thereto by Denmark (Period from 1 July 2004 to 30 June 2005), Council of Europe, Committee of Ministers, 972rd meeting of the Ministers' Deputies, 6 September 2006.

47 The priority for active placement in employment compared to the passive receipt of benefits in replacement of wages is inherent in the definition of the situation described in Article 20 of the Code, which occurs only in cases where it is impossible to obtain suitable employment. The priority given to rehabilitation in employment is also obvious in active labour market policies, envisaged by Article 24.6 of the Protocol and Article 25 of the revised Code, as a part of a modern unemployment benefits' system. In the same way, the ILO considers that the methods of granting unemployment benefits should contribute to the promotion of full employment, as a top priority, avoiding the erection of barriers to work or job creation (Convention No. 168, Articles 2, 7 and 14).

48 Resolution ResCSS(2006)3 on the application of the European Code of Social Security and the Protocol thereto by Denmark (Period from 1 July 2004 to 30 June 2005), Council of Europe, Committee of Ministers, 972rd meeting of the Ministers' Deputies, 6 September 2006; See also Resolution ResCSS(2003)11 on the application of the European Code of Social Security and the Protocol thereto by Norway (Period from 1 July 2000 to 30 June 2001), Council of Europe, Committee of Ministers, 833rd meeting of the Ministers' Deputies, 26 March 2003.

consideration of personal characteristics of the unemployed in the name of the goal of full employment.

b. The Absence of Criteria Related to Employment *in se*

We find absolutely no reference to criteria related to employment *in se*, neither in the Code and its Protocol, the Resolution of the Committee of Ministers, nor in the revised Code[49].

c. Flexibility of the Criteria According to the State of the Labour Market

At the second meeting of the Committee of Experts on Social Security (CS-SS) in March 2007, Committee members were asked to answer various questions on selected criteria for suitable employment and on the penalties applicable in case of refusal of a suitable employment.

Based on a synthesis of the answers provided, a working group drafted a Guide to the Concept of Suitable Employment in the context of unemployment benefit, which was published in 2010[50]. In this guide, the working group explains the aims pursued by the concept of suitable employment and its feature, and then makes some suggestions.

The working group asserts that the state of equilibrium between rights and duties is affected by the socio-economic context and by the situation of the labour market, which means that:

- These factors justify differences between countries, in the determination of the criteria for suitable employment, and in the implementation of these criteria by the employment agencies (when they propose jobs to the unemployed) and the unemployment insurance agencies (when they decide to apply a sanction following any refusal of a job by an unemployed person);
- These factors also imply that the application of the criteria for suitable employment can evolve in time[51].

Priority is clearly given to the economic objective in this guide. The concept of suitable employment must be adapted to the prevailing

---

49 The revised Code indicates that it is advisable to take account of the effects of the job on the personal situation of the unemployed. It is a matter of considering the personal situation of the unemployed (criterion related to the unemployed person). It is not a matter of fixing specific minimum standards relating to the job on conciliation working and on working life, that would be applied in the same way to all workers (parallel with Article 19.2 of ILO Convention No. 168).

50 Guide to the concept of suitable employment in the context of unemployment benefit, Council of Europe, December 2009, adopted by the Committee of Experts on Social Security (CS-SS), during the 4th meeting (Strasbourg, 24-26 March 2009).

51 Guide to the concept of suitable employment in the context of unemployment benefit, *op. cit.*, p. 10.

situation on the domestic markets in order to guarantee a sane economic development[52] and must be flexibly interpreted in the context of the European Code of Social Security.

The working group thus seems to endorse the position of Denmark and Norway, although it had previously been condemned by the Committee of Ministers, under the social objective of the concept of suitable employment. We are quite puzzled by the willingness of this group of experts to make more flexible the components of the concept of suitable employment. It should be noted, however, that on the nine members of the group representing the interests of the Member States, two were Danish and two Norwegian.

The guidelines adopted by the Group[53] are deliberately general so that States can take account of their own legislation and socio-economic situation at the time they transpose the guidelines into their policies and administrative procedures. It is no longer required that the personal characteristics of the unemployed (occupation, skills, qualifications, experience, level of wages of previous employment) be taken into account during an initial period. It is clear that this is only a possibility. The duration of a possible period of protection is left to the discretion of Member States.

During the second period (or immediately, if no initial period of protection is envisaged), very general and undemanding criteria are laid down in relation to employment status.

If the Committee of Ministers refers to these guidelines in its future resolutions, it is feared that it will no longer impose absolute consideration of the social and professional status of the unemployed during the initial period of unemployment, which is not imposed by the Code. This interpretation of suitable employment would be however contrary to ILO conventions and the interpretation thereof as given by the CEACR.

---

52 Guide to the concept of suitable employment in the context of unemployment benefit, *op. cit.*, p. 23.

53 Guide to the concept of suitable employment in the context of unemployment benefit, *op. cit.*, p. 25 et s.

d. Application of Table 2

Objective	Job of quality – Dignity	
Means	Security	Flexibility
Criteria related to the job (Quality of the job *in se*)	*Career and employment security*: - *Health and well-being*: -	*Reconciliation between working and non-working life*: - *Training opportunities and improved career prospects*: -
	Trade-union freedom and social dialogue: - *Equality and not discrimination*: -	
Criteria related to the personal characteristics of the unemployed (Quality of the job *in concreto*)	*Adequacy with the personal characteristics of the worker*: +	

Source: E. Dermine

C. The Concept of Suitable Employment within the European Union

The European Union does not have competence for harmonisation on social security. Only Member States are qualified for this matter.

In order to ensure a certain convergence of the industrial relations' policies and to adapt the social protection systems to new realities, the Member States set up the Open Method of Coordination (OMC) for Social Protection and Social Inclusion. They laid down common objectives and agreed on indicators. They make reports on the continuation of its objectives; the indicators make it possible to measure the progression compared with the objectives. This is about a non-constraining process of political co-operation with the underlying idea that the division of good practices will give an impulse to the convergence and the social modernisation of social security systems.

The objectives are as follows to:

- "*Promote social cohesion and equal opportunities for all through adequate, accessible, financially sustainable, adaptable and efficient social protection systems and social inclusion policies.*
- *Interact closely with the Lisbon objectives on achieving greater economic growth and more and better jobs and with the EU's Sustainable Development Strategy.*

- *Strengthen governance, transparency and the involvement of stakeholders in the design, implementation and monitoring of policy*"[54].

There are general indicators and specific indicators in three fields: "inclusion", "pensions" and "health care".

There are quantitative statistical indicators such as the long-term employment rate, the number of persons at-risk of poverty and living in jobless households. Thus, absolutely no account is taken of the definition of suitable employment as accepted by the Member States when evaluating the quality of the social protection systems within the framework of the OMC's primary goal.

The Commission reaffirmed its will that the OMC for Social Protection and Social inclusion be indissociable from the basic political orientations promoted in the Strategy of Lisbon and in particular from the improvement of the quantity and quality of employment[55].

At the present time, it is notable that the OMC for Social Protection and Social inclusion, by laying down quantitative objectives compared to the statistical indicators selected, prefers to increase the rate of employment via the active social inclusion of the unemployed (quantity aspect) than to play a part in the concept of quality of employment.

Finally, it is apparent that in Article 34 of the EU Charter of Fundamental Rights the EU includes a general recognition of the entitlement to social security benefits in the event of loss of employment.

---

54 Communication from the Commission to the Council, the European Parliament, the European Economic and Social Committee of the Regions, "*Working together, working better: a new framework for the open coordination of social protection and inclusion policies in the European Union*", Brussels, 22 December 2005, COM(2005) 706 final.

55 Communication from the Commission to the European Parliament, the Council, the European Economic and Social Committee and the Committee of the Regions, "*A renewed commitment to social Europe: Reinforcing the Open Method of Coordination for Social Protection and Social Inclusion*", Brussels, 2 July 2008, COM(2008) 418 final.

Application of Table 2

Objective	Job of quality – Dignity	
Means	Security	Flexibility
Criteria related to the job (Quality of the job *in se*)	*Career and employment security*: - *Health and well-being*: -	*Reconciliation of working and non-working life*: - *Training opportunities and improved career prospects*: -
	Trade-union freedom and social dialogue: - *Equality and not discrimination*: -	
Criteria related to the personal characteristics of the unemployed (Quality of the job *in concreto*)	*Adequacy with the personal characteristics of the worker*: -	

Source: E. Dermine

D. Conclusive Table 3: Guarantees Offered by the Concept of Suitable Employment, in Terms of Quality of Employment

Table 3

Objective	Job of quality – Dignity	
Means	Security	Flexibility
Criteria related to the job (Quality of the job *in se*)	*Career and employment security* *Health and well-being* ILO: - Council of Europe: - European Union: -	*Reconciliation between working and non-working life* *Training opportunities and improved career prospects* ILO: - The Council of Europe: - European Union: -
	Trade-union freedom and social dialogue *Equality and not discrimination* ILO: - The Council of Europe: - European Union: -	
Criteria related to the person of the unemployed (Quality of the job *in concreto*)	*Adequacy with the personal characteristics of the worker*: + ILO: + The Council of Europe: + European Union: -	

Source: E. Dermine

Conclusion

At the international level, the guarantees on the quality of the jobs proposed to the unemployed relate primarily to the adequacy of the job with the social and professional status and profession of the unemployed.

The concept of suitable employment seems more an economic tool for the adjustment of the offer and demand for work for an optimal allowance of the labour force than a lever for the quality of jobs.

A complete absence of guarantees at the level of the European Union is observed. In spite of the creed of the Strategy of Lisbon, "more and better jobs", social security is currently considered by the European commission as a lever for the quality of employment only for what it can contribute to the quantity of employment. The quantity of employment, described in terms of "inclusion and access to the job market", indeed constitutes one of the ten criteria to evaluate the *quality of work*. However, Europe must pay attention to the fact that the *quantity of employment* may go hand in hand with a deterioration in the *quality of jobs*.

Under pressure from the Strategy of Lisbon, there is a risk that States may be gradually demolishing the notion of suitable of employment, in favour of reinsertion in the labour market.

The Legal Status of the "Offer of Employment"

A French Concept of Suitable Employment?

Pascal CAILLAUD

Researcher – Law and Social Change (UMR-CNRS 6297)
Maison des Sciences de l'Homme Ange Guépin – University of Nantes

Introduction

Some ILO conventions relating to unemployment refer to the concept of suitable employment (see the contribution of Elise Dermine). Article 6 of ILO Convention No. 88, published in 1948, on "employment service" specifies "that the employment service shall be so organised as to ensure effective recruitment and placement, and for this purpose shall assist workers to find suitable employment and assist employers to find suitable workers, and more particularly shall, in accordance with rules framed on a national basis".

In the same way, Convention No. 102 of 1952, concerning minimum standards for social security, imposes that each Member shall provide the persons protected with unemployment benefit. But, at the same time, this text considers the possibility of suspending earnings, as defined by national laws or regulations, due to the inability to obtain *suitable employment* in the case of a person who is capable of and available for, work.

More recently, Article 21 of Convention No. 168 of 1988 on "Employment Promotion and Protection against Unemployment Convention", stated that "the benefit to which a protected person would have been entitled in the case of full unemployment may be refused, withdrawn, suspended or reduced, to the extent prescribed, when the person concerned refuses to accept suitable employment". Only the Conventions 88 and 102 were ratified by France.

If these texts have aim to define the obligations of national service employment, the concept of "suitable employment" identifies the rights but also obligations of the job seeker, especially when he refuses an employment (see E. Dermine in this book). Thus, in several European legislations (COE, 2010), declining an offer of "suitable employment" is specifically intended to restrict the right to job-seekers' allowance (Germany, Belgium, Spain, United Kingdom, Ireland and Luxembourg).

France does not explicitly include the notion of "suitable employment" in its national legislation. Until 2008, people were removed from the list of job-seekers when "without legitimate reason", they refused a job, whatever "the duration of employment contracts offered, *compatible* with their expertise or training, their geographical mobility opportunities with account made for their personal and family circumstances and mobility aids offered and paid the wage rate usually in operation in the professional sector and region." The absence of objective criteria and the concept of a "compatible offer of employment" could be appreciated in a very restricted way by the public employment service and was left to the discretion of each advisor in charge of monitoring a job seeker (Leclerc, 2008).

With the Act of 1 August 2008, about the "rights and duties of job seekers", are now removed from the list of job seekers, people who, without legitimate reason, twice refuse a "reasonable offer of employment", a concept based on the nature and characteristics of employment, the privileged geographical area and the expected wage (Article L. 5411-6-2 of the French Labour Code).

The introduction of this new concept in French law was the subject of much debate and another oldest concept of job offer was recalled: the "valid offer of employment" (Catala, 2008). Created in 1993, it had a different purpose than a "reasonable offer of employment" because it did not cover the relationship between the French administration of jobs and the job seeker, but the relationship between an employer who plans to lay-off workers and the employees whose contract of employment was threatened. "Valid offer of employment" was therefore intended to cover precisely those at risk of becoming a job seeker.

However *valid* or *reasonable*, the offer of employment does not have the same characteristics. The obligation of the employer is not defined in the first instance, it becomes, in the second, the job seeker's obligation of, and on which objective criteria were registered in the law in 2008. The successive analysis of these concepts will allow us to compare them and to confront them, finally, with a concept of suitable employment.

I. "Valid offer of employment": an Obligation for Employers to Avoid Unemployment of the Employee

In the French collective procedure for economic redundancies, the presence of "valid offers of employment" for employees whose jobs are threatened is currently and regularly noted in the rehabilitation measures contained in the "protection plan for employment" (PSE)[1] prepared by the employer (Favennec, 2010).

Curiously, this notion appears in none of the major texts of the French labour law, although the judges in the French Supreme Court (*Cour de Cassation*), in its jurisprudence are regularly verify whether the employer has strictly respected all of its obligations before proceeding with a redundancy.

A. *The "Valid Offer of Employment": the Administrative Origin of the Concept*

When we search in the databases of French law[2] for the concept of "valid offer of employment", it is noted that it only appears in two official documents, both belonging to the class of circulars (*Circulaires*), administrative acts whose legal value is limited.

Since the law of 2 August 1989, called the "Soisson Act", in the companies with more than 50 employees, any employer who wants to make at least 10 employees redundant over a period of 30 days, must establish and implement a "social plan"[3] to avoid these redundancies or limit their number, and to facilitate the redeployment of staff to avoid their redundancy. Older workers or workers with social characteristics or qualifications making them difficult to getting into work are principally concerned by this Act.

The Act of 27 January 1993 was finally necessary to define the content of the "social plan". The French legislator imposes on the employer four types of measures relating directly or indirectly to the objective of professional redeployment.

The first measure is the *creation of new activities* in the company or the group which can create new jobs. Also needed are *retraining measures or conversion measures* to adapt the employees affected by the proposed redundancies to the needs of the labour market. *Measures on working time* are also to be found in this social plan. More importantly, the social plan should include *measures of internal or external rede-*

1 "Plan de Sauvegarde de l'Emploi".

2 www.legifrance.gouv.fr.

3 "Plan Social".

ployment into the company, but the law does not specify the exact form of these measures.

A circular from the Ministry of Labour, on 28 January 1993, clarified what these redeployment measures are.

The employer is required, for economic redundancies and for whatever number of workers are affected and the size of the company, to search for any job that may be offered to employees with due account of their capabilities. This search must initially be made within the company and, if need be, within the perimeter of the group to which it belongs.

The measures for external redeployment cover all *the assistance mobilised directly or indirectly to facilitate the recruiting of employees by another employer*, when internal redeployment is not available on to them. These include commitments to provide each employee with one or more "*valid offers of employment*", "job-antenna", devices for a differential allowance to make up for loss of later wages, mobility aids, etc.

Two observations must be made on its text. On the one hand, a circular has a particular status in the French legal system. A circular usually explains the extent of the right resulting from the law to ensure an application as uniform as possible in the whole of the territory. Also, a circular cannot change the existing law by enacting new standards, or giving an erroneous interpretation. However, the "valid offer of employment" does not appear in any law. On the other hand, this circular, in particular, does not explicitly define what a "valid offer of employment" is.

Since the Social Modernization Act of 17 January 2002, the "social plan" has been replaced by the "Protection Plan for employment." If the legislator has specified the measures to be taken by the employer who proceeds with collective redundancies (Article L1233-62 of the French Labour Code), we found that there were no changes to be implemented in the employers' obligations:

– *Actions for the internal redeployment* of employees in the same job class or equivalent to those they already hold or, with the agreement of employees, on jobs of a lower category;

– *Creation of new activities by the company*;

– *Measures to promote external redeployment*, with the support for reinsertion in the local labour pool;

– *Measures to support the creation of new activities or the resumption of existing activities by employees*;

– *Training activities* to facilitate the internal or external redeployment of employees in equivalent jobs;

– *Measures to reduce the working time* and measures to reduce the volume of overtime.

In actions of external redeployment, the law does not always make explicit reference to the notion of "valid offer of employment." It was not until the circular dated 17 July 2007 on "redeployment cells" that this notion appears again. Indeed, if the French labour code gives only an indicative list of measures that may be included in the "Protection plan of employment", the creation by the employer of a "redeployment unit" set up to help redundant workers find new jobs, is the minimum basis of this plan (Favennec, 2010). These "redeployment units" may be internal in the company, intercompany, or be the object of a special agreement with the State if the company has substantial financial difficulties. In the definition of the relationship between employer and labour administration in this Circular, it is recalled that "public service employment may contribute to the definition of the concept of *valid offer of employment* in the redeployment operation", without this contribution being defined.

In the absence of a definition of the legal and objective criteria, the application of the employer's obligation to offer his/her employees a "valid offer of employment" is under the control of the courts of justice.

B. The "Valid Offer of Employment": an Obligation of the Employer under the Control of the Judge

An analysis of the jurisprudence of the French Supreme Court, on the "valid offer of employment" shows that the French judge is confronted by two different legal problems. What is the nature of the employer's and the redeployment unit's obligation to make a "valid offer of employment" to the employees whose economic redundancy is being considered? What are the criteria for the judge to consider an offer as *valid*?

In theory, in the "Protection Plan of employment", the Labour Code does not impose a duty to achieve a specific result[4] on the company (Catala, 2008). The obligation is one of best intent[5]: to search all means to avoid redundancies and facilitate the redeployment of redundant workers by mobilising specific measures. These measures must be implemented according to the resources available to the company or the group to which it belongs.

---

4 "Obligation de résultat".

5 "Obligation de moyen".

However, a recent judgement of the Supreme Court imposed a "quasi-duty" on the employer to achieve a specific result[6]. In this case, a company that had decided to close its head office and transfer its activities to another had started a process of collective redundancy for economic reasons. This procedure involved a "Protection Plan for Employment" and "an enterprise agreement for transferred staff". Both procedures provided that if any employee of the company, during the three years following the start of a new contract of employment, would lose his/her job or refuse a new geographical area of employment, would profit at his/her request from measures to promote redeployment and vocational training. One of the employees, whose contract of employment had continued with this new company, refused the geographical change suggested by his new employer who laid him off. He asked his original company for the benefit of external redeployment measures in the "protection plan of employment" for employees older than fifty years. Following an appeal from this employee, the French Supreme Court considered the enterprise agreement and the "protection plan for employment", which provided that the original company would guarantee four "valid offers of employment" to active employees of fifty years, in the period of two years after their adhesion. However, the original company did not propose it: its obligation was analysed as a *duty to achieve a given result.*

The Supreme Court also defined the content of the "valid offer of employment", especially in a series of judgements on 19 January 2010, all related to the "protection plan for employment" from the same company.

During the redundancy proceedings, this company (Capdevielle and Son) had set up a "protection plan for employment". This provided that two "valid offers of employment" should be offered to "active" candidates, i.e. those who participated in job search workshops, went to fixed appointments and recruitment interviews, and personally made efforts to find a job. The "valid offer of employment," defined in the "protection plan for employment", aimed to make an offer for a permanent contract or fixed-term contract, at a maximum distance of 50 km from home or involving not more than one and-a-half hours of daily transport. The proposed employment was to correspond to the profession, the skills, the capabilities, or the employee's career objective. Remuneration was to correspond to the wages practised in the "employment area" for the branch of industry of this employment. This device was to be deployed for a period of nine months.

---

6 French Supreme Court of Appeal, 21 November 2006, No. 05-40656.

Several former employees have said they had not received any such proposals. Believing that the company was not fulfilling its obligations, they legally disputed the device of redeployment in the Court. With these recent judgements, the Supreme Court clarified the extent of employers' obligations.

Initially, the French Supreme Court considered that it was not enough for the company to make proposals for employment to employees to fulfil its requirement for redeployment. It is necessary for these offers to be *serious*. But this was not the case when a single job offer was made to an employee and the employer named in this offer had not answered the request of the employee[7]. This is not the case when the prospective employer had given a refusal to some applicants before the job interview[8]. On the other hand, if the prospective employer had refused to recruit an employee after the interview, the Supreme Court admitted that the employment offer was valid[9].

The issue of employees who had already found jobs by their own means was also raised. The employer estimated that in such a case, he could not be blame for a failure of the obligation to provide a specified number of valid employment offers. For the French Supreme Court, it was not enough to exempt the employer from the obligation for redeployment: "*the employer is not released from his/her obligation to provide a specified number of valid offers of employment simply because the employee has found another job*"[10].

In a second case, the Court also considered the nature of the proposed job on offer. It estimated that the valid offer for employment defined in the "Protection plan for employment" was not only an offer for a job that meets the objective of professional employees but also that on employment in relation to *professional expertise, skills or capabilities* of the employee[11]. Under these conditions, the job can be considered valid and effective.

The analysis of case law and a synthesis of the "Protection plan for employment" in France (Ramonet, 2010) make it possible to identify the characteristics of a "valid offer of employment". It can be defined as an offer of employment or a second interview with the same employer after selection or obtaining a proposal for a contract. It could be a permanent contract or a fixed-term contract for more than six months. Concerning the workplace, the job offer is usually 50 km. maximum from the place

7 French Supreme Court of Appeal, 19 January 2010, No. 08-44316.

8 French Supreme Court of Appeal, 19 January 2010, No. 08-44313.

9 French Supreme Court of Appeal, 19 January 2010, No. 08-44302.

10 French Supreme Court of Appeal, 19 January 2010, No. 08-44306.

11 French Supreme Court of Appeal, 19 January 2010, No. 08-44315.

of residence to the job of the person, or a one and-a-half hour trip. Lastly, the suggested wage must correspond to the average wage paid by the employment pool for the sector concerned or at least 80% of the previous gross salary of the applicant (Raoul-Duval and Perrin, 2010).

Applicable only in economic redundancies, the "valid offer of employment" appears a quite unstable concept. The employer's obligation of is not defined at the legal level and is only controlled by the judge. However, it is sometimes difficult to generalise from the criteria that appear in the jurisprudence. This is not the case of the "reasonable offer of employment", created in 2008 to define the obligations of the unemployed person.

II. The Reasonable Offer of Employment: an Obligation for the Unemployed to Accept Jobs

The Act of 1 August 2008 on the rights and duties of the unemployed person, is considered as a major reform to the unemployment insurance system because, according to some authors, it does indeed fundamentally modify the vision of French unemployment compensation, by focusing on the duty to work, rather than on the right to work (Chauchard, 2010).

The central mechanism of the new legislation, the "reasonable offer of employment" determines the conditions under which an unemployed person may lose benefits by refusing proposals for work.

That does not mean that the obligation of the unemployed to accept a job did not exist in the previous system. Indeed, before the 2008 reform, people were removed from the list of job seekers, who "*without a legitimate reason, refused a job, whatever the duration of employment contracts offered, compatible with their specialty or their training, their opportunities for geographic mobility taking into account their personal and family circumstances and mobility aids that are offered, and paid the usual wage rate in effect in that sector and region*". But in the absence of objective criteria any decision was left to the discretion of any advisor in the employment administration (Leclerc, 2008).

In our analysis of the "valid offer of employment", we found that it was the judge who controlled whether the unemployed person had been wrongly or rightly removed from the list of those unemployed and receiving benefits. The French Council of State (*Conseil d'État*) which passed judgment in any legal dispute between the jobseeker and the public employment service solved problems of wages[12], the legal nature

12 Council of State, 2 November 2005, No. 272373.

of the employer[13], the situation of successive failures at job interviews, etc.[14]

Since the 2008 reform, the "compatible job offer" has given way to a "reasonable offer of employment" in French law. The introduction of this concept in the French Labour Code was above all the opportunity for Parliament to redefine or expand the obligations of the job seeker. On the other hand, the public authorities very precisely defined the criteria for a "reasonable offer of employment" to avoid a repetition of previous problems.

A. The Extent of the Obligations of the Unemployed Person

With the reform of unemployment insurance in 2008, unemployed persons now have three obligations (Camaji, 2010). Firstly, they must perform *positive and repeated attempts to search for a job.* Then they are obliged to participate in the definition and updating of a "*personalised plan for access to employment*"[15] (PPAE). This document describes the search criteria for the unemployed person, the nature and characteristics of employment, the favoured geographical area and the level of wages expected. To determine these search criteria, consideration is given to the training of the unemployed, the qualifications, knowledge and skills acquired during professional experience, personal and family circumstances and the situation of the local labour market.

The PPAE must be developed *jointly* by the unemployed person and the employment administration. However, this PPAE does not have a legal contractual nature. In the previous system of unemployment insurance, the judge ruled in any dispute concerning the nature of relationships between the employment administration and the unemployed. Did the approval which was regularly required reveal the existence of a contract? After much hesitation by the French Courts, the French Supreme Court rejected the contractual nature of these relationships[16].

Finally, the unemployed also have now an obligation to accept "reasonable offers of employment," and we shall return later to discuss the content of such offers. Since 2008, the refusal on two occasions of a "reasonable offer of employment" without legitimate reason is a reason for being struck off of unemployed register. This refusal of employment may take several forms. It may be a refusal of a formal relationship with the employer. It can also be non-attendance at a job interview when the unemployed was given the opportunity of an interview. Finally, this can

---

13 Council of State, 5 May 1995, No. 137028.

14 Council of State, 13 May 1994, No. 137753.

15 "Projet personnalisé d'accès à l'emploi".

16 Supreme Court of Appeal, 31 January 2007, No. 04-19464.

be an express refusal of a job by an unemployed person during a job interview.

If the unemployed person has a legitimate reason, this is not a formal refusal of a "reasonable offer of employment". But this reason must be given by the unemployed person and justified in writing. It should be noted that there is a risk to the unemployed in this provision because the notion of a "legitimate reason" is not defined in text. It is left to the discretion of the Employment Administration. If it rejects it, the unemployed person must take legal recourse against his/her removal, which is not suspensive. The unemployed will be deprived of benefits and will only regain them if he/she wins the case before a judge, and only after some years.

The refusal on two occasions of a "reasonable offer of employment" constitutes a reason for being struck off the unemployed register. However, the sanctions imposed by the French Labour Code are progressive. A double refusal prohibits the unemployed from being re-registered for a period of two months. In the event of a repeated refusal, this period can be increased to up to six months. Finally, in case of several refusals, the allocation may be suppressed from two to six months or even permanently.

It is necessary to point out that this new legal system did not obtain the unanimity of all social partners. In a collective bargaining agreement prior to the Act of 1 August 2008, the social partners negotiated a National and Interprofessional Agreement, on 11 January, 2008, on the modernisation of the labour market. Whilst this Agreement has several clauses relating to unemployment, there was no agreement between the employers' and union representatives of workers on the rights and duties of the unemployed and also the Employment Administration. Article 18 of the Agreement specifies only a declaration of intent, and calls upon the legislature to initiate reform.

B. A Qualitative Definition of Employment

According to Article L5411-6-2 of the French Labour Code, the nature and characteristics of employment, the favoured geographical area and expected salary mentioned in the PPAE, are components of the reasonable offer of employment. At first analysis, this new definition *a priori* relates to only the qualities of employment, but not to the specific characteristics of the unemployed person. This interpretation should be relativised: the "reasonable offer of employment" is part of the PPAE, whose elements should also feature the characteristics of the unemployed. A circular from the Ministry of Labour, 5 November, 2008, on the PPAE and the reasonable offer of employment also specifies that the personal situation of the unemployed should be taken into consideration.

Some elements of the definition of "reasonable offer of employment" are related to the particular situation of the unemployed.

The reasonable offer of employment, as defined in the PPAE, must consider the job seeker's profile. This profile consists of the training, qualifications, knowledge and skills acquired during professional experience.

The professional skills from previous jobs must be taken into account. These skills are not required to be recognised by a diploma or qualification (the French procedure for validation of experience or informal learning).

After three months of research, the link with the previous job disappears and the general qualifications and skills of the unemployed will be used as a reference to determine appropriate employment. The field of the job search is extended beyond professional expertise, considered as too narrow. This is to encourage the unemployed to look for employment related to their skills, but broadly defined.

The personal and family situation of the unemployed is also part of the criteria for defining the field of the job search. This makes it possible to appreciate mobility difficulties. In the reasonable offer of employment, jobs incompatible with the unemployed person's state of health will not be included. Similarly, jobs with staggered hours will be excluded from the definition of a reasonable offer for a single parent who has difficulties to look after his or her child. Moreover, any change in the family status of the unemployed may cause a redefinition of the employment criteria.

Other elements are related to the nature and characteristics of the employment.

The trade, the type of mission assigned, the level of responsibility, the type of contract, the contract duration and the working time are considered as the nature and characteristics of employment.

The working time is one of the characteristics of required employment. If the PPAE indicates that the employment required is a full-time job, the unemployed person cannot be obliged to accept part-time employment, whatever the period of his/her registration. Similarly, if the PPAE indicates a part-time job, the unemployed person can refuse to accept a full-time job.

The type of contract is also part of these characteristics. If the required employment is a permanent contract, a fixed-term employment shall not constitute a reasonable offer of employment. Similarly, if the PPAE relates to the search for a fixed-term contract for family reasons, a permanent contract can be refused.

The geographic area is now an objective element of a reasonable offer of employment. In the first six months of research, the unemployed person will determine freely his/her preferred search area. After six months of unfruitful searching, objective criteria are determined by the official texts; the employment offered is considered reasonable when it involves a maximum of one hour or a distance of thirty km. maximum between home and work. These two conditions are alternatives. If the employment offered is located more than thirty km. away but may be reached in less than one hour by public transport, it is reasonable. The presence of public transport is important (buses, trains, underground systems, etc.). Indeed, in the absence of public transport in some rural areas, the criterion for the time between home and work disappears. It is the same when there is public transport available but it is not operational during the hours of work proposed, especially in case of staggered hours (night work, early mornings, late at night, etc.).

Finally, the expected wage is that sought by the unemployed person. During the first three months after registration, the level of expected wage is fixed by the unemployed person. It may therefore be different from the rate of pay previously received. However, after 12 months' registration, the replacement income (if the job seeker receives an indemnity) is then taken into account to determine whether the offer of employment is reasonable. For the unemployed who have received benefits or who have nevertheless received a wage, a "reasonable offer of employment" can be 85% of their previous salary.

Conclusions

Although it has not integrated the concept of suitable employment into its internal law, the French legislation has two conceptions of any job offer – valid or reasonable.

One established the employers' obligations, and the other those of the unemployed. One is derived from the interpretation by the employment administration of old legislation (1993), another was sanctioned by a recent Act in 2008. One is characterised by the absence of criteria to define its objectives, leaving the difficult role of interpretation to the judge in the French Supreme Court; the other is based on objective elements relating to the nature of the employment proposed, the characteristics of the unemployed him/herself. One is founded on the freedom of refusal of employment by the employee, the other on the unemployed person's obligation to accept it.

Can these two concepts, apparently so different, coexist in the French legislation?

As recalled by authors (Catala, 2008), a "valid offer of employment" offered to employees whose redundancy is being contemplated, is perhaps the "reasonable offer of employment" to be suggested to an unemployed person.

The precise nature of the criteria for any "reasonable offer of employment", like its recent creation, begs that it should replace the "valid offer of employment" in the practical application of the "Protection plan for employment"". It might be considered logical that the employers' obligation to offer a job, as part of redeployment measures, has the same objective criteria and conditions as those which feature in relations between the employment administration and the unemployed, in terms of qualifications, wages, workplace, etc.

Should we consider this "reasonable offer of employment", as the informal translation of the concept of suitable employment in ILO Conventions 88, 102 and 168? If Conventions 88 and 102 do not precisely define the concept of suitable employment, this is not the case with Convention No. 168 of which Article 21.2 provides that

> In assessing the suitability of employment, account shall be taken, in particular, under prescribed conditions and to an appropriate extent, of the age of unemployed persons, their length of service in their former occupation, their acquired experience, the length of their period of unemployment, the labour market situation, the impact of the employment in question on their personal and family situation and whether the employment is vacant as a direct result of a stoppage of work due to an on-going labour dispute.

It is difficult not to see in the French law of 2008, the same inspiration as in ILO Convention No. 168. But, of the three conventions, only conventions No. 88 and 102 of 1948 have been ratified by France. It is note the case of the Convention No. 168.

PART IV

NON-DISCRIMINATION AND EQUALITY AT WORK

Family Friendly Employment as Quality of Employment

Laura CARLSON

Associate Professor at the School of Law, Stockholm University

Quality of employment has become an urgent aspect of European efforts in the field of employment and employment law. The original focus of the EC during the 1970s was on unemployment, transformed into quantity of employment in 1997 with the European Employment Strategy, a coordinated effort to implement policies and actions aimed at boosting labour market outcomes in the EU. Non-discrimination in employment was taken up in the 1998 declaration as pointed out by Vielle and Borelli in the Introduction above. Within the framework of the Lisbon *Growth and jobs* strategy launched in 2000, the overriding objectives of the European Employment Strategy were expanded to encompass not only full employment, but even quality and productivity at work (for a more detailed discussion as to quality of work, see Caillaud, Ghailani, Peña-Casas above). Europe 2020, A European Strategy for Smart, Sustainable and Inclusive Growth (European Commission 2010) has included an employment strategy, defining inclusive growth to be "fostering a high-employment economy delivering social and territorial inclusion" with the objective of 75% of the population between 20-64 years old being employed. As a facet of inclusive growth, the Commission states the need at the national level to promote new forms of work-life balance and to increase gender equality. Other facets of discrimination have been addressed in the subsequent chapters, see Canazza (age), Garcìa-Izquierdo and Ramos-Villagrasa (sex). The focus here is on work-life balance with respect to parenting as quality of employment must be seen as including balancing work and family.

Work-life balance historically has been an issue for women in their roles as mothers. One of the greatest challenges in modern times has been achieving equality between women and men, both in the workplace as well as at home. The path towards this objective has not always been straightforward. Women have always worked, but have not had the power, politically or socially, to always have this work recognised, nor to define the conditions of their work. This article explores the progression that has occurred since World War II with respect to family and work, from being singularly a women's issue, to the present day understanding that balancing family and work is an issue for both women and men, as both women and men are parents, not just women. Against this background, it can ultimately be argued that the ability to balance family and work has become an aspect of quality of employment.

As can be seen from the legal frameworks explored below, balancing family and work for mothers and fathers has now also become an issue for employers, particularly in light of the shift from the single male breadwinner family model to a dual income family dynamic. These progressions are cursorily traced in this article through the legal treatment of these issues in international public law, the European Union, Sweden and the United Kingdom. The role of fathers, and the need for both parents to be able to balance family and work, can be seen as a newly emerging aspect of quality of employment in modern workplaces. An aspect of work-life balance not addressed here, but one which will also become more urgent over time, is balancing work and care for the elderly, particularly in light of Europe's ageing population.

This article first traces the developments with respect to this issue of balance family and work on the international level, then the European level. This is followed by an examination of the development of this issue within two member states of the European Union, Sweden and the United Kingdom. The conclusion to this article addresses issues raised in the comparison, as well as future paths the law could take.

I. International Instruments: From Protections Against Unlawful Sex Discrimination (1948) to Facilitating Positive Parenting (2006)

World War II gave impetus to several international and regional instruments, addressing providing protection against unlawful discrimination as promulgated by the United Nations ("UN"), the Council of Europe and the International Labour Organisation ("ILO"). A progression can be traced in these instruments beginning with protection for equal treatment and equal pay between men and women, to facilitating work and family care for women, to facilitating work and family care for the best interests of the child, interpreted to mean active, or as seen below, even positive parenting by both parents.

A. UN Instruments

The first of these instruments was the UN Universal Declaration of Human Rights, adopted by the UN General Assembly in 1948, directly after World War II. Under it, all member countries (with the exception of six) declared in its Article 2 that "[e]veryone is entitled to all the rights and freedoms set forth in this Declaration, without distinction of any kind, such as race, colour, sex, language, religion, political or other opinion, national or social origin, property, birth or other status." Article 7 prescribes that "[a]ll are equal before the law and are entitled without any discrimination to equal protection of the law. All are entitled to equal protection against any discrimination in violation of this Declaration and against any incitement to such discrimination." Equal pay for equal work is protected in its Article 23(2), which states that "[e]veryone, without any discrimination, has the right to equal pay for equal work."

The first UN World Conference of Women was held in 1975 and the 1979 UN Convention on the Elimination of All Forms of Discrimination Against Women ("CEDAW") was subsequently drafted. CEDAW is seen as the first international treaty to address fundamental rights for women in politics, health care, education, economics, employment, law, property, marriage and family relations. The preamble takes up, however, the role of both parents in the family, "[b]earing in mind … the social significance of maternity and the role of both parents in the family and in the upbringing of children, and aware that the role of women in procreation should not be a basis for discrimination but that the upbringing of children requires a sharing of responsibility between men and women and society as a whole."

The preamble to CEDAW goes on to state "that a change in the traditional role of men as well as the role of women in society and in the family is needed to achieve full equality between men and women." Article 11(2) places obligations on the States Parties, in order to prevent discrimination against women on the grounds of marriage or maternity and to ensure their effective right to work, to take appropriate measures including to "encourage the provision of the necessary supporting social services to enable parents to combine family obligations with work responsibilities and participation in public life, in particular through promoting the establishment and development of a network of child-care facilities."

The next instrument relevant here is the 1990 Convention on the Rights of the Child. Under its Article 18, the State Parties are to "use their best efforts to ensure recognition of the principle that both parents have common responsibilities for the upbringing and development of the child" and that "the best interests of the child will be their basic concern." Under Article 18(3), the States Parties are to "take all appropriate measures to ensure that children of working parents have the right to benefit from child-care services and facilities for which they are eligible." The progression from solely protection as unlawful discrimination on the basis of sex to the involvement of both parents in the home and the subsequent need for both parents to be able to combine work and family is evident in these instruments.

B. *The Council of Europe*

The European Convention for the Protection of Human Rights and Fundamental Freedoms ("ECHR")[1] was signed in Rome in 1950 by the members of the Council of Europe. Under Article 14 ECHR, the signatories committed themselves to the principle that "[t]he enjoyment of the rights and freedoms set forth in this Convention shall be secured without discrimination on any ground such as sex, race, colour, language, religion, political or other opinion, national or social origin, association with a national minority, property, birth or other status." Article 8 of the ECHR protects the rights of individuals to a family life.

Several instruments issued by the Council of Europe have stressed the importance of families in Europe. Only one is mentioned here, due to space constraints, Recommendation (2006) 19 of the Committee of Ministers to Member States on policy to support positive parenting as adopted by the Committee of Ministers on 13 December 2006. "Positive parenting" is defined in this recommendation as "parental behaviour based on the best interests of the child that is nurturing, empowering, non-violent and provides recognition and guidance which involves setting of boundaries to enable the full development of the child." The Committee states in Article 5 of the recommendation that "[i]n the best interests of the child, the rights of parents, such as entitlement to appropriate support from public authorities in fulfilling their parental functions, must also be given prominence." It emphasises that "[t]he exercise by parents of equal and shared responsibility for their children makes a major contribution to the harmonious development of the child's personality. Particular attention should be paid to the important role of fathers in the care and rearing of their children, taking into account in particular the principle of gender equality." Article 6(3) addresses reconciling family and working life, stating that "[p]ublic authorities should create the necessary conditions – and employers should be encouraged –

---

1 For more information on the Convention, the European Council and the European Court of Human Rights, *see* the Council's website at www.coe.int and the Court's website at www.echr.coe.int.

to implement a better reconciliation of family and working life through legal and other provisions…" The article goes on to state that "[g]ood practices make it clear to employers that a comprehensive work/life balance policy creates a win-win situation within companies."

The recommendation also addresses the impact on families from the (lack of) reconciliation of work and family life and family breakdowns. One of the proposed objectives of governments as stated in Article 3 is "the removal of barriers to positive parenting, whatever their origin. Employment policy, in particular, should allow a better reconciliation of family and working life." The Committee summarises by stating that "[i]t is also essential to implement and further develop a suitable policy to bring about a change in social attitudes and patterns of life in order to accommodate more effectively the needs of children, parents and families and in particular to promote family-friendly working environments and services."

C. The ILO

The ILO was also an early actor both in the field of equality between women and men as well as reconciling family and work. The adoption of ILO Convention No. 100 on the Equal Remuneration for Men and Women Workers for Work of Equal Value of 1951 came three years after the signing of the UN Universal Declaration of Human Rights. The Equal Pay Convention was followed seven years later by ILO Convention No. 111 on discrimination (employment and occupation) adopted in 1958.

ILO Convention No. 156 on Workers with Family Responsibilities adopted in 1981 can be seen as a forerunner in the area of reconciling family and work, raising an awareness of the need for both parents to combine work and family, recognising in its preamble "the need to create effective equality of opportunity and treatment as between men and women workers with family responsibilities and between such workers and other workers." Article 3(1) states that "[w]ith a view to creating effective equality of opportunity and treatment for men and women workers, each Member shall make it an aim of national policy to enable persons with family responsibilities who are engaged or wish to engage in employment to exercise their right to do so without being subject to discrimination and, to the extent possible, without conflict between their employment and family responsibilities." A more recent example of reconciling family and work can be seen in the 2008 ILO Resolution Concerning Working Time, regarding the importance of accurately gauging work time, elaborated in order to "bring to light gender justice and reconciliation of work and family life." The parallel development from simply protections against unlawful discrimination on the basis of sex to the understanding of the involvement of both parents and the need to reconcile family and work is again evident.

II. The Progression in the EU from Equal Pay (1957) to Work-life Balance (2010)

EU efforts in the area of equal treatment began almost with its inception, with Article 119 of the Treaty of Rome mandating equal pay for equal work between women and men. Almost twenty years after the adoption of the equal pay provision in Article 119, a triad of directives was issued by the Council addressing issues of sex discrimination: the 1975 Equal Pay Directive requiring equal pay between men and women[2], the 1976 Equal Treatment Directive requiring equal treatment in employment between men and women[3] and the 1979 Social Security Directive prohibiting different treatment with respect to social security schemes on the basis of sex[4].

After a lull of almost two decades, there was a renewal of activity in the area of equal treatment between women and men during the 1990s on the European Union level, with several directives adopted addressing sex discrimination issues: The Pregnant Workers and Breastfeeding Directive[5], the Parental Leave Directive[6], the Burden of Proof Directive[7]

---

2 Council Directive 75/117/EEC of 10 February 1975 on the approximation of the laws of the Member States relating to the application of the principle of equal pay for men and women ("Equal Pay Directive"), OJ 1975 L 45/19, Celex No. 31975L0117. The Equal Pay Directive is now incorporated in the Discrimination Directive.

3 Council Directive 76/207/EEC of 9 February 1976 on the implementation of the principle of equal treatment for men and women as regards access to employment, vocational training and promotion and working conditions ("Equal Treatment Directive"), OJ 1976 L39/40, Celex No. 31976L0207. The 1976 Equal Treatment Directive was amended in 2002 by Directive 2002/73/EC of the European Parliament and of the Council of 23 September 2002 amending Council Directive 76/207/EEC on the implementation of the principle of equal treatment for men and women as regards access to employment, vocational training and promotion, and working conditions, OJ 2002 L 269/15, Celex No. 32002L0073. It is now incorporated in the Discrimination Directive.

4 Council Directive 79/7/EEC of 19 December 1978 on the progressive implementation of the principle of equal treatment for men and women in matters of social security ("Social Security Directive"), OJ 1979 L 6/24, Celex No. 31979L0007.

5 Council Directive 92/85/EEC of 19 October 1992 on the introduction of measures to encourage improvements in the safety and health at work of pregnant workers and workers who have recently given birth or are breastfeeding (tenth individual Directive within the meaning of Article 16 (1) of Directive 89/391/EEC), OJ 1992 L 348/1, Celex No. 31992L0085.

6 Council Directive 96/34/EC of 3 June 1996 on the framework agreement on parental leave concluded by UNICE, CEEP and the ETUC ("Parental Leave Directive"), OJ 1996 L 145/4, Celex No. 31996L0034. Later amended and extended to the United

and the Part-Time Work Directive[8]. This level of activity continued into the next millennium with the Equal Treatment Directive significantly amended in 2002[9], and the Equal Treatment in Access to Goods and Services Directive issued in 2004[10]. Ultimately, seven[11] of the twelve[12] directives issued with respect to sex discrimination, along with certain

---

Kingdom and Northern Ireland by Council Directive 97/75/EC of 15 December, Directive 96/34/EC on the framework agreement on parental leave concluded by UNICE, CEEP and the ETUC, OJ 1998 L 10/24, Celex No. 31997L0075.

7 Council Directive 97/80/EC of 15 December 1997 on the burden of proof in cases of discrimination based on sex ("Burden of Proof Directive") OJ 1998 L 14/6, Celex No. 31997L0080. Later extended to the United Kingdom and Northern Ireland by Council Directive 98/52/EC of 13 July 1998 on the extension of Directive 97/80/EC to the burden of proof in cases of discrimination based on sex to the United Kingdom of Great Britain and Northern Ireland, OJ 1998 L 205/66, Celex No. 31998L0052. This directive has been incorporated into the Discrimination Directive.

8 Council Directive 97/81/EC of 15 December 1997 concerning the Framework Agreement on part-time work concluded by UNICE, CEEP and the ETUC ("Part-time Work Directive") OJ 1998 L 014/9, Celex No. 31997L0081. Later extended to the United Kingdom and Northern Ireland by Council Directive 98/23/EC of 7 April 1998 in the extension to the United Kingdom of Great Britain and Northern Ireland, of Directive 97/81/EC on the framework agreement on part-time work concluded by UNICE, CEEP and the ETUC OJ 1998 L 131/10, Celex No. 31998L0023.

9 Directive 2002/73/EC of the European Parliament and of the Council of 23 September 2002 amending Council Directive 76/207/EEC on the implementation of the principle of equal treatment for men and women as regards access to employment, vocational training and promotion, and working conditions, OJ 2002 L 269/15, Celex No. 32002L0073.

10 Council Directive 2004/113/EC of 13 December 2004 implementing the principle of equal treatment between men and women in the access to and supply of goods and services, OJ 2004 L 373/37, Celex No. 32004L0113.

11 The seven directives now included in the Discrimination Directive are: the Equal Pay Directive 75/117/EEC; the Equal Treatment Directive 76/207/EEC as amended by Directive 2002/73/EC; Directive 86/378/EEC on the implementation of the principle of equal treatment for men and women in occupational social security schemes as amended by Directive 96/97/EC; and The Burden of Proof Directive 97/80/EC as supplemented by Directive 98/52/EC on the extension to the United Kingdom of Great Britain and Northern Ireland of Directive 97/80/EC on the burden of proof in cases of discrimination based on sex.

12 Five of the twelve directives with respect to discrimination were omitted from the proposal because of the belief that their integration would overcomplicate the system:

- The Equal Treatment in Social Security, Directive 79/7/EEC; The Equal Treatment of the Self-employed, Directive 86/613/EEC;
- The Protection of Pregnant Workers and New Mothers, Directive 92/85/EEC; and
- The Parental Leave Directive 96/34/EC as well as Directive 98/52/EC extending the Parental Leave Directive to the United Kingdom and Northern Ireland.

Also not included in the Discrimination Directive are the Part-Time Work Directive 97/81/EC and the most recent Directive 2004/113/EC on the equality of access to and supply of goods and services.

of the principles established in the case law of the Court of Justice, were codified into one, the 2006 Discrimination Directive[13].

The development in EU law with respect to women's rights can be seen as slowing evolving from a biological understanding of women as mothers with the male breadwinner in the background, to a gendered approach in which parenting is not tied to biology. The focus has also shifted from simply being women's issues to including and facilitating the ability of men to be active fathers. This can be seen in the Council Directive 2010/18/EU implementing the revised Framework Agreement on Parental Leave and repealing Directive 96/34/EC. Under the 2010 parental leave directive, the need to improve the reconciliation of work with private and family life is emphasised, and includes the possibility to introduce new types of family leave such as paternity leave, in addition to existing maternity leave and parental leave. A recent judgment by the Court of Justice further enforces this direction, where the Court found that an employer's refusal to allow a father to take breastfeeding leave was in violation of the principles of equality in EU law, in acceptance of the argument presented by Spain that it was "liable to perpetuate a traditional distribution of the roles of men and women by keeping men in a role subsidiary to that of women in relation to the exercise of their parental duties"[14].

Europe 2020, A European Strategy for Smart, Sustainable and Inclusive Growth (European Commission 2010) explicitly includes in its strategy with respect to inclusive growth the need at the national level to promote new forms of work-life balance and increase gender equality. Work-life balance is viewed as necessary for all employees in this strategy, not simply for women.

III. The Progression in Sweden from the Creation of Parental Rights (1976) to Specific Protections for Parenting (2008)

Due to a shortage of workers in one of the strongest economies in the world at that time, Sweden began facilitating women's work in the 1970s. There was little protection against discrimination in place at that time, and it was mostly in public employment[15]. The work of women

---

13 Directive 2006/54/EC of the European Parliament and of the Council of 5 July 2006 on the implementation of the principle of equal opportunities and equal treatment of men and women in matters of employment and occupation (redrafted).

14 See Case C-104/09, *Pedro Manuel Roca Álvarez v. Sesa Start Espanã* [2010] ECR, Celex No. 62009JO104 at para. 36.

15 There were a few provisions for discrimination prohibitions in place at this time, such as an act passed in 1945 prohibiting employment termination on the basis of marital

was, however, restricted by statute during this period, particularly with respect to night work and forced maternity leave for industrial workers, resulting in lawful discrimination on the basis of sex in certain areas of employment. The issue of whether legislation should be used as a means to promote equality between women and men in employment had been the object of general (and at times, heated) debate during the entirety of the 1970s in Sweden, spurred in part by the subsequent progressions in EC law as well as by the United States 1964 Civil Rights Act.

Efforts in Sweden were focused on the formal economic equality of a woman as financially independent of the family (i.e. her husband), with the objective of allowing women to participate in the labour market. To this end, family taxation was abolished, limited rights to pension sharing between spouses were adopted, and there was virtually no legal provision for spousal maintenance after divorce except in cases of destitution. A new constitutional act, the Instrument of Government was adopted in 1974. In its second version adopted two years later and still in force, Article 16 forbade the state from discriminating against any person by law or regulation due to gender with certain exceptions. A right to leave from employment to take care of children, encompassing both parents, was passed in 1976 in the effort towards formal equality between the sexes in the law, at the same time repealing the mandatory maternity leave that had been in place in the legislation since 1906[16]. The decision to take parental leave was left to the parents, with employers barred from refusing to respect the decision of a parent regarding the taking of leave. An ideological shift occurred with the passage of the act, with maternity leave as an obligation for certain women within industry transformed into a right for each parent to decide to exercise[17].

The 1976 parental leave act was already replaced by a new act in 1978[18]. An unequivocal right to leave was retained in the new act, introducing the right to reduced hours. However, the employer had the right to schedule the reduction of hours, and in the absence of any agreement, to do so unilaterally at the end and beginning of each day.

---

status or pregnancy, *Lag* (1945: 844) *av 21 dec. 1945 om förbud mot arbetstagares avskedande i anledning av äktenskap eller havandeskap*, a government regulation requiring equal pay for equal work in the Swedish state public sector was promulgated in 1948 after the UN Universal Declaration of Human Rights, *Statens allmänna avlöningsreglemente* (1948: 436), and a government regulation adopted in 1973 prohibiting discrimination on the basis of sex or age in state employment, *Kungörelse* (1973: 279) *om förbud mot köns- och åldersdiskriminering vid tillsättning av tjänst.*

16 *Lag* (1976: 280) *om rätt till föräldraledighet.*

17 The 1945 Act on protection against employment termination on the basis of marriage or pregnancy was simultaneously repealed.

18 *Lag (1978: 410) om rätt till ledighet för vård of barn, m.m.*

The right of the social partners to opt out of the legislative provisions through collective agreements was added. The 1978 Act was amended again in 1979, strengthening protection by making any unlawful decision by the employer invalid, and granting pregnant women the right to reassignment in the event of strenuous physical work[19]. The 1978 Act was amended seven times during the 1980s and a further six times in the 1990s, to be ultimately replaced by the 1995 Parental Leave Act, still in force, and which has been amended fourteen times since its adoption, mostly in efforts to increase the rights of employees.

An Equality Committee was appointed in 1976 and given the task of investigating and drafting legislation prohibiting unlawful sex discrimination in employment. Its mandate was based on the conviction that a law prohibiting sex discrimination was significant as one of several societal mechanisms for bringing about change[20]. In line with Sweden's legal model of self-regulation, the social partners, in response, entered into Equality Agreements, the first in 1977 covering large segments of the working population. In the private sector, all areas except transportation were covered in an effort to prevent subsequent regulation by the proposed legislation or the proposed Equal Opportunity Ombudsman, *JämO*. The social partners then argued that these agreements should be given time for their effectiveness to be assessed prior to the adoption of legislation or, as an alternative, that legislation would impede work with equality and increase the bureaucracy[21].

The Equality Committee appointed in 1976 issued its report in 1978[22] and the Government thereafter presented a first legislative bill with respect to prohibiting unlawful sex discrimination in employment[23]. This was only a "half-law" initially passed by the Swedish Parliament with a vote of 155 to 150, because it only included the paragraphs in the legislative bill containing the general prohibition against sex discrimination[24]. The proposed parts covering the creation and jurisdiction of the Equal

---

19 *Lag (1979: 645) om ändring i lagen (1978: 410) om rätt till ledighet för vård of barn, m.m.*

20 Its first report was Government Inquiry SOU 1978: 38 *Jämställdhet i arbetslivet med förslag till lag om jämställdhet mellan kvinnor och män i arbetslivet.* The Committee issued a second report, Government Inquiry SOU 1979: 56 *Steg på väg* concerning a national plan of action resulting from the 1975 United Nations Women's Conference in Mexico.

21 See Legislative Bill 1978/79: 56 *med förslag till lag om jämställdhet mellan kvinnor och män i arbetslivet, m.m.* at 9, 196.

22 Government Inquiry SOU 1978: 38.

23 Legislative Bill 1978/79: 175 *med förslag till lag om jämställdhet mellan kvinnor och män i arbetslivet, m.m.*

24 *Lag* (1979: 503) *om jämställdhet mellan kvinnor och män i arbetslivet.*

Opportunity Ombudsman, *JämO*, as well as the obligation for the employer to carry out active measures, were not adopted. There was some resistance against placing collective agreements within the jurisdiction of *JämO*, as evidenced by the 1977 Equality Agreement, a resistance that prevailed until 1994. A second legislative bill was submitted in 1979, which was to a large extent simply the same as the first proposal[25]. It was adopted in its entirety by Parliament, passing by only one vote. After decades of discussion and debate, the first Swedish act prohibiting unequal treatment of women and men at work finally came to pass, effective from 1 July 1980[26].

That the 1979 Equal Treatment Act was not a happy compromise is evident not only from the fact that the first proposal adopted did not have a chance to become effective before it was repealed. Only one year later, the second act was amended again, and rather significantly. Seven new paragraphs were added, due to factors both internal and external to Sweden[27]. Three legislative bills had already been submitted that year concerning sex equality, one with respect to the costs for the enforcement agency, *JämO* and the Equality Council, one for amendments to the 1979 Equal Treatment Act, and the third to ratify the CEDAW[28]. The 1979 Equal Treatment Act was amended three times during the 1980s.

The results of a ten-year evaluation of the 1979 Equal Treatment Act formed the basis for the 1991 Act concerning Equal Treatment Between Women and Men at Work ("1991 Equal Treatment Act")[29]. The 1991 Act kept much of the 1979 Equal Treatment Act, particularly its layout and enforcement mechanisms. A very central aspect of the Swedish model was retained in the 1991 Equal Treatment Act, namely that, under the self-regulation, collective agreements could replace the Act's provisions for active equality measures to the extent that the agreements were approved at central level by the social partners, however without any need for the arrangements to provide a greater degree of protection than the legislation.

---

25 Legislative Bill 1979/80: 56 *med förslag till lag om jämställdhet mellan kvinnor och män i arbetslivet, m.m.*

26 *Lag* (1979: 1118) *om jämställdhet mellan kvinnor och män i arbetslivet.*

27 *Lag* (1980: 412) *om ändring i lagen (1979: 1118) om jämställdhet mellan kvinnor och män i arbetslivet.*

28 See Legislative Bill 1979/80: 129 *om ändring i lagen (1979: 1118) om jämställdhet mellan kvinnor och män i arbetslivet*, Legislative Bill 1979/80: 92 *om bestridande av kostnader för jämställdhets ombudsmannen och jämställdhetsnämndens verksamhet* and Legislative Bill 1979/80: 147 *om godkännande av Förenta nationernas konvention om avskaffande av all slags diskriminering av kvinnor.*

29 *Jämställdhetslag* (1991: 433).

One of the new active measures employers would need to take under § 5 of the 1991 with respect to employment conditions was to "facilitate both female and male employees to combine work and family." However, the Equal Treatment Ombudsman at that time argued that he had no jurisdiction with respect to discrimination against men in their role as fathers. The 1995 Parental Leave Act was amended in 2008[30] to explicitly give the Equal Treatment Ombudsman the right to represent fathers in issues of unlawful discrimination with respect to rights to parental leave.

By the new millennium, Sweden had nine legislative acts covering different grounds for discrimination in different settings:

- The 1991 Equal Treatment Act;
- The 1995 Parental Leave Act;
- The 1999 Measures to Counteract Ethnic Discrimination in the Working Life Act[31];
- The 1999 Act prohibiting Discrimination in Working Life for People with Disabilities[32];
- The 1999 Act prohibiting Discrimination in Working Life based on Sexual Orientation[33];
- The 2001 Act on Equal Treatment of Students at Universities[34];
- The 2002 Act Prohibiting Discrimination on the Basis of Part-Time and Fixed-Time Work[35];
- The 2003 Act Prohibiting Discrimination with respect to Goods and Services[36]; and
- The 2006 Act Prohibiting Discrimination with respect to primary school children[37].

30 *Lag* (2008: 572) *om ändring i föräldraledighetslagen* (1995: 584).

31 *Lag* (1999: 130) *om åtgärder mot etnisk diskriminering i arbetslivet.*

32 *Lag* (1999: 132) *om förbud mot diskriminering i arbetslivet av personer med funktionshinder.*

33 *Lag* (1999: 133) *om förbud mot diskriminering i arbetslivet på grund av sexuell läggning.*

34 *Lag* (2001: 1286) *om likabehandling av studenter i högskolan.*

35 *Lag* (2002: 293) *om förbud mot diskriminering av deltidsarbetande arbetstagare och arbetstagare med tidsbegränsad anställning.*

36 *Lag* (2003: 307) *om förbud mot diskriminering.* This act was amended in 2004 by *lag* (2004: 1089) *om ändring i lagen* (2003: 307) *om förbud mot diskriminering* and in 2005 by *lag* (2005: 453) *om ändring i lagen* (2003: 307) *om förbud mot diskriminering.*

37 *Lag* (2006: 67) *om förbud mot diskriminering och annan kränkande behandling av barn och elever.* This act was amended in 2008 by *lag* (2008: 224) *om ändring i lagen* (2006: 67) *om förbud mot diskriminering och annan kränkande behandling av barn och elever.*

A universal act was passed in 2008, the Discrimination Act[38], coming into effect on 1 January 2009. The 2008 Discrimination Act forbids unlawful discrimination on the basis of sex, transgender identity or expression, ethnicity, religion or other belief, disability, sexual orientation or age. The protection against unlawful discrimination covers employment (both private and public), education, labour market policy, starting a business and professional recognition, membership in organisations such as trade unions, housing, the provision of goods and services both for the provider and the customer, social benefits, social insurance and military service.

The 1995 Parental Leave Act was not incorporated into the 2008 Discrimination Act. However, the 2008 Discrimination Act retained in its Chapter 3 section 5 the obligation that employers take the active measures necessary to allow both women and men to facilitate combining work and family.

IV. The Progression in the UK from Equal Rights (1975) to Paternal Leave (2006)

The struggle for equality for women in the United Kingdom took a path different from both Community law, which even in the 1950s focused on sex discrimination as an impediment to free trade in the guise of social dumping, and in Sweden, which focused on the maximisation of female participation in the workforce during the 1970s. The main impetus for the passage of the Equal Pay Act 1970 and Discrimination Act 1975 was the United Kingdom's contemplated EC membership, and the Equal Pay and Equal Treatment Directives. Legislation on sex discrimination was enacted in the form of the Equal Pay Act 1970 and the Sex Discrimination Act 1975. These acts were followed by a period of relative legislative inactivity, for almost twenty years. This reluctance to legislate gave way to a flurry of legislation beginning in

---

38 *Diskrimineringslag* 2008: 567. An English translation of this act can be found on the website of the Equality Ombudsman of Sweden at www.do.se. The 2008 Discrimination Act replaces:
- The 1991 Equal Treatment Act (on grounds of sex);
- The 1999 Act with measures to counteract Ethnic Discrimination in Working Life;
- The 1999 Act prohibiting discrimination in working life for people with disabilities;
- The 1999 Act prohibiting discrimination in working life based on sexual orientation;
- The 2001 Act on the equal treatment of students at universities;
- The 2003 Act prohibiting discrimination with respect to goods and services; and
- The 2006 Act prohibiting discrimination with respect to primary school children.

the 1990s that has continued to-date. The focus of the new legislation has been to facilitate the balancing between family and work.

The UK legislative regulation shares the same bifurcation as in Sweden with respect to efforts to eradicate sex discrimination, legislation specifically prohibiting sex discrimination and requiring equal pay, as well as legislation guaranteeing certain rights on parental leave. With the passage of the 2006 Equality Act, all the discrimination legislation has been merged under this one umbrella. As is the case in Sweden, UK legislation regarding discrimination and parental leave has been very much influenced by Community law. A marked difference, however, has been that in Sweden, efforts have been directed at the formal economic equality of women as independent from the family, women participating full-time in the labour market with individual based taxation, limited rights to pension sharing between spouses, and virtually no right to spousal maintenance after divorce except in cases of destitution. The efforts in the United Kingdom are focused on women having the option of more flexible work, such as part-time work, to facilitate combining family and work, along with provisions for family taxation, pension sharing and spousal maintenance. This difference in focus, a reflection both of ideology and political aspirations regarding the role of women in society as a whole, can be seen as a partial explanation for the different focus of the legislations, in Sweden towards full-time work, and in the United Kingdom towards facilitating part-time and more flexible work.

The Equal Pay Act 1970[39] passed into legislation as a result of the EC Equal Pay Directive. It did not originally contain an explicit provision guaranteeing equal pay for equal work. This was added after an adverse ruling from the European Court of Justice in 1983[40]. The Equal Pay Act basically includes a prohibition against unequal pay in the form of an equality clause, enforcement mechanisms before the employment tribunal, exceptions, and the employer's duty to provide information as well as a "questioning of the employer." The Sex Discrimination Act 1975 prohibited direct and indirect discrimination against women and men.

The same progression can be traced here as in the systems mentioned above, with an expansion of rights to include both men and women with respect to combining work and family in the Employment Rights Act of

---

39 The Equal Pay Act of 1970 came into force in 1975. The five-year period was to give employers the chance to adjust their practices. The act has been amended since its adoption.

40 *See Ms S Villalba v. Merrill Lynch & Co Inc & Others*, Appeal No. UKEAT/0223/05/LA, Employment Appeal Tribunal dated 31 March 2006.

1996 ("ERA"). The ERA has provisions for parental leave as well as flexible working, found mainly in Part VIII. The groundwork for Part VIII can already be seen in in its Part V, *Protection from Suffering Detriment in Employment.* According to Section 47C, an employee has the right not to suffer any detriment from his/her employer for a reason related to the exercise of rights associated with flexible working, pregnancy, childbirth or maternity, ordinary, compulsory or additional maternity leave, parental leave or paternity leave, as well as taking time off to care for dependents, to include a spouse, child, parent or person living in the same household who is not an employee, tenant, lodger or boarder.

Parts VIII and VIIIA are the heart of the provisions in the ERA with respect to family leave and flexible working. Part VIII sets out maternity leave, parental leave, and paternity leave. Maternity leave is divided into three categories: ordinary maternity leave (Section 71), compulsory maternity leave (Section 72) and additional maternity leave (Section 73). Ordinary maternity leave is taken in accordance with the regulations set out by the Secretary of State, but for a period of not less than 18 weeks, to be taken at the discretion of the employee. Compulsory maternity leave is the category of leave adopted to conform to the EU requirement for obligatory maternal leave in accordance with the EC Pregnancy Directive. The compulsory leave has not to be less than two weeks and has to fall within an ordinary maternity leave period. Additional maternity leave is also governed by the regulations as adopted by the Secretary of State with no minimum requirements as to length. The Secretary of State is also authorised under Section 76 to issue regulations concerning parental leave for a period of at least three months. Parental leave is to be taken under the same protection as that established for maternity leave.

The right to request a contract modification or flexible working is set out in Part VIIIA. An employee may apply to his/her employer for a change in the terms and conditions of employment relating to the hours required, the time required, the distance to work between the employee's residence and the employer's place of business, or other aspects as specified by the Secretary of State in the appropriate regulations. The purpose for the change must be to enable the employee to care for a child and the application must be made before the child reaches the age of six or if the child is disabled, eighteen. The employer can refuse the application on the following grounds: the burden of additional costs, a detrimental effect on the capacity to meet customer demand, inability to re-organise work between existing staff, inability to recruit additional staff, a detrimental impact on quality or performance, insufficient work, planned structural changes or other grounds as specified by the Secretary of State.

The Equality Act 2006[41] designated a list of "equality and human rights enactments" which the Secretary of State was empowered to add, remove or change[42]. The primary equality and human rights acts of interest on sex discrimination were the Equal Pay Act 1970, the Sex Discrimination Act 1975 and the Human Rights Act 1998 (the UK implementation of the ECHR), against which unlawful sex discrimination was to be assessed[43]. This act created a "gender duty" for public authorities to promote gender equality and prevent sex discrimination in the exercise of public functions[44] and was viewed as one of the most significant changes in discrimination law in thirty years. Instead of individuals prosecuting complaints against sex discrimination, this duty places the responsibility on public bodies to demonstrate that they treat men and women fairly and are taking active steps to promote gender equality, a form of heightened gender mainstreaming.

The Work and Families Act 2006[45] extends the period of Statutory Maternity Pay and Adoption Pay from 26 to 39 weeks and also allows the Ordinary Maternity Leave and Additional Maternity Leave to be taken for a combined 52 weeks without any length of service requirement. Entitlements to additional paternity leave now allow fathers to take 26 weeks leave as well as increasing the rights of fathers to mirror more closely those of mothers. These provisions introduce new rights for mothers to transfer part of their statutory maternity pay or maternity allowance to fathers. Employees will be able to go into work for up to ten 'Keeping in Touch' days without losing any entitlement to benefits.

As of October 2010, the Equality Act is the current statutory regulation of discrimination, passed in an attempt to simplify the system as described above and created by the 2006 Equality Act[46]. However, the explicit definitions of discrimination in the new act include pregnancy and maternity discrimination, but not parental or paternal discrimination.

The Secretary of State for Trade and Industry is empowered to issue statutory instruments, regulations, to carry out and enforce the above

41 The Equality Act 2006 is available at the UK Office of Public Sector Information: www.opsi.gov.uk/acts/acts2006/20060003.htm.

42 Equality Act 2006, Chapter 3, Part 1, Sections 33(1) and (3).

43 *Id.* at Section 33.

44 *Id.* at Section 82.

45 The Work and Families Act 2006 is available at the UK Office of Public Sector Information at www.opsi.gov.uk/acts/acts2006/20060018.htm.

46 The Equality Act 2010 is available at the UK National Archives at www.legislation.gov.uk/ukpga/2010/15/contents.

acts. Those statutory instruments of interest here can be placed into three categories: the regulations on family leave (maternity, parental and paternity), flexible working and enforcement mechanisms. The amended Maternity and Parental Leave etc. Regulation of 1999 as provides entitlement to statutory ordinary maternity leave for a period of 26 weeks, additional maternity leave of up to 26 weeks, compulsory maternity leave for a two-week period and parental leave of up to thirteen weeks. The Statutory Paternity Pay and Statutory Adoption Pay (General) and the Statutory Paternity Pay and Statutory Adoption Pay (Weekly Rates) (amended) Regulations of 2006, as a result of the Work and Families Act 2006, establish paternity leave as well as further requirements and rights. A male employee is entitled to one or two weeks' paternity leave with Statutory Paternity Pay, and also 26 weeks Additional Paternity Leave, if he is the biological father of the child, spouse or partner of the child's mother, or if he expects to have responsibility for the upbringing of the child. The Additional Paternity Leave gives entitlement to a cash benefit only if the mother has cash benefits for her outstanding leave.

The Flexible Working (Eligibility, Complaints and Remedies) Regulations 2002 and the Flexible Working (Procedural Requirements) Regulations 2002 set out the framework for the right to flexible working as protected in the Employment Rights Act 1996. An employee is entitled to request a contract modification for flexible working if he/she has been employed for 26 weeks and either is a parent, foster parent or guardian of a child or spouse or partner to such a person[47].

In contrast with the approach taken by Sweden on the economic independence of spouses as well as the emphasis on both spouses working full-time, the approach in the UK has been more focused on facilitating flexible working for parents, with the father's right to take leave gaining momentum in the past decade.

V. Reconciling Family and Work as an Emerging Quality of Employment

As can be seen from the legal frameworks examined above, a tangible movement can be detected in the law within each of these systems, from a focus on equal treatment between men and women at work, to reconciling family and work for both parents, i.e., for both mothers and fathers. At the international level, this issue has been treated from a perspective of human rights as well as societal good. At the two national levels examined here, the focus in Sweden has been on the economic

[47] The Flexible Working (Eligibility, Complaints and Remedies) Regulations 2002, Sections 3-7.

independence of the spouses, as well as the full-time employment of women, the ways of achieving equality between men and women, whilst the focus in the United Kingdom has been on facilitating women's work through more flexible work arrangements, regardless of whether the work is part-time or full-time. The protection is markedly stronger for women, as witnessed by the definitions of discrimination in the 2010 Equality Act, explicitly including pregnancy and maternity, but not explicitly parenthood or paternity.

Reconciling work and family for women has always been a feature of their lives. The legal frameworks presented above demonstrate that this balancing is a quality of employment in all of these systems, at least for mothers. Reconciling work and family for men as fathers is a new aspect of this issue that can be seen to be gaining ground, perhaps not as quickly as for women, but still slowly and surely. This in its turn will increase the already existing pressure on employers to take the balancing act between work and family even more into account as a quality of employment.

The issue facing the future is defining the necessary contribution of the law with respect to work-life balance, an issue addressed more generally below with respect to quality of work by Bonvin, Cianferoni and Widmer in the conclusion. Their general conclusion as to quality of work is that a combination of both substantive rights and procedural rights with a focus on a capabilities approach are necessary to promote a fair conception of "job quality" and its effective enforcement. In the issue of work-life balance, the necessary combination can be seen instead as both substantive law and procedural law with a focus on access to justice, the ability to successfully invoke the rights as granted under the law. As work-life balance in essence is not a diffuse concept, but rather concrete, whether a parent can combine work and taking care of a child, the key factor here becomes giving both parents, men and women, the means necessary to invoke their rights without fear of any sanctions by employers in the forms of employment termination, lower wages, or worse working conditions.

Quality of Work within the Active Ageing Strategy

Christine CANAZZA

Lecturer at the Université catholique de Louvain

This chapter depict the effectiveness of the legal norms that shape the "quality of work" notion. Its purpose is to examine the "quality of work" framework as a major aspect to be taken into account within the active ageing strategy and with special regard to the principle of unlawful age discrimination.

The first part recalls the international and European legal context regarding the principle of unlawful age discrimination and examines to what extent this principle is part of the quality of work (I). The second part focuses on the utility of quality of work and the struggle against unlawful age discrimination to achieve the goals of the European Employment Strategy in terms of active ageing – and the specific objectives for older workers launched after the "Lisbon Strategy" (II).

This chapter explores the "quality of work" notion from a legal point of view. The results could then potentially be used to complement the legal framework for this particular notion[1].

I. Non-discrimination as Part of the Quality of Work

This chapter retraces the international and European legal context regarding the principle of discrimination, and in particular discrimination based on age (1.1.). It then examines the extent to which this principle is part of the quality of work (1.2.).

A. Non-discrimination in International and European Law

The principle of non-discrimination is established both at international and European levels. Protection against discrimination for all persons

[1] The author wants to thanks Professor J. Macnicol from the London School of Economics for his precious remarks on this contribution.

is a universal right recognised by a wide range of internationally agreed human rights instruments[2] and signed by EU Member States.

For each of these levels, I will first examine discrimination at work, which implies a denial of equality of treatment and opportunity at work from different angles **(a) The principle of non-discrimination**. This can be directed against individuals in their own right or as members of social groups. Many countries have enacted a wide variety of laws and mechanisms to combat discrimination at work. A growing number of countries are moving away from legal approaches, based exclusively on the prohibition to discriminate (negative duty), to a broader approach that tends to prevent discrimination and promote equality (positive duty).

Second, I will focus on the legal instruments against unlawful age discrimination at work **(b) The specificity of unlawful age discrimination**. Indeed, if some of the instruments provide for a generally applicable prohibition of discrimination covering several instances of discrimination (e.g. age, gender or nationality)[3], others focus on a single instance. Discrimination on the basis of age is a very recent criterion, although there have been some cases before the EUC.J. during the last few years that could help to define this specific type of discrimination. It is also important to bear in mind that age is not defined in the legal instruments relating to discrimination. Besides, though widespread in practice, this discrimination is extremely difficult to prove.

---

2 E.g. the Universal Declaration of Human Rights, the United Nations Convention on the Elimination of all forms of Discrimination Against Women (CEDAW), the International Convention on the Elimination of all forms of Racial Discrimination (CERD), the United Nations Covenants on Civil and Political Rights (ICCPR) and on Economic, Social and Cultural Rights (ICESCR) and the European Convention for the Protection of Human Rights and Fundamental Freedoms (ECHR).

3 Other works have examined "quality of work" in relation to other characteristics. For example:

– For a study on quality of work in relation with employment security, health and well-being, skills development and work life-balance, see *Quality of work and employment in Europe* European Foundation, Dublin, 2007.

– For a study on job quality and gender equality, see M. Smith *et al.*, "Job quality in Europe", *Industrial Relations Journal*, 2008, pp. 586-603.

– For a study on quality of work related to wage inequality, gender equality and industrial relations, see Ana M. Guillen. *et al.*, *Quality of Work in the European Union. Concept, Data and Debates from a Transnational Perspective*, Brussels, P.I.E. Peter Lang, 2009.

1. Non-discrimination, a Fundamental Right in the ILO Legal Instruments

a. The Principle of Non-discrimination

The promotion of equality of opportunity and treatment has been of fundamental importance to the ILO since its very creation. The ILO Constitution in 1919 incorporated the first international treaty with reference to the principle of equal remuneration for men and women workers for work of equal value. The Declaration of Philadelphia, now part of the Constitution[4], further developed the principle of non-discrimination and recognised the human rights' dimension and its fundamental role in achieving social justice at work. The Declaration asserts that the principle of non-discrimination is one of the principles that "should inspire the policy of its Members"[5].

International labour standards are legal instruments drawn up by ILO constituent members[6] and adopted at the ILO's annual International Labour Conference. They set out basic principles and rights at work. They are either *conventions*[7], or *recommendations*[8]. A convention lays down the basic principles to be implemented by ratifying countries, while a related recommendation complements the convention by providing more detailed guidelines on how it could be applied[9]. ILO Conventions and Recommendations are important sources of protection for working people all over the world.

Eight conventions have been identified as "fundamental"[10], covering subjects that are considered fundamental principles and rights at work. One of these fundamental principles is the elimination of discrimination in respect of employment and occupation. This principle is also covered in the ILO Declaration on Fundamental Principles and Rights at Work

---

4 Annex to the ILO Constitution – entitled "Declaration concerning the aims and purposes of the ILO" (10 May 1944).

5 Article II states that: "*all human beings, irrespective of race, creed or sex, have the right to pursue both their material well-being and their spiritual development in conditions of freedom and dignity, of economic security and equal opportunity*". Article III states that the Conference recognised the ILO obligation to ensure equality of educational and vocational opportunity.

6 Governments, employers and workers.

7 Legally binding international treaties that may be ratified by Member States.

8 Serve as non-binding guidelines.

9 However, recommendations can also be autonomous (i.e. not linked to any convention).

10 Currently, around 90% of these conventions have been ratified.

(1998)[11]. As a follow-up to the ILO Declaration on Fundamental Principles and Rights at Work, the ILO has published two global reports that are key resources for the principle of non-discrimination:

- *Equality at work: tackling the challenges*[12] provides a global picture of discrimination in work, including a study of progress and failures in the struggle to fight discrimination, ranging from traditional forms (such as sex, race or religion), to newer forms (based on age, sexual orientation, HIV/AIDS status and disability);
- *Time for equality at work*[13].

The ILO has also established international norms defining rights according to the principle of non-discrimination, and elaborating on conditions and guidelines to protect and promote these rights including Convention No. 111 on Discrimination in Respect of Employment and Occupation (1958) and Recommendation 111 concerning Discrimination in Respect of Employment and Occupation (1958).

Article 3 of the ILO Convention 111 on Discrimination in Respect of Employment and Occupation (1958) (hereafter called "Convention 111") states that each Member *undertakes to declare and pursue a national policy designed to promote equality of opportunity and treatment in respect of employment and occupation, with a view to eliminating any discrimination in respect thereof.* The grounds for discrimination include *race, colour, sex, religion, political opinion, national extraction or social origin*, but not age.

However, it has to be specified that any distinction, exclusion or preference in respect of a particular job, based on its inherent requirements, are not deemed to be discriminatory. Moreover, special provisions for protection or assistance provided for in other Conventions or Recommendations adopted by the International Labour Conference are not to be deemed to be discriminatory. In this regard, Article 6 of Recommendation 111 concerning Discrimination in Respect of Employment and Occupation (1958) (hereafter called "Recommendation 111") states that: *Application of the policy of non-discrimination should not adversely affect special measures designed to meet the particular requirements of persons who, for reasons such as sex, age, disablement, family re-*

11 The aim of this Declaration is to ensure respect for fundamental rights at work (and their promotion and realisation in economic and social practice) and to provide the Organization with a clearer framework for development.

12 *Equality at work: tackling the challenges*. Global report as a follow-up to the ILO Declaration on Fundamental Principles and Rights at Work. Report of the Director-General, 2007.

13 *Time for equality at work*. Global report as a follow-up to the ILO Declaration on Fundamental Principles and Rights at Work. Report of the Director-General, 2003.

sponsibilities or social or cultural status are generally recognised to require special protection or assistance.

b. The Specificity of Unlawful Age Discrimination

As stated above, age criteria can be found in two ILO legal instruments: Article 6 of Recommendation 111 relating to positive policies and Articles 3 of Recommendation 162 concerning Older Workers (1980) (hereafter called "Recommendation 162") which states, *Older workers should, without discrimination by reason of their age, enjoy equality of opportunity and treatment with other workers*[14].

The Committee of Experts on the Application of Conventions and Recommendations publishes a yearly report. The reports for the 1988 and 1996 looked in depth at the application of Convention 100 and its Recommendation.

In the 1988 report, the Committee recalled that age is viewed as "a physical condition for which there are particular needs and in respect of which special protection and assistance are recognised as being necessary". However, it also stated that the issue of age, and particularly that of older workers, must be raised in the context of the promotion of equality of opportunity and treatment, and no longer considered exclusively within the framework of protection and assistance. The Committee's view is that discrimination on the basis of age should be considered in relation to a compulsory retirement age and the employment conditions both for older and young workers. Finally, the report revealed that if an exception for *bona fide* occupational requirements had been made in a series of occupations, for reasons involving the safety or health of the worker or of third parties, the courts are less inclined to automatically consider age to be a *bona fide* occupational requirement in categories of employment without proof of the impact of age.

The report issued in 1996 placed emphasis on the emergence of new criteria. It stated that age was one of the grounds referred to in Article 5 of Convention No. 111, but it was also increasingly the subject of legislation in many countries. The Committee concluded that with regard to the changing nature of discrimination and the promotion of employment, it might be appropriate to include age discrimination in an additional protocol, subject to specific ratification, which was not already contained in Article 1 of the Convention.

---

14 See also Article 2: *Employment problems of older workers should be dealt with in the context of an overall and well balanced strategy for full employment and, at the level of the undertaking, of an overall and well balanced social policy, due attention being given to all population groups, thereby ensuring that employment problems are not shifted from one group to another.*

2. *EU Law Regarding Age Discrimination*

a. The Principle of Non-discrimination

All EU Member States have adopted legislation that prohibits discrimination, and they are all parties to the main human rights conventions prohibiting discrimination, concluded under the auspices of the United Nations and the Council of Europe.

Since the Lisbon Treaty, reference to the principle of non-discrimination has become even more important in European legal instruments:

– Articles 2 and 3 of the consolidated versions of the Treaty of the European Union introduced new social targets related to discrimination:

The Union is founded on the values of respect for human dignity, freedom, democracy, equality, the rule of law and respect for human rights, including the rights of persons belonging to minorities. These values are common to the Member States in a society in which pluralism, non-discrimination, tolerance, justice, solidarity and equality between women and men prevail. The Union shall combat discrimination and promote solidarity between generations.

– Article 10 of the Treaty of the Functioning of the European Union also required that the Union combat discrimination when defining and implementing its policies and activities.

– The Charter of Fundamental Rights of the European Union[15] prohibits *any discrimination based on any ground such as sex, race, colour, ethnic or social origin, genetic features, language, religion or belief, political or any other opinion, membership of a national minority, property, birth, disability, age or sexual orientation.*

There is a long tradition of non-discrimination in the EU Treaty regarding two specific criteria: gender and nationality. More recently, Article 13 of the EU Treaty – introduced by the Amsterdam Treaty[16] – gives the Community specific powers to take action to combat discrimination based on sex, racial or ethnic origin, religion or belief, disability, age or sexual orientation. Based on Article 13, the European Community enacted two Directives that prevent people in the European Union from being discriminated against on grounds of race and ethnic origin[17], and on grounds of religion or belief, disability, age or sexual orienta-

---

15 Implemented in December 2009, with the same legal value as the treaties.

16 Implemented in 1999.

17 Council Directive 2000/43/EC implemented the principle of equal treatment between persons irrespective of racial or ethnic origin.

tion[18]. The purpose of these Directives is to lay down a general framework for combating discrimination, with a view to putting into effect in the Member States the principle of equal treatment (defined in the Directives as absence of direct and indirect discrimination). The Directives define a set of principles that offer every individual in the EU a common minimum level of legal protection against discrimination. A few cases have already been adjudged by the EUC.J. on the basis of these Directives.

In a similar vein as in international norms, the Employment Framework Directive 2000/78 (hereafter called "Directive 2000/78") acknowledges that, in some circumstances, it is justifiable to allow exceptions to the non-discrimination principle. Differential treatment may therefore be justifiable where a particular characteristic (e.g. age or ethnic origin) constitutes a genuine and determinant occupational requirement[19]. Moreover, a difference in treatment on the grounds of age may not constitute discrimination if this difference is justified by some other legitimate aim – such as employment policy – provided that the means of achieving that aim are appropriate and necessary. Finally, the possibility to make provision for positive measures may also sometimes call for distinctions to be made.

b. The Specificity of Unlawful Age Discrimination

There is a growing body of evidence in different EU countries showing that older workers are frequently discriminated against in the labour market. Despite the changes that have occurred in Member State policies, the reality of the labour market and the experience of older workers in most EU countries show that exclusion from employment still exists. In most countries, older workers tend to occupy a relatively low status in the labour market, experience discrimination with regard to work recruitment and training and are disproportionately represented among the long-term unemployed.

Directive 2000/78 has several provisions on age discrimination, mainly related to the limit of the principle of unlawful age discrimination. Most Member States have decided to exercise this option. As a consequence, there is a great deal of uncertainty across the Member States as to which forms of age discrimination will be treated as justifiable by national courts and/or the EUCJ. In fact, Directive 2000/78 permits national law to include a range of exceptions in relation to both

---

18 Council Directive 2000/78/EC established a general framework for equal treatment in employment and occupation.

19 For example, age could constitute a legitimate occupational requirement when a man over 60 years is needed to play the part of a grandfather in a TV series.

direct and indirect age discrimination[20]. For example, Article 6(1)[21] lists examples of differences which could be allowed, including the fixing of minimum conditions for age, professional experience or seniority for access to employment. This article enables national laws to promote the vocational integration or protection of young people and older workers; such laws are quite common in the EU Member States. In the *Mangold* case[22] in 2005, the EUCJ stated that the principle of non-discrimination on grounds of age must be regarded as a general principle of Community law merely because the source of the principle underlying the prohibition of discrimination can be found in various international instruments and in the constitutional traditions common to Member States. In fact, the specific criteria for age can only be found in two ILO instruments (Recommendations 111 and 162) and in one European constitution (in Finland). After the *Mangold* case, it seemed that the existence of a general principle of equal treatment, particularly in respect of age, has been reconsidered by the EUCJ but this principle was then reasserted in the recent *Kücükdeveci* case[23] in 2010. In my opinion, the court should be cautious when it examines age discrimination, in particular in regards with the possibility for Member States to determine the social policies that suit their own national situation.

In 2005 and 2008, the European Commission[24] published reports on the transposition of Directive 2000/78, stressing the difficulty of transposing age discrimination protection in national legislation due to its consequences for labour markets, and also the fact that the major problem regarding discrimination is the respect of this principle in practice. However, in 2008 the European Parliament asked the European Commission to propose a horizontal directive covering all the criteria for discrimination (including age) in both the private and professional

---

[20] Fixing minimum and maximum age requirements in access to employment can be described as direct age requirements, whereas a required number of years of experience constitutes an indirect age requirement.

[21] *Member States may provide that differences of treatment on grounds of age shall not constitute discrimination, if, within the context of national law, they are objectively and reasonably justified by a legitimate aim, including legitimate employment policy, labour market and vocational training objectives, and if the means of achieving that aim are appropriate and necessary.*

[22] EUCJ, 22 November 2005, *Mangold*, C-144/04.

[23] EUCJ, 19 January 2010, *Kücükdeveci*, C-555/07.

[24] Report on the Implementation of Directive 2000/78/CE (2005), 28 September 2005; Report on the Implementation of Directive 2000/78/CE (2008), 19 June 2008. See also M. Bell, I. Chopin and F. Palmer, *Developing Anti-discrimination Law in Europe*, 2007 – the 25 EU Member States compared which is a comparative review of the transposition of the EC Racial Equality and the Employment Equality directives in the national law of 25 EU Member States.

sectors and to incorporate the non-discrimination policy in the Lisbon strategy[25].

All EU countries have had to transpose Directive 2000/78 into their legal systems, and their laws must fulfil the obligations under international law. Consequently, both international and EU instruments ought to have had a major impact on their domestic laws. However, the international and European standards define only the minimum level of protection against discrimination, and many countries have gone beyond these requirements and have extended the protection. A. Nayer[26] points out that there is a distinction between non-discrimination in international law and in European law[27]. Whereas international legislation seeks to prohibit all kinds of discrimination in order to protect the fundamental rights of workers[28] and only gives criteria as examples, European legislation has a very narrow field of non-discrimination, and gives the criteria as well as the scope.

B. Non-discrimination, a Fundamental Right Within the Quality of Work

Since the mid-1990s, there has been great interest in the issue of quality of work. There is also a growing awareness that developments in the labour market should be analysed on the basis of a comprehensive set of indicators reflecting qualitative and quantitative aspects of the world of work[29]. To satisfy the need to develop policies to improve work quality, both the ILO and the EU have developed quality of work frameworks. The quality of work conceptual frameworks of the EU and the European Foundation are more specifically geared towards high-income countries (EU Member States), while the ILO's concept of decent work also includes the poorest and most vulnerable countries[30].

---

25 Proposal for a Council Directive on implementing the principle of equal treatment between persons irrespective of religion or belief, disability, age or sexual orientation, 2 July 2008, COM(2008) 426 final.

26 A. Nayer *et al.*, *Le droit à l'épanouissement de l'être humain au travail: Métamorphoses du droit social*, Brussels, Bruylant, 2007, pp. 223 et s.

27 The first being more social and the second more economic.

28 Non-discrimination is a right of its own and a constitutive element of all human rights (i.e. the enjoyment of all rights must be guaranteed on a non-discriminatory basis).

29 R. Pena-Casas, "Quality of Work and Employment in EU Policy Arena: Conceptual Frameworks and Monitoring Indicators", Paper for the RECWOWE Network, 2007.

30 In English one of the first interpretations of the word "decent" is "satisfactory, of an acceptable standard". In everyday language, a decent job is at least *sufficient in quality and quantity.* The word "*decent*" has this connotation, with respect to the need for workers to have "*acceptable*" or "*adequat*e" work and working conditions.

The Decent Work Agenda of the ILO brings together the goals for employment, social protection, social dialogue and rights at work in a vision which guides economic and social policy choices[31]. Fundamental rights play an essential role in promoting decent work. As mentioned above, one of these fundamental rights is the principle of non-discrimination (1.2.1.).

In Europe, the promotion of quality of work is a guiding principle in the Social Policy Agenda of the European Union. In 2000, the Heads of State and Governments of the EU met in Lisbon to launch a series of reforms. At this meeting, a new overall goal of moving to full employment through creating not only more, but also better jobs was set; job quality became a priority for Europe. One aspect of quality is related to the principle of non-discrimination (1.2.2.).

1. Decent Work, Equity and Fair Treatment (ILO)

The notion of 'decent work' was first defined by the ILO Director-General in the 1999 Report to the International Labour Conference[32]. The report emphasised the fact that "decent work" not only aimed to create more jobs, but also to create better jobs (jobs of acceptable quality/quality of employment). One of the six dimensions included in the initial definition[33] of decent work – equity in work – is related to the workers' need to have fair and equitable treatment and opportunity in work. It also includes the absence of discrimination at work and in access to work.

The notion of decent work is also linked to the four strategic objectives set within the 2000-2001 ILO programme, i.e. employment, social protection[34], workers' rights and social dialogue[35]. While the first two components refer to opportunities, remuneration, security and conditions of work, the last two emphasise on the workers' social relations. In

---

31 While the objectives behind decent work in these Conventions are of universal validity, the content and the mechanisms for attainment must be adapted to countries' structural and institutional characteristics: D. Ghai, "Decent work: Concept and indicators", *International Labour Review*, 2003, Vol. 142, No. 2.

32 *The primary goal of the ILO today is to promote opportunities for women and men to obtain decent and productive work, in conditions of freedom, equity, security and human dignity.* J. Somavia, *Decent jobs for all in a global economy; an ILO perspective*, document submitted to the Third WTO Ministerial Meeting (30 Nov.-3 Dec. 1999), available at www.ilo.org.

33 Decent work means productive work in which rights are protected and which generates an adequate income, with adequate social protection. It also means sufficient work, in the sense that all should have full access to income-earning opportunities.

34 E. Dermine contribution.

35 F. Dorssemont contribution.

particular, the notion of decent work incorporates the fundamental rights of workers of freedom of association and non-discrimination in work.

In 2002, R. Anker[36] built a system of statistical indicators[37] in order to measure decent work. He identified ten general characteristics of work that individuals from around the world would consider important elements of decent work. Within the ten indicators proposed is included 'Fair treatment in employment', which has been expressed in terms of equality of opportunity in employment and occupation, and equal pay for work of equal value[38].

The ILO continued to campaign for the decent work goal[39] and has put even more emphasis on decent work policies after the global economic crisis in September 2008[40].

2. Quality of Work, Diversity and Non-discrimination (EU)

The goal to "create more and better jobs" appeared at the European Lisbon summit (2000) with specific reference to the need to improve the level and quality of employment. This goal of a "better job" has been a central part of the European Employment Strategy since 2001. The notion of *Quality in Work*[41] has been defined in the Communication from the European Commission: *Employment and social policies: a framework for investing in quality* (2001). It included work dimensions

---

36 R. Anker *et al.*, *Measuring Decent Work with Statistical Indicators*, Working Paper No. 2, 2002, p. 42 et s.

37 R. Anker added to these ten indicators of decent work an eleventh group of indicators that summarise key aspects of the "economic and social context of decent work": he assumed that it is important to consider the economic and social context within which decent work occurs.

38 R. Anker suggested concentrating the indicators for fair treatment in regard to gender differential treatment and he did not include age as a subject for study. However, he recognises that *Segregation and discrimination are obviously not limited to gender. There are many other grounds for differentiated treatment and discrimination in the labour market.*

39 Ministerial Declaration of the High-level Segment of ECOSOC, World of Work Magazine No. 57, September 2006. See also the ILO Fundamental Declaration on Social Justice for a fair Globalisation, *Working out of crisis: Strategies for Decent Work in Europe and Central Asia*, Conclusions of the Eighth European Regional Meeting of the ILO, Lisbon, 9-13 February 2009, Leaders' Statement: The Pittsburgh Summit, September 24-25, 2009.

40 Report of the Director-General, *Tackling the global jobs crisis. Recovery through decent work policies*, International Labour Conference, 98th Session 2009, Report I(A).

41 The concept of Quality of jobs is broader than Quality of work: it refers to the characteristics of a job in itself: it calls for a set of characteristics of a job, which determine the level of satisfaction of workers and enable them to talk in terms of "good" or "bad" jobs.

and indicators in this context. The 2001 Commission Communication identified ten "dimensions" of job quality, although it stated that quality was a multifaceted concept[42]. These indicators were approved by the Council[43] and communicated to the Laeken European Council in December 2001. The ten dimensions[44] of quality contained in this concept cover not only the characteristics of individual jobs but also those of the wider work environment and context. In addition to indicators referring to the characteristics of a job[45] a set of context indicators[46] were identified. One of the ten agreed dimensions of quality in work[47] is "Diversity and non-discrimination".

As mentioned above, the EU Treaty and legislation establish the principle that all workers must be treated without discrimination in terms of sex, age, disability or ethnic origin. Equality and non-discrimination between workers are essential pillars of the European legislation, and the European Council adopted indicators in relation to the rate of employment of vulnerable groups, e.g. older workers. It defines 'diversity management' as (...) *meeting the needs of a culturally diverse workforce and of sensitising workers and managers to differences associated with gender, race, age and nationality in an attempt to maximise the potential productivity of all employees.*

---

42 The Employment Committee (EMCO) discussed and agreed a list of indicators on quality in work under the 10 dimensions: Indicators of Quality in Work, Report by the Employment Committee to the Council, 14263/01, 23.11.2001.

43 In 2001, the Council agreed to assess progress using a set of indicators for quality built on the ten dimensions of quality in work identified by the European Commission.

44 1. Intrinsic job quality; 2. Skills, lifelong learning and career development; 3. Gender equality; 4. Health and safety at work; 5. Flexibility and security; 6. Inclusion and access to the labour market; 7. Work organisation and work-life balance; 8. Social dialogue and worker involvement; 9. Diversity and non-discrimination; 10. Overall work performance.

45 Such as those on pay gaps and transitions by pay level, adult participation in education and training, temporary contracts and accidents at work.

46 Among these last indicators we find those on employment and unemployment gender gaps, employment rate of older workers, youth employment ratio, labour market gaps for disadvantaged groups and growth in GDP per person employed and per hour worked.

47 It has to be noted however that the concepts of both *Quality in Work* and *Decent Work* have been adopted by the European Union *Promoting decent work for all. The EU contribution to the implementation of the decent work agenda in the world*, COM(2006) 249 final, 24 May 2006: The conclusion of the report stated that [...] *Decent work is an element of the internal and external dimension of the EU Lisbon strategy for growth and jobs*, report on the EU contribution to the promotion of decent work in the world, Commission Staff Working Document, COM(2008) 412 final, 2 July 2008.

Diversity and non-discrimination are related to the issue of adopting comprehensive national strategies to promote integration in the employment market for disadvantaged groups such as older workers. However, despite the focus on quality of work within the European Union since 2001, not much has been done to evaluate the quality of work itself, above all, regarding that of older workers.

II. Discrimination and Quality of Work with Regard to the Goals of the Active Ageing Strategy

It has been demonstrated above that the struggle against discrimination is a significant aspect of quality of work. In this last part, these two objectives are examined in order to determine how useful they are – or should be – in order to achieve the goals of the European Employment Strategy and the targets determined at the Lisbon and Barcelona Councils as well as in Europe 2020 (2.1.). Finally, I will try to work out what does the concept of quality of work entail precisely for older workers (2.2.).

A. Quality of Work is Part of European Employment Policies

The ageing of the European population is reducing the labour force in Europe and social protection budgets are in jeopardy. The existing employment gap for 55-64 year olds makes it necessary to reinforce the preventive and active policy measures to promote the integration of this group into the labour market. But this cannot be done without appropriate working conditions. Emphasis should be placed on recruitment policies for older workers as well as anti-discrimination policies.

In order to raise the employment rates of older workers, some Member States have introduced incentives for employers to retain or recruit these workers, with penalties to discourage their dismissal, and/or have implemented reforms of pensions and introduced stricter conditions for early retirement. However, there is a need to put in place global national strategies and a policy for targeted action[48] in order to increase the employment rate of older workers.

The attention paid to the ageing of the workforce in policies has increased in the last decade. In the EU, the sustainability of pensions, economic growth and the future labour supply have stimulated a series of social policies that support the aims of longer working lives and later retirement. The Luxembourg Job Summit in November 1997 launched the European Employment Strategy (hereafter called "EES"). The EES establishes a multilateral surveillance framework to encourage Member

[48] Financial incentives, life-long learning strategies, adapted working conditions.

States to implement effective policies. The EES aims at strengthening the coordination of national employment policies. Its main objective is to involve Member States in a series of common objectives and targets, focused on four pillars[49].

Active ageing has been an integral part of the EES since 1999. In its conference paper *Towards a society for all ages. Employment, Health, Pensions and Intergenerational Solidarity*[50], the European Commission stated that there were different demographic trends – depending on the age band – that implied different policy challenges for the EU – namely an increase in the need for social policy reforms for the age band of 65 years and over and active ageing for the age band of 50-64 year olds, particularly for labour market policy and pension reform.

The 2001 Employment Guidelines stress the importance for Member States of developing active ageing policies[51] while the 2002 Employment Guidelines call for 'in-depth changes in the prevailing social attitudes towards older workers' and emphasise the importance of the quality dimension[52]. Improving quality in work appeared as a key priority in the 2001 and 2002 Employment Guidelines and is one of the three overriding objectives in the Employment Guidelines for the period 2003-2005[53]. The 2008-2010 Employment Guidelines encourage a continuation of action against discrimination and the establishment of an intergenerational approach in order to cope with the ageing population[54].

Furthermore, there was a strong appeal for an active ageing strategy after the Report of the Employment Taskforce in 2003. In its Communication in 2003, the Commission pointed out that [...] *more determined policy action is needed especially with respect to encouraging invest-*

---

49 Employability, entrepreneurship, adaptability and equal opportunities.

50 European Commission, *Towards a society for all ages. Employment, Health, Pensions and Intergenerational Solidarity*, Conference paper, European Symposium, Vienna, 1999.

51 Council Decision of 19 January 2001 on Guidelines for Member States' employment policies for the year 2001, p. 50.

52 "The promotion of quality in work should also be considered as an important factor in maintaining older workers in the labour force". Member States are expected to develop policies on active ageing by: adopting positive measures to maintain working capacity and skills of older workers, in particular through sufficient access to education and training, introducing flexible working arrangements including, for example, part-time work if workers so choose, and raising employers' awareness of the potential of older workers; and reviewing tax and benefit systems to reduce disincentives and make it more attractive for older workers to continue participating in the labour market (European Commission, 2001b).

53 Together with full employment and social cohesion.

54 Council Decision 2008/618/EC, 15 July 2008, on guidelines for the employment policies of the Member States.

ment of firms in training and promoting active ageing through better adapted working conditions and greater financial incentives to remain in work.

Improving job quality is directly related to three objectives of the EES: full employment, quality and productivity at work and social cohesion and inclusion. Regarding these objectives, the European Commission[55] points out the fact that quality in work is crucial to re-attract older people into the labour market[56] and that there is a strong link between low quality in work and social exclusion and poverty[57]. An inclusive labour market implies that it is possible for all citizens of working age who are willing and capable of work to enter and remain in the labour market.

Special attention has to be paid to the concept of flexicurity and its possible consequences for older workers. The 2007 Joint Employment Report stated that flexicurity policies should aim to raise the quality of work. Non-discrimination and the employment rate of older workers are key indicators of these quality dimension within the EES. However, some dimensions which are important in relation to flexicurity, are not part of the EU indicators like for example: job content, autonomy and working conditions[58].

In order to cope with ageing populations, the European Union has set specific objectives for older workers since the launching of the Lisbon Strategy.

– The first objective laid down by the Lisbon Council of March 2000 was to make Europe *the most competitive and most dynamic knowledge-based economy in the world, capable of sustainable economic growth accompanied by quantitative and qualitative improvement of employment and greater social cohesion* within ten years. The EES is a key component of this global strategy. The Lisbon Council decided that there should be an employment rate of 50% for older workers by 2010.

– In March 2002 the Barcelona European Council called for reinforcement of the EES as an instrument of the Lisbon strategy in an

55 Communication from the Commission to the Council, the European Parliament, the European Economic and Social Committee and the Committee of the Regions of 26 November 2003: *Improving quality in work: a review of recent progress*, COM(2003) 728 final – Not published in the Official Journal.

56 The withdrawal from the labour market of older workers in low quality jobs is up to four times higher than that of older workers in jobs of higher quality.

57 E.g. previous inactivity reduces the likelihood of a transition back into the labour market, particularly among older workers.

58 M. Smith *et al.*, "Job quality in Europe", *Industrial Relations Journal*, 2008, pp. 586-603.

enlarged Europe. It also raised the average effective exit age from the labour market by 5 years, for 2010.

The Europe 2020 strategy places emphasis on demographic ageing, stressing that the combination of a smaller working population and a higher number of old people will place strains on European welfare systems. One of the three new targets is to increase the employment rate for the active population (20-64 year olds) up to 75%, by including a greater involvement from older workers (women as well as migrants). A part of the Europe 2020 strategy includes "An Agenda for new skills and jobs". This agenda aims to make labour markets more flexible, give workers the skills they need, improve working conditions and create jobs. However, the improvement of quality in work and on working conditions only tends to review existing laws on working time, health and safety and the integration of non-EU workers, and does not incorporate the working conditions of older workers even though one of the flagship initiatives put forward by the Commission is the promotion of active ageing policies. These objectives are complemented by action on different fronts which are part of the active ageing strategy: reform of pensions, an extension of the active working life, the encouragement of lifelong learning, an improvement in working conditions and the struggle against unlawful age discrimination.

However, although the EU stresses the need to improve the quality of work, the Member States have interpreted this narrowly in terms of labour supply. Most of the measures taken by the EU Member States aim at providing incentives to remain in employment or reducing primes for early retirement, but there are very few initiatives aimed at enhancing the possibility for older workers to remain in employment, and those that exist are of a preventative nature[59]. In fact, there is no clear understanding of the disincentive and/or inability to continue working resulting from poor employment conditions for older workers. Neither is there a global strategy for active ageing within the Member States.

Moreover, it seems that since 2005, the EU has insisted more on intergenerational equality rather than the rate of employment of older workers. One of the tasks set by the Social European Agenda[60] for the period 2005-2010 is an analysis of the consequences of an ageing population, and the future of intergenerational relations.

---

59 A. Walker, *Towards Active Ageing in the European Union*, a paper for the Millennium Project Workshop – *Towards Active Ageing in the 21st century*, The Japan Institute of Labour, 2001.

60 Communication from the Commission on the Social Agenda, 9 February 2005, COM(2005) 33 final.

Promoting quality of work and the principle of non-discrimination with regard to age are important aspects in order to reach employment rate targets within the EES. The quality in work concept and related indicators are essential instruments as a follow up to the EES implementation in EU Member States. Access to good quality jobs for older workers could raise the employment rate, as the decision to stay in the labour market depends mostly on the quality of work[61]; a synergy must be found between quality and quantity of work.

B. What Does Quality of Work Entail for Older Workers?

1. The Importance to Improve Working Conditions and to Struggle Against Age Discrimination

While the quality of work for older workers implies the improvement of both theirs working conditions and action against age discrimination (2.2.1.), the question remains to determine which are the key areas where this quality can be increase for this group of workers (2.2.2.).

The 1995 Resolution on the employment of older workers made by the Council and the representatives of the governments of the Member States underlines two major principles:

1. The demographic trend towards ageing of the working population necessitates increased efforts to adjust the conditions in which workers in the latter part of their working lives work and are vocationally trained, taking account also of the competitiveness of undertakings.

2. Older workers must benefit from adequate resources and from measures to prevent their exclusion from the labour market. In this respect, due account should be taken, in pay systems, of workers' experience and, in general, the best possible use should be made of professional experience.

It thus points out two major strategies aimed at increasing the employment rate of older workers: the improvement in their working conditions and the development of anti-discrimination measures.

These two components are also present in the ILO Director General's report for 1999, in which he identified four objectives, which were also reiterated in the Director-General's 2009 report. Both of these reports put employment and labour market issues, together with social protection and respect for workers' rights, at the heart of national policies. The 2009 report also suggested fourteen converging policy areas to be

61 N. Burnay, *Travailleurs âgés: d'une politique de réduction du chômage à une politique du vieillissement actif*, Brussels, P.I.E. Peter Lang, 2005.

analysed: some of the components in the ILO Global Job Pacts are consistent with an ageing population[62].

– *Improving working conditions*

The quality of employment and working conditions, including efforts to adapt working life to the demands of life outside work, are crucial aspects of the quality of work. The Dublin Foundation reports, issued in 2005 and 2008, show that improving working conditions leads to better job sustainability over a working life, which in turn can prevent an early exit from the labour market and encourage a greater participation from older workers. It is clear that the improvement of working conditions has an effect on the capacity and will of older workers to prolong an active working life, and could be an important tool to help raise the employment rate[63].

– *Action against age discrimination throughout working life*

In order to prolong an active working life, it is important to pay attention to age discrimination in employment. The principle of non-discrimination is a transversal aspect in the improvement of working conditions.

The last part of this chapter examines the key areas were these two policies should play a role in order to achieve "quality of work".

2. *Key Areas Regarding Older Workers' Quality of Work*

Various key areas are significant in any improvement in the quality of work for older workers:

1. In order to raise the quality of employment, employers who demand the freedom to adapt their workforce and employment conditions to prevailing market conditions and especially the flexibility of labour markets, must also respect broad universal principles, such as non-discrimination.

2. Some groups of workers are particularly vulnerable to labour market inequality, in particular that group of older workers who are moved from regular, protected jobs and are often excluded prematurely from work, or end up in insecure jobs. In order to obtain quality in access to employment, it is particularly important to develop the skills, expertise, training and employability of older workers (as well as those of younger workers). The importance of education and training for both economic and social reasons, especially to overcome some forms of discrimina-

---

62 Report of the Director-General, *Tackling the global jobs crisis. Recovery through decent work policies*, International Labour Conference, 98th Session 2009, Report I(A), pp. 13, 15-17 and 20-22.

63 V. Michaud, *Welfare and the Labour Market in the EU*, ENEPRI paper, No 7, 2004.

tion, has to be recognised[64]. Employment policies are required which favour universal access to jobs and incomes, both to reduce poverty and exclusion and to take full advantage of human capabilities in the creation of income and wealth.

3. Another aspect which is important in order to improve the quality of work is to maintain the health, well-being and working capacity of older workers[65].

4. The fourth area is related to suitable working conditions and employment opportunities for ageing workers in order to keep them in the labour market. This area implies, for example, flexible working, reconciliation between the work-life balance, recruitment conditions, a decent wage, etc. The Foundation has analysed cases of good practice in age management[66] that have improved working conditions for older workers. Each case study describes how enterprises approached the issue and presents its findings in the medium to long term. Additionally, the Foundation has published a database of good practice, examples of which may be useful for employers.

5. The last aspect is the reintegration of older workers using social and financial incentives in order to reach employment rate targets. However, as A. Supiot has stated, social policies alone are not sufficient if they only serve as financial means to reinsert older workers[67].

Most of these areas are related to working conditions and, on the basis of the new article 153 in the Treaty on the Functioning of the European Union, the EU can adopt directives – to support and complement the activities of the Member States – regarding workers' health and safety, working conditions and the protection of workers when their employment contract is terminated.

64 Fourth European Working Conditions Survey (2005). This survey demonstrates that older workers receive less training and have more limited access to 'new' technologies than younger workers.

65 There is a trend towards a reduction in exposure to physical risks with increasing age. However, workers aged 45-55 report higher exposure to risks associated with physical position, repetitive movements and heavy workloads Workers over 55 years of age have a high level of job autonomy and comparatively low levels of work intensity: Fourth European Working Conditions Survey (2005).

66 Eurofound, *A guide to good practice in age management*, Luxembourg, 2006.

67 A. Supiot, *Le droit du travail, que sais-je?*, Presses universitaires de France, 2004, p. 123.

Conclusion – Improving Quality of Work is Necessary in Order to Achieve the Active Ageing Strategy

In the EU, the active ageing strategy is based on both non-discrimination and the quality of work. However, it seems that less attention has been given to active ageing within the EES since 2005 and the same trend can be observed at the international level, where the ageing population was regarded as a programme priority in the 1999 report, but this was no longer the case in the 2009 report issued just after the financial crisis. The aim of the Lisbon strategy was to increase the participation of older workers in employment. The target has been redefined since the Europe 2020 growth and jobs strategy; the main goal is now to achieve an employment rate of 75% for all persons between 20 and 64.

In this paper, two major goals have been identified in order to achieve quality of work for older workers. These are the improvement of working conditions and applying the principle of non-discrimination (which is a side issue of the first goal).

Age discrimination is clearly an important barrier to an active ageing strategy and it is difficult to achieve active ageing goals in an ageist labour market and society[68]. Member State intervention is required to combat age discrimination for both social[69] and economic[70] reasons. This article has demonstrated that an awareness of the need to combat age discrimination is present in all of the key areas which tend to improve working conditions. There should be policies establishing conditions and practices for hiring, assignment of tasks, working conditions, promotions and termination of employment with regard to older workers. These policies can aim at managing diversity, and improving working conditions for all workers – in particular, access to good quality employment – by promoting non-discrimination. The achievement of a high level of employment depending on non-discrimination has become an objective with a high priority at political level. The legal framework to fight against discrimination is stronger than ever. However, legal norms are not sufficient; non-discrimination legislation mainly imposed negative obligations on employers and there should be a comprehensive approach to combat discrimination.

---

68 A. Walker and P. Taylor, "The Ageing Workforce: Employers' Attitudes Towards Older Workers", *Work, Employment and Society*, Vol. 8, No. 4, 1994.

69 Because it creates stigma, social exclusion and the denial of full citizenship.

70 If older people are discriminated against on grounds of age, they are denied the chance of making an economic contribution. The ageing of the workforce reinforces the moral and economic imperatives for action against age discrimination. A. Walker, *Towards Active Ageing in the European Union*, *op. cit.*

With regards to the question of quality of work, if at the beginning of the last decade the EU and ILO devoted a lot of attention to quality of work, this dimension has disappeared from the Europe 2020 strategy, although there is a need for a social agenda to focus on this issue[71]. Basically, older workers with poor work capacity tend more often to be unemployed or to leave the labour market. Therefore, quality of work provides an integrated framework for different dimensions of work and could help bolster employment rates. Moreover, we have seen that the key areas identified above as part of the quality of work for older workers converge with the indicators of quality taken into account by the EU[72], the ILO and in the legal norms.

EU policies and practices to improve opportunities for older workers and to extend working life have recently advanced significantly. The improvement in working conditions is essential to ensure better job and social security sustainability over the working life cycle and prevent an early exit from the labour market.

In order to improve the rate employment of older workers, there has to be involvement by all parties concerned. Governments, companies and social partners have to take proactive measures to improve working conditions and to tackle discrimination, while older workers have to accept the idea of working longer and to acquire – or to keep – their skills. Furthermore, in order to achieve quality of work for older workers, the age specificity has to be taken in account in order to determine the working conditions for workers throughout their working lives and proactive strategies have to be considered over the entire working life (for example, for health and education).

The year 2012 has been designated as the "European Year for Active Ageing". Lots of work has been done in the struggle against age discrimination but little regarding the improvement in working conditions for older workers. There is still a need to concentrate on the quality of work – and in particular the working conditions for older workers – both by the Member States with their national tools and by the EU through for example the use of article 153 of the Treaty on the Functioning of the European Union.

---

71 P. Pochet, 'What's wrong with EU2020?', *ETUI Policy Brief*, Issue 2/2010.

72 Indicators refer to the characteristics of job and also context – such as indicators on employment and unemployment gender gaps, employment rate of older workers, youth employment ratio, labour market gaps for disadvantaged groups and growth in GDP per person employed and per hour worked.

Equality Employment Opportunity Legislation in Europe

Organisational Barriers and the Organisational Justice Framework for the Promotion of Women at Work

Antonio L. García-Izquierdo
Senior Lecturer, University of Oviedo

Pedro J. Ramos-Villagrasa
Researcher, University of Oviedo

I. Introduction: the Quality in Work Perspective

Nowadays, Europe is facing dramatic changes concerning several work issues related to the globalisation process since the ending of the second century. In consequence, the European Union (EU) has developed some proposals. One is the European Employment Strategy (EES) to coordinate employment policies of the Member States and the associated and candidate countries. In March 2000, the EES was extended by the Lisbon Strategy, where the European Council proposed to achieve more and better jobs. One year later the Stockholm European Council established quality in work as a general horizontal objective of the EES. This means that all the guidelines of the EES must take into account quality in work.

On March 2010 the European Strategy 2020 was launched as a replacement for the Lisbon Strategy, and put the stress on quantity over quality of jobs. However, we can see in the introduction of the present book[1], the debate about quality in work is still ongoing and present in the institutional and legal framework of the EU (e.g. Treaty of Lisbon art. 3, par. 3 and Treaty on the Functioning of the European Union, art. 9).

[1] See P. Vielle and S. Borelli, Introduction to this book.

But, why quality in job is so important? According to the Commission of the European Communities[2], quality in work contributes to full employment, higher productivity growth and better social cohesion. The link between quality in work and full employment is strengthened with improved access to employment and an upward occupational mobility for workers in low quality jobs. Moreover, it is necessary to improve working conditions to increase productivity, taking advantage of lower absenteeism and unhealthy rates as a consequence of better working conditions. So it is important to remark job quality is a mean to reach sound job outcomes, a well-established principle in quality of working life literature (García-Izquierdo & Ramos-Villagrasa, 2009). Lastly, quality in work is recognised as essential for preventing social exclusion, unemployment and poverty and thus maintaining regional cohesion in Europe. Moreover, the Communication from the Commission on employment and social policies tackling with quality in work links the dual goals of competitiveness and cohesion in a sustainable way, with clear economic benefits flowing from investing in people and strong, supportive social systems[3]. This Communication clarifies quality in work construct, as well. Quality in work means better jobs not only fair pay and minimum standards but includes the desired objectives related to employment (the environment and the specific features of the job), the workers' individual characteristics, the reconciliation between these characteristics and job requirements, and person's individual job satisfaction. The proposed definition of quality in work is measured in two dimensions covering different but related facets: the characteristics of the job itself (intrinsic quality, skills, life-long learning and career development), and the work and labour market contexts (gender equality, health and safety at work, flexibility and security, inclusion and access to the labour market, work organisation and work-life balance, social dialogue and worker involvement, diversity and non-discrimination, overall economic performance, and productivity).

The quality in work concept (EU) is quite similar to the concept of decent work[4] (ILO), but there are some remarkable differences[5]. Those differences tackle with their aims and significance attached to legal

---

2 Communication from the Commission to the Council, the European Parliament, the European Economic and Social Committee and the Committee of the Regions "Improving quality in work: a review of recent progress" [COM(2003) 728 final].

3 Communication from the Commission to the Council, the European Parliament, the European Economic and Social Committee and the Committee of the Regions "Employment and social policies: a framework for investing in quality" [COM(2001) 313 final].

4 See Caillaud, Ghailani and Peña-Casas chapter for a complete comparison.

5 See Vielle and Borelli, for going deep in this issue.

rights at work[6] and their focus in the tension between stability *vs.* flexibility[7]. The Decent Work Agenda has as the main objective the promotion of rights at work, employment, social protection and social dialogue (Ghaï, 2003), so it is centered on intrinsic values; whilst, quality in work put first achieving economic objectives.

This chapter is centred on the second dimension of quality in work following the Communication's definition. Concretely in how legal dispositions could be improved taking in account some initiatives from Equal Employment Opportunities (EEO) at work. EEO relates to several aspects of quality in work, such as gender equality, inclusion and access to the labour market, diversity, and non-discrimination at job. In the decent work model, EEO is directly related with employment dimensions of fair treatment.

Policies that are beneficial to EEO are still scarce throughout Europe. Nevertheless, the general movement in favour of these measures renders a revision of this issue crucial. Moreover, access to the labour market and to qualified jobs by means of personnel selection and promotion policies are core procedures implemented by human resources departments, but which are too often discriminatory. In the present chapter we wish to contribute to the scarce literature regarding gender discrimination and job access procedures, enhancing good practices for improving organisational conditions and opportunities.

EEO mainly concerns equality. Equality is a fundamental right[8], a common principle in some EU[9] fundamental dispositions, and a central aspect of quality in work[10]. Moreover, it is a necessary condition for the achievement of the EU objectives on productivity growth, full employment, and social cohesion.

As inequalities do still exist, however, this situation will be analysed by examining the EEO principles and relating them to the legal provisions under which personnel selection and promotion is carried out in employment access procedures. We have reviewed at length some of the difficulties in job access for women, and finally propose the organisational justice framework as a promising approach towards inclusion in

6 See Vielle and Borelli chapter in this book.

7 See Deumer chapter in this book.

8 Chapter III of the Charter of Fundamental Rights of the European Union [2000/C 364/01].

9 See as example the Constitution of the Member States, *e.g.*: Basic Law for the Federal Republic of Germany art. 3; Constitution of the Italian Republic, art. 3; Constitution of France, art. 1; and Constitution of Spain art. 14.

10 Communication from the Commision to the Council, the European Parliament, the European Economic and Social Committee and the Committee of the Regions "Improving quality in work: a review of recent progress" [COM(2003) 728 final].

European legislation and recommendations, to combat these problems and, therefore, improving the quality in work.

II. Equal Employment Opportunities and Legislation in Europe

A. The EEO Perspective

The EEO frames measures directed towards *giving a voice* to all people involved in organisations (Folger, 1977), the possibility to give one's own opinion and arguments on organisational processes. The EEO ensures impartiality and equality, and when applied to personnel selection and promotion, facilitates access to the labour market for all collectives and social groups. In addition, adopting EEO measures conveys certain advantages, such as conflict prevention and a better organisational image (Cropanzano & Greenberg, 1997). Studies on this topic show that these measures help both supervisors and applicants, and that procedures considered as fair are related to individual satisfaction and attachment to the company; furthermore, they contribute to job offers being accepted (Anderson, 2003; Gilliland & Chan, 2001), may convey a better organisational image of a potential employer (Bauer *et al.*, 2001; Schmitt & Gilliland, 1992), and may even have a possible impact upon the attitudes, motivation, and job performance of candidates accepted into an organisation (Ryan & Ployhart, 2000).

The current trend towards EEO, according to Schmidt, Ones and Hunter (1992), can imply a conflict when decisions have to be taken, since EEO should be combined with a hierarchy of merit, competitiveness and efficiency; all elements possible, legal, and valid should be examined – which is no easy task. In effect, how these three conditions can be met at the same time remains to be resolved. The question of whether to give priority to individual or group interests becomes really complex when a decision has to be reached affecting people in focus in an individual group. This also affects academics and practitioners, as managers in organisations demand from both groups that workers' rights are respected and, simultaneously, that company objectives be met.

B. European EEO Legislation

Organisations such as the EU and ILO require equality based on several grounds, such as sex, age, nationality, etc. Some of these aspects have been reviewed previously in this book. However, sex is the main issue in discrimination legislation in the EU. The Treaty of establishing a Constitution for Europe, the Treaty on the Functioning of the European Union (TFEU) and the Charter of Fundamental Rights of the European

Union, all of them state the non-discrimination principle, including sex and the equality of men and women[11]. Moreover, the TFEU encourage correcting inequities in every country (art. 157). Insofar, the largest body of European legislation related to EEO is dedicated to equality between women and men. Consequently, we are going to focus on gender here in after.

The policy objectives of the EES in 2001 were encompassing a mainstream perspective on gender and non-discrimination. These are intertwined concepts. Gender mainstreaming could be seen, as a principle that mobilises all general policies and measures for achieving equality between men and women, even the development of policies that may have significant differential impact on each gender (Commission of the European Communities, 1996). But we will back to this later.

Tackling with equality, as previously[12] stated, gender equality it is considered a cross-cutting dimension that we put closely related to other quality of work and employment dimensions: inclusion and access to labour market, work organisation and work-life balance, and diversity and non discrimination.

Equality between women and men is governed by some treaty provisions and directives on various issues as access to employment, equal pay, maternity protection, parental leave, social security, occupational social security, the burden of proof in discrimination cases, and self-employment. The case law of the European Court of Justice might be added as another key element.

The more relevant Directives summarising the legislation in force we want to outline are the following: the Discrimination Directive 2006/54/EC[13] on equal opportunities and equal treatment of men and women in matters of employment and occupation (replacing European Directives 76/207/EEC[14] and 2002/73/EC[15] on equal treatment for men

---

11 Treaty establishing a Constitution for Europe, arts II-80, II-81, II-83; Treaty on the Functioning of the European Union, art. 8; and Charter of Fundamental Rights of the European Union, arts. 21 and 23 [2000/C 364/01].

12 See the chapters of Caillud, Ghailani and Peña-Casas, that of Carlson, and that of Canazza for a complete view.

13 European Parliament and Council Directive 2006/54/EC on the implementation of the principle of equal opportunities and equal treatment of men and women in matters of employment and occupation, OJ 2006, L 204/23.

14 Council Directive 76/207/EEC of 9 February 1976 on the implementation of the principle of equal treatment for men and women as regards access to employment, vocational training and promotion and working conditions, OJ 1976, L39/40.

15 Directive 2002/73/EC of the European Parliament and of the Council of 23 September 2002 amending Council Directive 76/207/EEC on the implementation of the principle of equal treatment for men and women as regards access to employment, vocational training and promotion, and working conditions, OJ 2002, L 269/15.

and women as regards access to employment, vocational training and promotion, and working conditions, 75/117 EEC[16] on Equal Pay, and 97/80/EC[17] on the burden of proof in cases of discrimination based on sex), Directive 2004/113/EC[18] implementing the principle of equal treatment between men and women in the access to and supply of goods and services, and Council Directive 2000/78/EC[19] establishing a general framework for equal treatment in employment and occupation.

European legislation defines discrimination as an unlawful different treatment based on prohibited criteria. EU law distinguishes between direct and indirect discrimination. Following Directive 2000/78/EC, direct discrimination, consists of treating someone differently, solely on the basis of age, sex, skin colour, national origin or disability, among other factors. Concentrating on sex discrimination, Directive 2006/54/EC states direct discrimination takes place where one person is treated less favourably on grounds of sex than another is, has been or would be treated in a comparable situation. The same Directive states indirect discrimination takes place where an apparently neutral provision, criterion or practice would put persons of one sex at a particular disadvantage compared with persons of other sex, unless that provision, criterion or practice is objectively justified. This is of the utmost importance to clarify the type of justifications that may be legally alleged by employers. As Directives 2000/43/EC[20] (art. 14) and 2000/78/EC (art. 5) stated, it is possible to justify indirect discrimination if that provision, criterion or practice is objectively justified by a legitimate aim and the means of achieving that aim are appropriate and necessary by reason of the nature of the particular occupational activities concerned or of the context in which they are carried out, such a characteristic constitutes a genuine and determining occupational requirement, provided that the objective is legitimate and the requirement is proportionate. "Assumptions are those of: a) professional activities for which sex is a factor because of its nature or conditions of its exercise, b) the protection of women, particularly in pregnancy and childbirth, and c) to promote equal opportunities

---

16 Council Directive 75/117/EEC of 10 February 1975 on the approximation of the laws of the Member States relating to the application of the principle of equal pay for men and women, O J 1975, L 45/19.

17 Council Directive 97/80/EC of 15 December 1997 on the burden of proof in cases of discrimination based on sex OJ 1998, L 14/6.

18 Council Directive 2004/113/EC of 13 December 2004 implementing the principle of equal treatment between men and women in the access to and supply of goods and services, OJ 2004, L 373/37.

19 Council Directive 2000/78/EC of 27 November 2000 established a general framework for equal treatment in employment and occupation, OJ 2000, L 303.

20 Council Directive 2000/43/EC implemented the principle of equal treatment between persons irrespective of racial or ethnic origin OJ 2000, L 180.

between men and women" (art. 2.6 EU Directive 76/207 on Equal Treatment).

The two Directives summarising the legislation in force relevant to these issues are the following: the Discrimination Directive 2006/54/EC on equal opportunities and equal treatment of men and women in matters of employment and occupation (replacing European Directives 76/207/EEC and 2002/73/EC on equal treatment for men and women as regards access to employment, vocational training and promotion, and working conditions, and 75/117 EEC on Equal Pay, 97/80/EC on the burden of proof in cases of discrimination based on sex) and Directive 2004/113/EC implementing the principle of equal treatment between men and women in the access to and supply of goods and services.

Respect to EEO, the purposes of the Discrimination Directive 2006/54/EC (recast) is the implementation of EEO and the equal treatment in the access to employment, including promotion and vocational training. In the art. 14 this Directive forbids discrimination both in public and private sector in some cases: access to employment and promotion (including selection criteria and recruitment conditions), access to vocational guidance and vocational training; employment and working conditions, including dismissals; and membership an organisation of workers or employers[21]. We could outline art. 27 where Member States may introduce or maintain provisions which are more favourable to the protection of the principle of equal treatment than those laid down in the Directive art. 29, on gender mainstreaming.

Gender mainstreaming was defined in the Treaty of Amsterdam as a principle that mobilises all general policies and measures for achieving equality between men and women, even the development of policies that may have significant differential impact on each gender. Gender mainstreaming was developed through some Communications[22], as the relevant 2000/C 150 E/05 Proposal for a Council Decision on guidelines

---

21 For further details regarding the freedom of association in EU see the Dorssemont's chapter.

22 Communication from the Commission of 21 February 1996 "Incorporating equal opportunities for women and men into all Community policies and activities" [COM(96) 67 final]; Communication from the Commission to the Council, the European Parliament, the Economic and Social Committee and the Committee of the Regions towards a community framework strategy on gender equality (2001-2005) [COM(2000) 335-1]; Decision No. 1554/2005/EC of the European Parliament and of the Council of 7 September 2005 mending Council Decision 2001/51/EC establishing a programme relating to the Community framework strategy on gender equality and Decision No. 848/2004/EC establishing a Community action programme to promote organisations active at European level in the field of equality between men and women.

for Member States' employment policies for the year 2000, where we can see in the appendix (pp. 57-58):

"Women still have particular problems in gaining access to the employment market, in career advancement, in earnings and in reconciling professional and family life. It is therefore important, *inter alia*:

- to ensure that active labour market policies are made available for women in proportion to their share of unemployment;
- to reduce tax-benefit disincentives, wherever identified, because of their negative effects on the female labour supply;
- to give particular attention to obstacles which hinder women who wish to set up new businesses or become self-employed;
- to ensure that women are able to benefit positively from flexible forms of work organisation on a voluntary basis. Therefore, the Member States will adopt a gender-mainstreaming approach in implementing the Guidelines of all four pillars. In order meaningfully to evaluate progress on this approach, Member States will need to provide for adequate data collection systems and procedures."

These proposals have been influencing in the National Action Plans (Pollack and Hafner-Burton, 2011). However, gender mainstreaming may be considered as a fuzzy concept (Booth & Bennet, 2002; Debusscher, 2011), so it needs to be clarified. Even, the relationship between gender mainstreaming and positive action measure could be negative, even a counterproductive role in the development of legally enforceable rights (Pollack & Hafner-Burton, 2011).

Otherwise, Directive 2004/113/CE state the principle of equal treatment (art. 4), but no the differences in treatment if the provision of the goods and services exclusively or primarily to members of one sex is justified by a legitimate aim and the means of achieving that aim are appropriate and necessary.

Besides this, recognise the possibility of implementing affirmative actions (art. 6): "With a view to ensuring full equality in practice between men and women, the principle of equal treatment shall not prevent any Member State from maintaining or adopting specific measures to prevent or compensate for disadvantages linked to sex".

Respect to affirmative actions, Directives 76/207/CEE and 2002/73 EC, now replaced by Directive 2006/54/EC, providing the basis for legal considerations of actions such as Affirmative Action Measures (AAMs). The AAMs are particular measures for women to correct those situations of inequality in comparison to men, like quotas and merit exemption. According to Kravitz (1995) we can distinguish four different kinds of AAMs:

a) opportunity enhancements AAMs, helping the target groups in the processes previous the selection decisions (e.g. in recruitment or training);
b) equal opportunities AAMs (elimination of discrimination by banning the undervaluation of target groups);
c) tiebreak AAMs (the target group receive preferential treatment when their qualifications are equal to those of non-target group members); and
d) strong preferential treatment AAMs (target group members are given preference even if their qualifications are inferior to non-target group members).

These measures have been the subject of a passionate debate in many countries and different reactions were apparent, depending on the kind of measure (Moscoso, García-Izquierdo, & Bastida, 2010). For example, strong preferential treatment AAMs are more negatively assessed by both men and women, and are even illegal in many countries. For these reasons, taking care about the way in which AAMs are implemented is needed. In this sense, it is necessary to recall now some Case Law from the European Community Justice Court cases, as the Kalanke, Marshall, Abrahamsson and Anderson, and Briheche (García-Izquierdo & García-Izquierdo, 2007).

Backing to Directive 2004/113/CE (art. 7) we can see, as in the Discrimination Directive 2006/54/EC (art. 27), the following *minimum* requirements: art. 9, regarding burden of proof; art. 12, regarding bodies of promotion of equal treatment; and the art. 16, regarding reports. The art. 9 states Member States shall ensure that, when persons who consider themselves wronged because the principle of equal treatment has not been applied to them, the respondent must prove that there has been no breach of the principle. The art. 12 of the Directive compels Member States to create a body for the promotion, analysis, monitoring and support equal treatment regarding sex, including providing independent assistance to victims of discrimination in pursuing their complaints about discrimination; conducting independent surveys concerning discrimination; and publishing independent reports and making recommendations on any issue relating to such discrimination. Finally, (art. 16) establish Member States shall communicate all available information concerning the application of the Directive to the Commission every five years since the end of 2009.

All the above refers to the employer's professional evaluation of the employee, since it is a core duty under his/her responsibility. Therefore he or she must prove that discrimination has not been committed and that his/her decision relied on objective and relevant instruments to explain the choice when hiring a person. To ensure a better legal protection against discrimination, Member States shall take the measures necessary to ensure that any laws, regulations, and administrative provisions contrary to the principle of equal treatment shall be abolished.

C. The Gap Between Legislation and Reality

As stated above, the EU is trying to achieve quality in work. The EES and the Lisbon Strategy aimed at raising equality, and EEO legislation helps this aim. In this sense, European Pact for Gender Equality, pretend closing gender gaps and combating gender stereotypes in the labour market promoting a better work-life balance and reinforcing governance through gender mainstreaming and better monitoring. These fields are closely linked to equal opportunities in the labour market (Council of the European Union, 2006).

As a consequence, EEO is a more than adequate HR policy. Given its advantages, EEO could be a strategic policy besides a legal constraint. But, surprisingly, some top organisations, i.e. quoted companies, include potentially discriminatory questions in their selection procedures (García-Izquierdo, Aguinis, & Ramos-Villagrasa, 2010). Additionally, Fagan & Burchell (2002) have reported several gender differences over time in working conditions.

What are the causes of the gap between legislation and reality? Gender-policies in Europe must cope with two "needles eyes". The first one consists in its adoption by the EU, and the second one is the implementation in Member States (Ostner & Lewis, 1995). Moreover, we mustn't forget the psychosocial nature of organisations. In that sense, Campa, Casarico & Profeta (2011) shows that the view of gender roles in society explains significantly the gender gap in employment. The way in which workers perform their tasks is affected by the socially-constructed reality of organisations (Wilpert, 1995), a network of shared meanings sustained by the workers' social interaction. This interaction facilitates how workers share values and ideas about their organisation, for example, the way in which tasks must be realised and many other procedures, including how to implement and perform personnel selection and promotion procedures. In the following section we present a review of these kinds of organisational barriers to the promotion of women at work.

III. Organisational Barriers to the Promotion of Women at Work

Despite legal provisions concerning EEO, women continue to endure difficulties in job access and companies continue to use potentially discriminatory selection procedures. The causes for this are related to bias, values and shared constructive nature of organisations. Here the primary ones are described: the glass ceiling phenomenon, discrimination and stereotyping against women, and gender bias.

A. The Glass Ceiling Phenomenon

The term *glass ceiling* was coined to describe the structural barriers that prevented women from reaching the top of corporate hierarchy. The US Department of Labour stated in 1991 that the glass ceiling is made up of barriers based on bias in attitude or in the organisation that prevent qualified individuals from being promoted to management level positions. All of which highlights the issue that the higher the organisation level, the lower the percentage of women in governance (Claringbould & Knoppers, 2007). These authors demonstrate that men control boards by affirming and negating affirmative action policies and by framing the process of recruitment and selection in such a way as to reproduce a male-dominated culture on the board of directors. On the other hand, women, tend to negotiate their entry by distancing themselves from their gender and proving their fitness. Sheridan and Milgate (2003) contend that, as most directors previously had been senior managers, the lack of women in boards can be attributed directly to the relatively low number of women senior managers. The case of management is particularly interesting since it has traditionally been seen as a male domain requiring specific sets of skills. Management sets (Wilson, 2004) a punishing pace with 60-hour working weeks being the norm; long days followed by heavy drinking sessions as a means of letting off steam. As Schein (2007, p. 10) points out, apart from the necessity of such long hours, "last minute meetings, urgent requests, and unscheduled high priority business trips appear to be a fact of corporate life" and have serious consequences for women. On the other hand, women need to comply with masculine norms of behaviour if they are to break through the glass ceiling, acting as masculine manager stereotypes, and exceeding male cultural norms. Furthermore, Liff and Ward (2001, p. 20) point out that "organisations are also the site within which women come to understand the requirements of senior jobs and their own career options. Organisational cultures, structures, and practices provide the context within which this occurs and can lead women to decide that such jobs, or the process they would have to go through to get them, are not for them." This can lead to a generalised managerial assumption that women are satisfied to continue in their present position, whilst male peers indicate much more strongly to the head in charge of promotion their readiness for the next step up. The traditional women's family responsibilities could hinder their commitment to the organisation and their lack of involvement in corporate networks that provide access to senior jobs. Other barriers are based in gender social systems, where work has considered in terms of male working roles, leading to direct discrimination and stereotyping. Recruitment and promotion could also operate in a gender-biased way. Other explanations place those barriers at individual level.

We can conclude that women are by-passed for promotion and are therefore under-represented at senior levels. The reasons why women are by-passed have been identified as follows (Gust, 2006). During their formative years, women receive less investment that would qualify them for promotion; because of occupational segregation, women largely compete among themselves for relatively few jobs with lower pay, have less job security and limited opportunities for advancement; women are concentrated in occupations with limited career prospects (gender stereotyping); in their 30s and 40s, when major strides are being made in individual careers, women have to endure the multiple burden of work and domestic demands; and finally, men receive preferential treatment based on their being perceived as leaders or decision makers.

B. Gender Bias

The gender bias seems to rest on employers' notions of women, as (more) trustworthy, honest, meticulous and patient (Aganon, 1999). Other explanations present women as better than men at team-building and communication and bringing underrated skills to the business process. Based on these attitudes, women and men are therefore matched to different jobs, jobs that are themselves stereotyped as requiring different kinds of traits, consistent with the views of the dominant group holding that job. Thus, the job of senior manager as held predominantly by men is viewed as requiring characteristics associated with men. Outstanding research by V. Schein and colleagues over a period of more than 20 years showed that the role of a manager has been associated with male traits, not only in the United States but in several other countries as well (Schein, 1973; 1975).

Yet the fact remains that white men hold a disproportionate number of the highest paying jobs and account for the best opportunities for advancement. Therefore, white men will be less disadvantaged at this stage than white women. This situation sustains the social perceptions accorded to masculine and feminine characteristics, creating an enduring male/female dichotomy: the association of women with *soft* or personnel skills and men with *hard* or technical competences. Recent research demonstrates that women are more likely to be appointed to leadership positions to take over companies that have a consistent record of poor performance (Ryan & Haslam, 2005; 2007). In consequence, gender bias is related with the glass-cliff phenomenon. This leads us back to the glass-cliff phenomenon: women in such positions are likely to be exposed to unfair criticism and are in danger of being held responsible for negative events that were set in motion before their appointment. On the other hand, we should also bear in mind that while glass-cliff positions hold an element of risk, they can, indeed, be seen as an opportunity for advancement. Moreover, it seems that the glass-cliff is a relatively robust and widespread phenomenon. Initial research into the glass-cliff looked specifically at poorly performing companies but more recent research places the focus on other factors constraining their performance after a precarious appointment; constraints such as: lack of information and support, lack of appropriate resources in dealing with everyday tasks, and ineffective networks of support in the organisations in which women operate (Ryan & Haslam, 2005; 2007).

C. Discrimination and Stereotyping

The reasons for the scarce presence of women in managerial positions are manifold: stereotypes, social group norms in incumbent managers, the perceived lack of suitability, and personal barriers (family work conflicts, lower earnings that yield to lower self-esteem, and identity work). All of the above facts stem from discrimination against women from the bottom to the top of the organisation. There is a growing interest in theories that account for wide variability in perceptions of events and people, such as discrimination and stereotyping.

Following Fiske (1998), some related concepts such as discrimination and stereotyping can be differentiated. Discrimination could be defined as differential treatment based on membership of a social grouping. Discrimination in employment takes place because of individual decisions by employers due to their attitude and on evaluating employees rather, than a purposive company policy. Stereotypes are beliefs about particular social groups. We have the possibility of differentiating prescriptive from descriptive stereotypes (Burgess & Borgida, 1999). Prescriptive stereotypes specify how somebody should behave, whereas descriptive stereotypes specify how somebody does behave. Consequently, people may be punished if they do not behave as expected.

Stone-Romero and Stone (2005) present a model that examines discrimination from the decision-maker's point of view. It underlines discrimination as a result of categorising individuals according to group membership, so decision-making is influenced by stereotypes. In general, the stereotypes of minorities are less likely to be consistent with the perceived requirements for high status professional and managerial jobs than are the stereotypes of whites, men and middle-aged workers. The fact that these demands are key to access high-status managerial and professional jobs contributes to the problem; even more so, since women are associated with allegedly female skills such as communication, organisation, and emotional support instead. Therefore, criteria for job access are presumably fostered and biased because of such a stereotyping (Schein, 2007).

In summary, the discrepancy between legislation and reality exists in the context of equality between women and men. The glass-cliff phenomenon, gender bias, discrimination and stereotyping, are at the basis of these phenomena. In consequence, legal provisions should take advantage of all of the social investigations into equality, to try to prevent such bad practices and illegal decisions. In this direction, we suggest the organisational justice framework as a promising approach to overcoming organisational barriers for the promotion of women at work.

IV. A Promising Approach: An Organisational Justice Framework

The prevention of discrimination can lead to a better understanding between organisations and applicants, and personnel selection could be viewed as a process beneficial to all parts involved. Organisational justice has been argued to be an important determinant of attitudes, decisions and behaviour, thus improving job performance, fostering behaviour that promotes the effective functioning of organisations, and as a consequence builds customer satisfaction and loyalty (Cropanzano, Bowen & Gilliland, 2007). We must stress that the meaning of justice in the organisational justice framework is different from the legal meaning, as is related to perceptions of fairness in the workplace.

The organisational justice concept arises from Adam's equity theory (Adams, 1965) and fairness theory (Folger & Cropanzano, 2001). According to Adams (1965), a perceived inequity creates a psychological tension that motivates individuals to restore justice: the greater the perceived inequity, the greater the psychological tension that motivates action. Equity deals with resource allocation as merit criteria are fulfilled. Moreover, the fairness theory suggests that negative situations prompt people to search for explanations and create what if scenarios, called counterfactuals (Folger & Cropanzano, 2001). According to these, we can only attempt fairness through decision-making processes based on objective criteria.

Organisational justice has three dimensions (Cohen-Charash and Spector, 2001): the distributive justice and procedural justice proposed by Gilliland (1993) and the interactional justice developed by Bies and Moag (1986). Distributive justice refers to the perceived fairness in decisions on resource assignment (perceived fairness in the outcome). Procedural justice refers to the perceived fairness in the ways to determine outcome within the process of decision-making (perceived fairness in the way to determine outcome). Finally, Bies and Moag (1986) introduced the concept of interactional justice (interpersonal treatment during the enactment of a procedure), which includes truthfulness and sensitivity in interpersonal treatment.

We are going to concentrate on procedural justice. Gilliland (1994) found that procedural justice could mitigate the negative effect of a non-distributive decision, like selection and promotion procedures. Procedural justice is the ability to control a process and the ability to make a standpoint in front of others. Leventhal (1980) checks whether procedural justice is fairly administered from the satisfaction or violation of the following procedures: avoiding bias, consistency in administration/implementation, accounting for management decisions on grounds of accurate information, capability to correct unfair decisions, representativity and ethics. When procedural justice is absent, this may cause employees to engage in actions against the organisation, but for more distinct reasons than from distributive injustice. Among the most compelling arguments are:

(a) that employees value procedural justice as a social norm, whose violation threatens important normative standards (Cropanzano, Goldman, & Folger, 2003);

(b) the voice effect, which argues that employees value the opportunity to have their opinions heard in the organisation and

(c) that it provides evidence of social standing, therefore, if the outcome is perceived to be unfair it may lead to fears of social ostracism (Cropanzano, Rupp, Mohler, & Schminke, 2001).

Substantial research reports that organisational justice is related to both perceptions of employment discrimination and reactions to it (Goldman, Gutek, Stein & Lewis, 2006).

Regarding the workplace, certain recommendations for personnel selection and promotion may be feasible. Gilliland (1993) distinguished ten procedural justice rules in personnel selection issues that he classified in three categories. The first category is formal characteristics. It includes job relatedness of measurement instruments, the opportunity to give a display of knowledge, skills and abilities, opportunity to check tests scores, and the consistency of test administration that relates to the standardisation of administrative procedures for people and techniques. The second category is information provided, including the supply of timely and informative feedback regarding selection performance and its outcome, the adequacy of information provided to applicants regarding the selection process and the organisation's integrity during the selection process. Finally the last category is interpersonal treatment, regarding the interpersonal effectiveness and interest of the recruiter, the extent to which conversation flows in a normal pattern and applicants are given the opportunity to ask questions and the appropriateness of the questions asked.

Procedural justice rules (Gilliland, 1993)

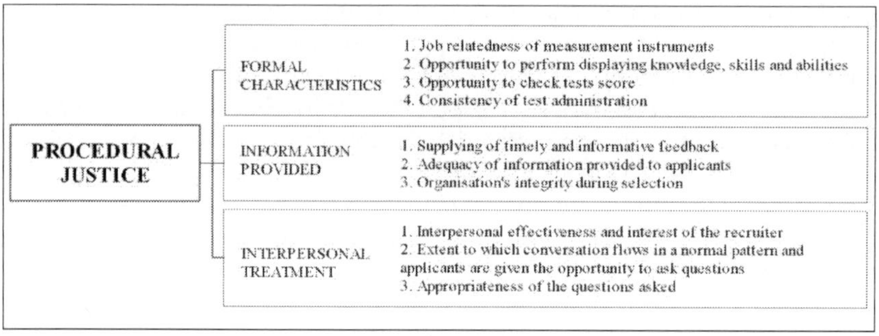

Moreover, Anderson, Born, and Cunningham-Snell (2001) state that an applicant's reaction to test-taking is more favourable when the following needs are met: "(i) more job-relevant, (ii) less personally intrusive, (iii) not contravening the candidates procedural or distributive justice expectations, and (iv) allowing the candidate an opportunity to meet in person with selectors" (Anderson *et al.*, 2001, p. 205).

Besides the recommendations derived from psychosocial research, we also want to stress the work of the *ISO PC230* Committee founded to develop an ISO standard related to procedures and methods used to assess people in work and organisational settings, including the maintenance of fairness and ethical principles. The standard is called *ISO 10667* and covers assessment service delivery: procedures and methods to assess people in work and organisational settings. There are two parts: one for service providers and one for client organisations that use assessments. There are two closely related parts in the standard and it sets out good practice and guidelines in areas such as: agreeing procedures between different stakeholders in the assessment process, formal planning assessment delivery, getting informed consent from assessment participants, privacy and data protection on assessment results, security and confidentiality, ensuring that reports arising from the assessment are based fairly on the assessment measures, providing appropriate assessment feedback, and guidelines on rights and responsibilities of assessment participants. ISO 10667 is the result of many years' work by an international committee with representatives from many countries including the US and several in Europe. The standard will help to increase the quality of recruitment, personnel selection and promotion processes, and will be able to contribute to the professionalisation of the entire industrial sector.

To sum up, we think that adopting some organisational procedures in legal provisions based on Gilliland's rules (1993), the Anderson *et al.* (2001) suggestions and the future standard ISO 10667 should improve transparency in human resource practices and increase confidence and the commitment of workers to their companies. For example, the recently published British Standard BS 8877 in September 2011, sets out best practice for all those operating in the online recruitment sector. It gives recommendations that apply to all methods of candidate attraction, screening, storage and selection using internet-based technology up to the point of offer or rejection. The standard identifies the roles and responsibilities of those involved. It also encourages transparency and helps to improve the candidate experience.

V. Conclusions

Quality in work is a horizontal objective of the EES, and can be achieved, at least partially, through gender equality, inclusion and access to the labour market, and diversity and non-discrimination in the workplace. All of this is part of EEO policy, so the legislation may consider advances in psychological and social investigation in order to improve the real and applied quality of jobs.

European EEO legislation shows that most Directives are oriented towards equality promotion, stressing sex discrimination. Despite the legislation in force discriminatory practices are taking place in organisations. In fact, in EU economies, women's employment is not equal to men, and a variety of disperse and scarce debates about equal opportunities exists in each country (Griffin, 2002). Some of the causes for these illegal practices are an organisational culture, where the thought processes of people that compose the organisations is contrary to the legislative constraints. Moreover, European legislation has concentrated on conditions of direct and indirect discrimination, but not on the specific criteria and practices. For example, indirect discrimination (adverse impact) is calculated in USA by means of statistical methods as the 80% rule, z Test, Fisher's probability test and chi square. All these methods compare the pass ratio of the focal group against the majority one, looking for differences in the ratios. For instance, the 80% rule states that a ratio of .80 or greater indicates that there is no adverse impact (Tippins, 2010.)

This can lead to specific doubts as to the true commitment of European institutions on equality (Davoine, 2006), as would be a great tool for human resources practitioners and for employers in avoiding organisational barriers and promoting equality at work. We recognise hard law must be completed with soft law, but this does not avoid the necessity of improving measures and principles to implement in every day cases. In this sense, the Strategy for Equality between Men and Women 2010-2015 follows the dual approach of gender mainstreaming and specific measures (European Commission, 2010), but employment agents could improve the quality of work and employment through everyday decision-making processes which take part in the organisational arena. These decisions are better decisions when criteria are clear and easy to implement. Tackling job access, personnel selection and promotion in organisations, these can be rendered more transparent, using adequate measure instruments that are additionally job-relevant and less personally intrusive. Recent dispositions like AAMs contribute to correcting the inequalities but are criticised because they raise sensitive moral, economic, and political issues (Faundez, 1994). In consequence, more effort is needed to develop legal dispositions that conciliate the guarantee of equality and its compliance. Legal measures must be taken under EES and the European Strategy 2020, as an appropriate vehicle to implement the best science-based practices for equality. A capital point is how people evaluate their working experience and deal with equality in the workplace. So, our proposal is to adopt some organisational justice procedures in legal dispositions which should improve transparency in human resources practices and increase the workers' trust in their companies. We can summarise these recommendations in four specific points:

1) the use of procedures free of bias, based on accurate information and upholding ethical standards in accordance with workers' expectations;
2) maintain the consistency in procedures;
3) allow workers the expression of their views and feelings during the procedures;
4) ensure that employees feel that they have had a chance to voice their opinion of the process (Brown, Bemmels and Barclay, 2010).

These kinds of proposals will made important improvements in the quality of jobs, specifically in outcomes as higher satisfaction, organisational climate, performance, and the prevention around stress problems.

Another point is the need to ensure the implementation of organisational justice framework into the organisations. In our opinion, one of the best ways is through collective bargaining and workers involvement[23]. The reason is the necessity to adopt effective and explicit measures, easy to understand and to implement, avoiding complex interpre-

23 See Dorssemont's chapter.

tation of abstract principles that finally could lead to the helplessness of focal groups. Moreover, the effectiveness of collective agreements is favoured fulfilled by the surveillance and monitoring of employers, employee representatives and union delegates.

Last but not least, we like to point out that although the present chapter is centred on equality between women and men, but a conjoint view with other chapters in this book examining other sources of discrimination will result in a complete pool on discrimination grounds[24]. The EES, the European Strategy 2020 and the legislative reforms derived from it are the very opportunity to incorporate and to develop the best science-based practices, for widing up different and complementary points of view about equality.

[24] See several chapters: that of Carlson, that of Canazza, and the one regarding atypical forms of work by Borelli.

Promoting Quality of Employment in the European Union and Beyond

The Necessary Contribution of Law

Jean-Michel BONVIN
Professor, University of Applied Sciences Western Switzerland (HES-SO), and Co-Director of the Centre for the Study of Capabilities in Social and Health Services (CESCAP)

Nicola CIANFERONI
Junior Researcher, CESCAP

Frédéric WIDMER
Senior Researcher, Co-ordinator of the CESCAP

In a globalised context, the issues of employment regulation and "job quality" raise new challenges. In the light of the preceding chapters, the objective of this conclusion is to examine the potential contribution of law in this respect. The issue of "job quality" includes the four key dimensions emphasised in the "Decent Work Agenda" developed by the International Labour Office: employment, working conditions, social protection and social dialogue. Thus, what matters is that the following four targets are met as closely as possible: there are jobs for everyone; these are of good quality; they are linked with entitlements to cash and in-kind benefits; social dialogue and its two pillars (the right to organise and the right to develop collective action, as advocated by ILO Conventions 87 and 98) are decisive tools to settle all these issues. Obviously, compromises are needed (some would say trade-offs) to reconcile these four dimensions as much as possible. The content and scope of such compromises vary significantly overtime and according to national institutional settings. At the present time, characterised by wide-ranging transformations of the labour market and its modes of regulation, there is a large agreement that the issue of "job quality" needs to be somehow reframed (Supiot, 1999; Gazier, 2003). Many authors contend that state regulation is no more the adequate tool to guarantee job quality in a context of globalised competition. Rather, other actors, be they at the transnational level (NGOs, consumer movements, international organisations, etc.) or at the local level (mainly enterprises, but also other local stakeholders such as public authorities, workers' representatives, etc.), ought to be actively involved to guarantee the fairness and efficiency of labour market regulation. This is justified in two main ways: the necessity to develop a global level of regulation in line with the global reality of the labour market on the one hand, the need to involve local actors, especially those in enterprises, in order to dissuade them to choose the "exit option" (i.e. delocalisation) on the other hand. This transformed context casts doubts on the place of law, esp. national law, within the regulation of the labour market in three main respects: a) what locus (or combination of loci) is the most appropriate for regulating the labour market and what actors should be mobilised in this task? b) what content (hard or soft, substantial or procedural) is to be designed? c) what ways or paths should be privileged for its effective implementation? This is really a matter of determining who is responsible for what, e.g. who ought to define and/or implement the working conditions, wages, levels of social protection for jobless people, etc.

In order to tentatively address these questions, this conclusive chapter is articulated as follows: Section I identifies the main changes with regard to flexibilisation of employment relations (I.1), collective bargaining (I.2), and the welfare state (I.3), and the challenges these represent in terms of "job quality". Section II focuses on some actual strategies that have been developed. Within a market framework, strategies such as corporate social responsibility, socially responsible investment, pressures by consumer movements or codes of conduct have proven to be insufficient (section II.1). Thus, Sections II.2 and II.3 suggest alternative conceptions inspired by the capability (Sen, 1999) and "capacitas" (Deakin and Supiot, 2009) frameworks. This part of the chapter will rely on the theoretical and empirical work conducted within the Capright project[1]. The last part of the chapter briefly synthesises the main findings.

---

[1] The Capright project was funded by the EU 6th framework (grant number: CIT4-CT-2006-028549). It argued that the relations between the labour market, employment and welfare regimes have to be analysed in terms of the promotion of individual and collective capabilities based on a fair and efficient use of rights to monetary and institutional resources for individuals (esp. sustaining wages and welfare). It gathered 25 teams coming from all over Europe and South America. For more information, see www.capright.eu.

I. Transformations of the Labour Market and its Regulation

Three main trends have had a deep impact on job quality and its regulation in European countries: the "flexibilisation" of employment relations, the erosion of collective bargaining, and the transformation of the welfare state. Whereas the first two trends are concerned with private arrangements in labour markets, the latter reflects a shift towards more market-oriented public policies (or "market-making" instead of "market-steering" policies to use Levy's words – (Levy, 2006)).

A. The Flexibilisation of Employment Relations

The mass production model of the post-war period presupposed the sharing of productivity gains between capital and labour taking the form of real wage growth, employment security and the development of welfare provisions in the fields of illness, disability, unemployment, old age insurance, etc. (Bihr, 1991). This "Fordist compromise" also involved the regulation of markets and the legitimisation of collective bargaining actors (Lallement, 2008). But "Fordism" was also criticised for the hard conditions it imposed on workers: strong subordination at work and repetitive tasks. The economic crisis of the 1970s revealed the gradual exhaustion of this mass production model. Since the mid-1960s, the declining productivity gains resulted in a lower corporate profitability. The abandonment of the fixed exchange rate (1971) and the oil shock (1973) reinforced this trend. The emergence of a financial capitalism oriented towards the interests of shareholders at the expenses of the traditional "insiders" in the firm (family owners, top managers) pressed for higher profitability rates in the short term (Batsch, 2002). For most exporting companies, reducing costs and improving their reactivity appeared to be a necessary condition to increase their competitiveness. Many of these, in industry as well as in services, started to decentralise low value-added activities and to implement lean production methods. The outsourcing of peripheral activities went together with the development of more precarious jobs and a growing number of working poor. Employers also imposed more temporal flexibility in order to align work volume with the demand, and higher wage flexibility. A side effect of this trend was the psychological distress of employees (Sennett, 1999).

This new economic context has had a deep impact on traditional employment relations and the characteristics of jobs. New and more flexible forms of employment have gradually emerged in all European countries since the 1980s, following the American trend of the 1970s. Managers started to recruit the workforce under temporary and/or part-time contracts. This "periphery" of low skilled workers with often precarious jobs and low wages allowed for quicker adjustments of the firms' productive capacity and resulted in a new distribution of entrepreneurial risks between workers, employers and shareholders, imposing a significant part of the growing risks emerging from international and competitive markets on workers (Mangan, 2000). This is envisaged as a counterpart for the continuing employment stability of the core skilled workers still enjoying employment security and higher wages, whose work is considered more essential for the productivity of enterprises and less easily replaceable (Atkinson, 1984; Hassel, 2007). This plurality of employment relationships poses a serious challenge in terms of job quality and employment regulation. All the more so since conventional mechanisms of workers' representation have traditionally tended to focus on core workers. This core/periphery distinction is also often associated with gender segregation (Deery and Jago, 2002). Along with the fragmentation of employment statuses, technological progress reduced the number of medium skilled jobs, and increased the polarisation between high (conception and organisation) and low (production and distribution) skilled jobs (Manning, 2004). This broad picture corresponds to a general trend that affects all "advanced" economies. Such a diversification of employment relations can be observed in all countries, but to varying degrees, and reflects adjustments to similar changes in the economy (Boyer, 2001).

However, important differences between countries are to be mentioned. From the point of view of labour regulation, dualism (core/periphery) appears to be one specific response to the flexibilisation trend, a response that is observable in countries like Germany, France, Spain and most continental European States. In this kind of system, employment regulations provide strong employment protection, good employment conditions and generous welfare support for the core workforce, whereas non-standard contracts do not allow such advantages. But at least two other types of arrangements are observable, depending on the power relationships (notably the role of trade unions) at stake in each country (Gallie, 2007). In the US and in Anglo-Saxon countries in general, flexibility has spread to all categories of workers (Kalleberg, 2009). In this variety of "market employment regimes", labour has no significant role in decision-making, individual employers are free to define work and wage conditions, and state intervention is weak, both in creating jobs and in providing social-security benefits. At the other extreme, the "inclusive employment regimes" of Scandinavia and Finland are based on high employment rates, a strong public sector, work-family policies, high levels of support to the unemployed and extensive employment rights (notably participation rights in firms). Hence, common trends towards flexibilisation have been filtered by institutional contexts providing workers with very different levels of job security. Whatever the differences, the growing plurality of employment relationships poses a serious challenge with respect to the adequate regulation of job quality for all categories of workers.

B. Collective Bargaining

Collective bargaining is the second dimension of employment regulation that has been under strong pressure over the last twenty years in Europe. Supiot (2002) observes a process of "proceduralisation" of labour law: concrete and qualitative issues that were once regulated by law are being increasingly transferred into the contractual sphere. Collective agreements between employers and workers (or their organisations) introduce a permanent negotiation of labour regulations, and create an opportunity for contesting these regulations. They can bring the conditions for a more situated and reflexive mode of regulation, more open to quick adjustment and presumably closer to the firm actors' concerns, provided however that workers are given real capacities to efficiently represent their point of view at the negotiating table. But the fragmentation of employment statuses, together with the current decentralisation trend, is challenging workers' solidarity, since similar job positions are increasingly exposed to diverging working conditions.

Again, decentralisation is not a uniform process in all EU countries. In their research on Germany, Sweden and Japan, Thelen and Kume (2006) showed that the most widely encompassing institutions of coordination (at national or sectoral levels) in these countries eroded significantly, whereas an intensification of the cooperation between workers' representatives and managers took place at enterprise level. In Sweden, social partnership has been transferred from the national to the sectoral level. In other countries like Germany, regulations are evaporating at the sectoral level both qualitatively and quantitatively (with enterprises leaving their associations and the collective bargaining system), giving an increasing role to enterprise actors (Hassel, 2007). Market-like or contractual mechanisms are thus gaining importance in the definition of wages and work conditions, but, apart from Anglo-Saxon countries, they are still combined with non-market forms of coordination at lower levels. Under these circumstances, not only are workers integrated in an increasingly dual employment system, with more and more employees remaining out of collective agreements and legal protections, but there is also a retrenchment of rights and advantages through decentralised collective agreements for the core of the workforce. In this context, collective agreements may act as an instrument of legitimisation of labour market deregulation and welfare state retrenchment (Coates, 2000). The Italian company Fiat is a case in point. This company decided to externalise two factories, creating two legally separate entities still under the control of Fiat (Cella, 2011; Quadruppani, 2011). This strategy implied the recruitment of the same employees under a new employment regime, outside the collective agreements applying to Fiat. To make such a deterioration in working conditions (possibility of ten-hour days for six days a week, increase from 40 to 120 overtime hours without compensation, shorter daily breaks, and the possibility of suspending unilaterally the reimbursement of sick leaves) more acceptable, the company committed itself to investment in the Italian production sites. The action of the EU often goes in the same direction of deregulation and weakening trade unions, as is evidenced by recent judgments of the European Court of Justice (e.g. the Viking (2007), Laval (2007) and Ruffert (2008) cases) that condemned the collective action carried out by workers against companies that, in conformity with the Lisbon treaty, had relied on the freedom of movement of capital, goods, services and workforce to deteriorate working conditions and impose lower wages (Dufresne, 2009; Supiot, 2010). Another issue in terms of collective bargaining relates to multinational companies and derives from the difficulty to organise a global representation of workers. The cases of Rio Tinto-Alcan in Switzerland or Volkswagen in Belgium, both conducted in the framework of the Capright project, illustrate the difficulties faced by local trade unions or workers' councils trying to defend workers' interests in the face of global economic interests. Existing provisions in terms of the right to be consulted or informed have not resulted in an increase in bargaining power because decisions were made elsewhere, in the absence of the workers' representatives. The global reality of firms is a challenge for local and national trade unions, even when they are able to build EU workers' councils.

Moreover, multinational firms and employers' associations are increasingly organised in networks, and trade unionism is forced to adapt to this network structure (Supiot, 2002). Union mergers and restructurings, international coordination between trade unions, the unionisation of new sectors are common, but still tentative, responses to such contemporary challenges.

C. The Recommodification of Social Policies

In most EU countries, entitlement to welfare benefits is closely tied to jobs, and thus constitutes an integral component of job quality. Unemployment, disability, old age, maternity, occupational accident and sometimes health insurances are strongly dependent on jobs. The possibility of accessing welfare benefits when out of labour markets is thus an important dimension of labour market regulation. The increasing precariousness of jobs tends to weaken the financial basis of the welfare state, and endangers the entitlement to welfare benefits of those holding a precarious job or those without a job. The challenge in terms of job quality is then how to maintain access to social rights when the traditional basis of social solidarity, i.e. full-time work, is weakened.

The possibility of combining private and professional life, i.e. the reconciliation between family, leisure, etc. and work, is also a challenge for the continuity of welfare benefits. Such reconciliation often implies that new equilibriums between work and other spheres of life, as well as other distributions of work and welfare along gender lines, are designed. While the Keynesian welfare state was often based on the male breadwinner model, this issue calls for other models such as that of the dual earner family. What matters then, in terms of job quality, is that part-time jobs or any atypical employment relationship (i.e. not in the line of the full-time and open-term contract) also include entitlement to adequate cash and in-kind social benefits.

Another challenge is linked with the emergence of the so-called "active welfare state" (Vielle *et al.*, 2005). In post-war welfare states, in line with the "decommodification" logic, social risks were socialised, i.e. systems of solidarity were set up in order to protect those losing their job under certain circumstances (disability, unemployment, occupational accident, etc.). But the new supply-side paradigm of the 1980s, emerged in a context of increasing globalisation pressures, brought in a new conception focusing on the "recommodification" of benefit recipients, the increase in overall employment rates and the reduction of public budgetary deficits and debts. Most European countries started to promote employability among the unemployed and the non-working population, notably social assistance beneficiaries and disabled people. From that time on, full employment and social integration have no longer been enhanced by public investments in a Keynesian line, but pursued via the improvement of the employability of non-working people, considered as a potential workforce. Instead of compensating for the incapacity to work, social policies are increasingly oriented towards the promotion of the working capacity (Bonvin and Moachon, 2005). This move implies a deep-seated transformation of the logic of social security systems, which are increasingly subordinated to the objective of recommodification. Hence, the conditions under which such recommodification takes place are quite important in terms of job quality. Measures such as job subsidies or pressure to take any job in order to reduce social expenditure (see for example the Hartz IV reforms in Germany), might create the conditions for unfair competition on the labour market, which in turn may push towards more flexibilisation and deregulation for "periphery" or even "core" workers on the labour market. Furthermore, unemployment also has a negative impact on job quality because the probability of having good job conditions is lower after having experienced long-term unemployment.

Thus, in terms of job quality, the issue of social protection raises at least two challenges: on the one hand how to ensure to those holding atypical jobs, or those without a job, the access to adequate social benefits (that would also increase their freedom of choice when it comes to balancing work and other activities); on the other hand how to guarantee that the present trends toward activating welfare recipients do not contribute to a deterioration in working conditions on the labour market.

II. What Regulation for the Contemporary Labour Market?

Faced with these challenges, the role of national States in defining labour market regulation is getting more complex, incorporating norms from both international institutions and more decentralised (regional or sectoral) levels. However, national States did not lose their central role, even though in all countries, strong pressures from domestic lobbies and international organisations such as the OECD pressed for the liberalisation of labour markets. Despite labour law reforms, European continental labour markets are still more regulated than their Anglo-Saxon counterparts, and some projects have been abandoned in the face of strong popular opposition (the French "*contrat première embauche*" is an obvious example). Thus, if flexibilisation of labour law is taking place in Europe, it still incorporates welfare considerations as is illustrated by the debate on the "flexicurity" concept at European level or the "decent work" agenda proposed by the International Labour Organisation (see part I in this volume). These agendas have been extensively reviewed in this volume. Let us underline here that both the flexicurity strategy and the "decent work" programme insist on the need to involve corporate actors in the pursuit of "job quality". The idea is that in a global context, corporate actors cannot be compelled to pursue "job quality", and therefore should be somehow stimulated in this direction. Two main strategies can be identified in this respect.

A. Disembedded Markets and Their Pitfalls

First, a "managerialist" perspective insists on market mechanisms such as corporate reputation and the idea that corporate social responsibility may be considered as a win-win strategy, insofar as socially respected workers, enjoying extensive entitlements, are more committed and motivated, which contributes to increase corporate profitability. The motto "Ethics pays" summarises this perspective. Empirical case studies conducted in the framework of the Capright project have demonstrated the frailty of such a concept. It may promote job quality in times of economic prosperity, but as soon as the situation deteriorates (i.e. as soon as ethics does no longer pay or appears to be too costly), job quality might easily be neglected by employers. Cases in the UK, Belgium or Switzerland clearly illustrate this point: if market pressure prevails over other concerns, then job quality is not the primary goal, at least not in times of difficult economic circumstances. For instance, such a managerialist perspective on corporate social responsibility prevailed in the case of the Swiss firm Tornos (Bonvin, 2007), but as soon as the firm came into economic trouble, the commitment to CSR was forgotten and nearly half of the workforce was dismissed without any social plan (there is no obligation related to this issue in Swiss labour law and in the collective labour agreements of the metalworking sector in Switzerland). Hence, trust in market mechanisms is not enough to guarantee that CSR will be the enterprise's constant strategy; it needs to be complemented by other mechanisms to contribute at all to the promotion of job quality.

To this purpose, pressures can certainly be exerted by consumer movements or by other means of self-regulation such as codes of conduct or ethical charts, but in the absence of any institutional tools for enforcement, the continuing effectiveness of these instruments can be cast into doubt. Indeed, codes of conduct often boil down to declarations of intent; and consumer movements may be quite selective in the issues they defend (e.g. child labour seems to be more conducive to such action than, say, infringements on trade union freedom – Bonvin, 2000; Diller, 1999), while their long-term efficiency depends to a large extent on their capacity to raise and sustain public attention in the long run, which certainly does not happen very often. It could also be imagined that shareholders might exert pressure on firms to push them into ethical behaviour. This is the idea behind the so-called "socially responsible investment" that has been incited, amongst others, by authors such as Aglietta, advocating salaried workers to become shareholders of their enterprises in order to influence their practices. However, the mechanisms governing shareholder assemblies (where votes are distributed according to the financial input of every shareholder) are not genuinely democratic and guarantee a stronger voice to the most powerful investors. Hence, a deep-seated reform of the legislative or regulative provisions concerning shareholders' rights is needed if such "ethically responsible investment" is to produce effective outcomes in terms of job quality. This clearly shows that, if left to market mechanisms alone, tools such as CSR, codes of conduct, consumer labels and ethically responsible investment, may well miss their target.

So the conclusion seems to be that institutions, i.e. law and legal bodies, cannot be discarded altogether. Somehow law is needed, but not the same kind of law. And part of the Capright project was precisely devoted to analysing the avenues that could be taken to reform law in order to adapt it to the new context. By adaptation, we do not mean that law has to be subordinated to market considerations such as competitiveness or productivity, but that it needs to be reformed in order to be able to efficiently pursue the defence of workers' rights and freedoms in the globalised context. In other words, the reform of law and labour law should aim at providing them with the means of taming or curbing the market logic, so as to effectively promote job quality for all workers on the labour market. The ILO "decent work" agenda pursues a similar line, calling for the restoration of what Supiot (2010) calls "the Spirit of Philadelphia" embodied in the ILO Declaration of Philadelphia adopted in 1944. This resonates as a reminder that law is needed if markets are to be subordinated to human development and not the other way round. This is also the essence of the difference between the capability and the human capital approach (Sen, 1999).

Hence, markets need to be somehow embedded in institutions if they are to work properly, i.e. in a sense that promotes job quality. Case studies conducted during the Capright project unambiguously demonstrated that self-regulation without legal or judicial institutions is not a satisfactory solution. The following subsections will focus on two complementary aspects of the necessary contribution of law to the issue of job quality: firstly (section II.2) as a "goals-rights-system" (Sen, 2003), secondly (section II.3) as a way to develop the "capacitas" or "capability for voice" of social partners, thus advocating a concept of procedural rights that complement substantial rights (Browne *et al.*, 2005; Supiot, 2009, 2010).

B. Bringing Law Back into the Globalised Context

The first aspect focuses on the distinction between soft law and hard law. Two questions are key in this respect. The first one refers to the distinction drawn by Amartya Sen between "rights as goals" or "goals-rights-system" on the one hand, and the "constraint view of rights" on the other hand (Sen, 2003, 2009; Alexander, 2004; De Munck, 2010). With this notion of "goals-rights-system", Sen develops an original conception of law that does not boil down to an imposition of duties or perfect obligations, but can also encompass the assertion of principles resulting in so-called 'imperfect obligations': "Loosely specified obligations must not be confused with no obligations at all. They belong, rather, to an important category of duties, (…) which Immanuel Kant called 'imperfect obligations', and which can coexist with other – more fully specified – imperatives of 'perfect obligations'" (Sen, 2009: 374). In his view, the absence of precise laws or legislative provisions does not coincide with the absence of any kind of duty. This applies to the field of human rights, and consequently also to the economic and social rights within them: it is not because there are no constraining laws imposing specific duties in terms of job quality on economic actors such as multinational companies that they have no duties whatsoever. Hence, normative shopping by firms (choosing the most favourable legal setting, i.e. the one coinciding with the lowest production costs, to settle their productive factories) is acceptable only insofar as it complies with the imperfect obligations contained in documents of "soft law" such as the Declarations of Human Rights. In Sen's view, soft law requires "trying to do what one reasonably can in the circumstances" (*ibid.*: 376). This point may be better apprehended by the "soft" vs. "fuzzy" law distinction introduced by Delmas-Marty (1998). According to her, the lack of precision or "fuzziness" of economic and social rights, so-called "second generation human rights", allows their adjusted implementation in different national or regional contexts; it does by no means imply that they are facultative. Soft law or, to use Delmas-Marty's words, "fuzzy law" does not coincide with the absence of law.

The second issue relates to the governance mechanisms used to implement soft law. At present, the privileged tool is "governing by indicators", as is illustrated by the EU open method of coordination for instance, where rules (or best practices) emerge via the benchmarking or comparison of performances against the indicators designed by the competent EU Committee (Salais, 2004; Bonvin, Moachon & Vero, 2011). In the field of job quality, the Employment Committee is responsible for designing such indicators. As Supiot (2010) points out, under such circumstances "government by laws", based on general and abstract rules, is being replaced by a new type of "governance by numbers" or indicators following a logic of self-regulation. In this new paradigm, Supiot claims, normativity is no longer vertical and referring to laws, but emerging from the supposedly objective and scientific measurement of facts. So-called "evidence-based policies" are the logical outcome of such a perspective. According to this approach, statistical measurement against indicators allows fully objective or "evidence-based" policy-making. New public management principles also contribute to this trend. States, in this perspective, should act as enterprises in competitive markets and react to quantitative indicators. Employment and unemployment rates, growth rates and other indicators (concerning women's participation, the distribution of vocational training, etc.) are examples of quantitative indicators that impose a predefined objective on national or local authorities and restrict the autonomy of decision of people both in and out of labour markets. By contrast, soft law envisaged as "goals-rights-systems" calls for democratic implementation, insofar as the incompleteness of principles requires democratic and public reasoning in order to be translated into enforceable legislative provisions. While "goals-rights-systems" imply democracy, "governing by indicators" often coincides with technocracy and the neglect of politics (since policy-making is a matter of measurement and evidence, experts, and not citizens or policy-makers, are the most adequately equipped to implement it)[2]. This also means that quantifiable outcomes (i.e. those that can be measured against indicators) will be privileged over qualitative concerns, which might be detrimental in terms of "job quality". Indeed, such a neglect of politics means that the democratic debate about values and norms is discarded and that the quantitative concerns pushed by experts can be imposed as the yardstick for good policy-making. This often results in privileging quantitative indicators such as employment quantity or financial equilibriums over "job quality" (as is illustrated e.g. in the EU Broad Economic Policy Guidelines).

Hence, there are two conclusions to be drawn with respect to this first aspect when it comes to designing adapted regulatory processes for the globalised labour market: firstly, soft law coincides with imperfect obligations, secondly its implementation calls for democratic and public reasoning, that does not boil down to "governing by indicators".

C. Promoting "Capacitas" and "Capability for Voice"

The second aspect deals precisely with the conditions to be implemented in order to put democracy at the core of labour market regulation and "job quality". In other words, the promotion of "job quality" requires a genuinely democratic negotiation between all stakeholders, especially employers and workers (and their representatives). Indeed, in the face of legal and conventional deregulation, workers' participation at enterprise level appears as a (necessary but non-sufficient) prerequisite for allowing them to defend themselves against the tendency to impose the burden of risks and market uncertainties on them (via imposed flexibilisation and precariousness). To this purpose, the EU law provides a basic core of rights that applies to all countries, but Member States have generally more extensive rights. Three categories of rights are usually differentiated: information, consultation (giving an opportunity to express an opinion before a measure is implemented) and co-determination (the consent of workers' representatives is required before implementing particular measures). The capacity of workers to influence employment conditions varies substantially along national lines: a weak "capacitas" or "capability for voice" in market regimes, a consultative involvement in dualist countries, and more extensive rights enhanced by strong unionism in Nordic countries (Gallie, 2007). However, this categorisation is very rough, and there are some exceptional cases, such as the dual German system which provides among the most extensive participation

---

2 This trend can also be observed at corporate level. Indeed, within the firm, "governing by indicators" is very often the norm, as managers are called to constantly monitor their performance against financial and economic indicators.

rights. In this country, workers' representatives occupy half of the seats on the supervisory board of firms with more than 2000 employees. This characteristic may explain why German firms experience less radical restructurings than firms in otherwise comparable institutional contexts (Widmer, 2011). But it is doubtful whether co-determination really contributes to democratic control and power-sharing in the interest of workers. Höpner (2001) observed that the German co-determination system in fact gives way to a cross-class alliance aiming at improving productivity and workers' commitment to the enterprise. This kind of arrangements can produce conflicts between workers' councils who identify with the enterprise, and trade unions that are more preoccupied with class cleavages. Co-determination alone can lead to the fragmentation of labour not only between different companies and sectors in the same country, but also between subsidiary firms of the same company in different countries, as is evidenced by the case of Volkswagen in Belgium (De Munck *et al.*, 2010).

As a matter of fact, reflexive and negotiated law at company level does not necessarily coincide with increased "job quality". Sectoral, national and EU levels are still needed to allow for more organised forms of bargaining, with States and organised interests participating in the regulation process. Even if the power asymmetry between labour and capital remains, labour associations provide a better bargaining capacity than enterprise-level participation within a direct, face-to-face contractual framework. This has been particularly true since the 1990s and the rising importance of financial capital in corporate governance systems, and the corresponding decline of workers' power in their enterprise (Batsch, 2002). However, the de-unionisation trend in Europe (Ebbinghaus, 2002) constitutes a serious challenge. Under such circumstances, the contribution of the State remains key in order to ensure the fairness of bargaining processes by promoting the "capacitas" or "capability for voice" of all people around the negotiating table, and to see that the collectively and democratically decided provisions are effectively enforced.

"Capability for voice" insists on each participant's real freedom to express his/her viewpoint and make it count in the collective decision-making process, it thus requires that the conditions for such effective participation are met. In much the same way, "capacitas" encompasses "the sum total of the preconditions of effective participation in market relations" (Deakin, 2009: 28). In this perspective labour rights are not only seen as a way to protect workers against the negative consequences of the market, but also as a tool to empower them and to make them genuine partners in the social construction of a fair and equitable market order. The prerequisites of "capability for voice" or "capacitas" are not met in the current state of affairs. As a matter of fact, the ILO focus on social dialogue, as well as the EU insistence that concrete flexicurity strategies be negotiated between social partners, cannot be fully implemented until collective negotiation takes places in a fair arena, allowing all negotiators to effectively influence the final outcome of the bargaining process. A series of conditions needs to be fulfilled in order to guarantee such a "capability for voice" or "capacitas" (Deakin and Supiot, 2009).

Firstly, cognitive abilities are needed, which implies access to information and adequate education to be able to produce appropriate information and knowledge bases and properly defend one's own interests. As a matter of fact, cognitive capabilities do not boil down to access to already available information, but also imply the free use of this information and, most significantly, the ability to produce one's own information. Indeed, those who master the production of information and knowledge enjoy more power, insofar as they are able to impose their own specific viewpoint on the issue of "job quality". For instance, the setting up of an Observatory on Stress and Constrained Mobility by the trade unions in the Orange conflict in France allowed workers to produce their own information on working conditions, which impacted significantly on how "job quality" was subsequently framed (Du Roy, 2009). Secondly, political abilities, e.g. the ability to build strategic alliances in order to get more influence in the decision-making process, also matter. In this respect, the rights to form trade unions and to develop collective action are crucial. As Supiot emphasises, when it comes to transforming power relationships into fair legal and judicial decisions, the capacity to effectively organise and negotiate is decisive. Indeed, workers need to build collectives in order to equilibrate power relationships and claim for more equitable regulations. Thirdly, adequate means of action should be available, such as the right to strike or other means to put pressure on employers. By contrast, such provisions as the Swiss Labour Peace agreement may be detrimental to workers, since they restrict to a large extent the right to strike and thus prevent workers from setting the conditions for more equilibrated power relationships. Fourthly, adequate social entitlements are needed, insofar as negotiators that do not enjoy such rights are in the same situation as Marx's reserve army used to be: if market solutions, i.e. having a job whatever its quality, are the only way to get an income, then the bargaining power of workers is considerably reduced; they have no alternative or exit option and are constrained to accept the conditions imposed by employers. To promote "capacitas", social entitlements are a necessary prerequisite.

Thus, the development of "capacitas" requires that these four conditions – cognitive capabilities, political capacities, the right to strike and to use other means of collective action, social entitlements – are met so that "job quality" can be framed and implemented in a more equitable way. Such procedural rights are needed to enhance the workers' "capability for voice" or their effective participation in the definition of "job quality". Moreover, this should be promoted at all relevant levels of employment regulation: the enterprise, the branch, the national level, and the international level, so as to prevent any normative shopping by enterprises.

III. Conclusion

We identified three main trends that have a strong impact on job quality and its regulation in European countries. First, the flexibilisation of employment relations gives birth to a growing plurality of job conditions and security levels. This trend poses serious challenges to regulations aiming at promoting job quality for all categories of workers. Second, collective bargaining institutions are undergoing a process of erosion leading to more market-like or contractual mechanisms. The dualisation of employment systems, with more and more employees remaining out of collective agreements and legal protections, is thus accompanied by a retrenchment of rights and advantages through decentralised collective agreements for the core of the workforce. The weakening of labour organisations is also linked to the EU action (see the Viking, Laval and Ruffert cases) and the necessity (and difficulties) to organise at international levels. Traditional defences against job quality erosion are thus starting to crumble. Last, the transformation of social protection through the recommodification of social policies significantly interacts with job quality and generates new challenges. On the one hand, atypical jobs do not allow adequate access to social benefits. On the other hand, activation trends may contribute to a worsening of working conditions on the labour market. Faced with these challenges, different answers are available in terms of regulation.

We showed that market solutions such as corporate social responsibility, socially responsible investment, pressures by consumer movements or the elaboration of codes of conduct are not convincing responses. As this conclusive chapter and more generally this book have demonstrated, markets need to be embedded in institutions as far as the promotion of job quality is considered as a public goal.

A combination of substantial rights (soft law but also conventional hard law) and procedural rights ("capacitas" or "capability for voice") is needed to promote a fair conception of "job quality" and its effective enforcement in the globalised context. Soft law, envisaged as a complement – by no means a substitute – to hard law, should define "imperfect obligations" built on democratic and public reasoning (instead of "governing by indicators"). The "capability for voice" of employees should be considered as the cement of procedural rights and depend on the four conditions mentioned above: cognitive capabilities, political capacities, the right to strike and use other means of collective action, and the effective and unconditional guarantee of social entitlements. Interpreted in this way, "capability for voice" paves the way for innovative social practices allowing workers to participate in the definition of their working conditions and of job quality. What is advocated by a capability approach to workers' rights as well as by the "capacitas" framework developed by Deakin and Supiot is not an illusory return to the Fordist compromise, but an adaptation of labour law in order to enable it to efficiently promote "job quality" and thereby contribute to the enforcement of Article 31 of the EU Charter of Fundamental Rights, that states that "Every worker has the right to working conditions which respect his or her health, safety and dignity". This would be a significant step toward the implementation of what is maybe the most fundamental principle in the Declaration of Philadelphia, namely that "Labour is not a commodity".

Bibliography

Adams J.S., "Inequity in social exchange", in L. Berkowitz (ed.), *Advances in experimental psychology*, New York, Academic Press, 1965, pp. 267-299.

Aganon M., "Women workers and unions in the formal sector: Adjusting to the crisis", in J. Frances, I. Illo, and R. Pineda (eds.), *Carrying the burden of the world: women reflecting on the effects of the crisis on women and girls*, Quezon City, Center for Integrative and Development Studies, 1999, pp. 69-83.

Albert M., "Le rôle économique et social de l'assurance", *Encyclopédie de l'assurance*, Paris, Economica, 1998, p. 9.

Alexander, J., "Capabilities, human rights and moral pluralism", *The International Journal of Human Rights*, Vol. 8, No. 4, 2004, p. 451-469.

Aliprantis N., "Les droits sociaux au-delà du niveau national", in Aliprantis N. (ed.), *Les droits sociaux dans les instruments européens et internationaux. Défis à l'échelle mondiale*, Brussels, Bruylant, 2009.

Alston P., "'Core Labour Standards' and the transformation of the International Labour Rights Regime", *European Journal of International Law*, 15, p. 457.

Anderson N.R., Born M., Cunningham-Snell N., "Recruitment and selection: applicant perspectives and outcomes", in Anderson N.R., Ones D.S., Sinangil H.K., Viswesvaran C. (eds.), *Handbook of Industrial, Work and Organizational Psychology*, London and New York, Sage, 2001, pp. 200-218.

Anderson N., "Applicant and recruiter reactions to new technology in selection: A critical review and agenda for future research", *International Journal of Selection and Assessment*, 2003, 11, pp. 121-136.

Anker R. *et al.*, "Measuring decent work with statistical indicators", *International Labour Review*, Vol. 142, No. 2, Geneva, 2003, p. 147-177.

Arpaia A., Curci N., Meyermans E., Peschner J., Pierini F., *Short time working arrangements as response to cyclical fluctuations*, European Union, 2010.

Atkinson J., "Manpower strategies for flexible organisations", *Personnel management*, Vol. 16, No. 8, 1984, p. 28-31.

Auer P., Berg J., Coulibaly I., "Is a stable workforce good for productivity?", *International Labour Review*, Vol. 144, No. 3, Geneva, 2005, p. 319-343.

Auer P., Gazier B., *The future of work, employment and social protection. The dynamics of change and the protection of workers*, International Labour Organisation, International Institute for Labour Studies, Geneva, 2002, 265 p.

Barbier M., "Les relations entre l'Église catholique et l'organisation internationale du travail", *Politique étrangère*, 1972, Vol. 37, No. 3, pp. 351-387.

Barnard C., *EC Employment Law*, Oxford, Oxford University Press, 2006.

Batsch L., *Le capitalisme financier*, Paris, La Découverte, 2002.

Bauer T. N., Truxillo D. M., Sánchez R. J., Craig J., Ferrara P., Campion M. A., "Applicant reactions to selection: development of the selection procedural justice scale (SPJS)", *Personnel Psychology*, 2001, 54, pp. 387-419.

Baverez N., "Assurance et protection sociale", *Encyclopédie de l'assurance*, Paris, Economica, 1998, p. 471.

Bedrac J., "What makes a good company? Employee interest representation in European company law: reflections and legal provisions", Report 94, ETUI-REHS, 2006.

Bell M., Chopin I., Palmer F., *Developing Anti-discrimination Law in Europe – the 25 EU Member States compared III*, 2007.

Bercusson B., "The European Community's Charter of Fundamental Social Rights of Workers", *The Modern Law Review*, 1990/09, Vol. 53, issue 3, pp. 624-644.

Bercusson B., "Les temps communautaires", *Droit Social*, 2000, pp. 248-256.

Bercusson B., *European Labour Law and the EU Charter of Fundamental Rights*, Baden-Baden, Nomos, 2006.

Bercusson B., "Qu'attendre de la promotion de la Charte des droits fondamentaux par le Traité de Lisbonne?", *Revue de Droit du Travail*, 2008, p. 74.

Bercusson B., *European Labour Law*, Cambridge, CUP, 2009, p. 376.

Berra J., *La structure des systèmes de sécurité sociale*, Etude de droit comparé, Lausanne, 2000.

Bescond D. *et al.*, "Seven indicators to measure decent work: an international comparison", *International Labour Review*, Vol. 142, 2003/2

Besson E., *Flexicurité en Europe: éléments d'analyse*, Secrétariat d'État à la prospective et à l'évaluation des politiques publiques, Paris, 2008, 46 p.

Bessy C., "La diversité des contrats de travail", *La qualité de l'emploi*, Centre d'études de l'emploi, Paris, La Découverte, coll. Repères, 2006, p. 64.

Beveridge F., "Implementing Gender equality and Mainstreaming in an Enlarged European Union: Prospects and Challenges", in Beveridge F., Velluti S. (eds.), *Gender and the Open Method of Coordination. Perspectives on Law, Governance and equality in the EU*, Dartmouth, Ashgate, 2008, pp. 11-34.

Bies R.J., Moag J.S., "Interactional justice: communication criteria of fairness", in R.J. Lewicki, B.H. Sheppard, M.H. Bazerman (eds.), *Research in negotiation in organizations*, Greenwich, JAI Press, 1986, pp. 43-55.

Bihr A., *Du "grand soir" à "l'alternative": le mouvement ouvrier européen en crise*, Ivry-sur-Seine, l'Atelier, 1991.

Bonnechère M., "L'optique du travail décent", *Droit Ouvrier*, 2007, p. 57.

Bonvin J.-M., "Le droit social à l'épreuve de la mondialisation", in J. Delcourt *et al.* (eds.), *Les défis de la globalisation*, Presses universitaires de Louvain, 2001.

Bonvin J.-M., "Corporate Social Responsibility in a Context of Permanent Restructuring: A case study from the Swiss metalworking sector", *Corporate Governance*, Vol. 15, No. 1, 2007, p. 36-44.

Bonvin J.-M. & Moachon E., "L'activation et son potentiel de subversion de l'État social", in Vielle, P., Pochet, P. & Cassiers, I. (dir.), *L'État social actif: vers un changement de paradigme?*, Brussels, P.I.E. Peter Lang, 2005, p. 63-92.

Bonvin J.-M., Moachon E. & Vero J., "Déchiffrer deux indicateurs européens de flexicurité à l'aune de l'approche par les capacités", *Formation et emploi*, No. 113, janvier-mars 2011, p. 15-32.

Boubli B., "Le plan de départs volontaires dans un Plan de Sauvegarde de l'emploi multifonctions", *La semaine juridique sociale*, No. 39, 2010, p. 1383.

Boyer R., "Du rapport salarial fordiste à la diversité des relations salariales", in *CEPREMAP Working Papers*, 2001.

Boyer R., *La flexicurité danoise, quels enseignements pour la France?*, CEPREMAP, Paris, éd. Rue d'Ulm/Presses de l'École normale supérieure, 2006.

Brown E., "Protecting Agency Workers: Implied Contract or Legislation?", *Industrial Law Journal*, 2008, p. 178.

Brown G., Bemmels B., Barclay L.J., "The importance of policy in perceptions of organizational justice", *Human Relations*, 2010, 63, pp. 1587-1609.

Browne J., Deakin S. and Wilkinson F., "Capabilities, Social Rights and European Market Integration", in R. Salais and R. Villeneuve (eds.), *Europe and the Politics of Capabilities*, Cambridge, Cambridge University Press, 2005, p. 205-221.

Burgess D., Borgida E., "Who women are, who women should be: Descriptive and prescriptive gender stereotyping in sex discrimination", *Psychology, Public Policy, and Law*, 1999, 5, pp. 665-692.

Burgoon B., Dekker F., "Flexible employment, economic insecurity and social policy preferences in Europe", *Journal of European Social Policy*, 2010, p. 126

Burnay N., *Travailleurs âgés: d'une politique de réduction du chômage à une politique du vieillissement actif*, Brussels, P.I.E. Peter Lang, 2005.

Camaji L., "Le demandeur d'emploi à la recherche de ses obligations", *Droit social*, No. 6, 2010, p. 666.

Campa P., Casarico A., Profeta P., "*Gender culture and gender gap in employment*", *CESinfo Economic Studies*, 2011, 57, 156-182.

Canals V., *Formation-insertion et transformation de la relation salariale*, coll. Logiques économiques, Paris, L'Harmattan, 2001, p. 37 et s.

Caracciolo di Torella E., Masselot A., *Reconciling work and family Life in EU Law and Policy*, Basingstoke, Palgrave Macmillan, 2010.

Catala N., "Offres valables et offres raisonnables d'emploi: rupture ou continuité?", *La semaine juridique générale*, No. 39 et 41, 2008, p. 193.

Cavalier G., Upex R., "The Concept of Employment Contract in European Union Private Law", *International and Comparative Law Quarterly*, 2006, Vol. 55, p. 587.

Cella G.P., "L'accord de Fiat Pomigliano et les relations professionnelles italiennes", *Chronique Internationale de l'IRES*, No. 128, 2011, p. 25-34.

Céras, *Le discours social de l'Eglise catholique de Léon XIII à Benoit XVI*, Paris, Bayard Edition, 2009, 1056 p.

Chauchard J.P., *Droit de la sécurité sociale*, LGDJ, Paris, Lextenso éditions, 2010, 694 p.

Cieslar A., Nayer A., Smeesters B., *Le droit à l'épanouissement de l'être humain au travail: métamorphoses du droit social*, Brussels, Bruylant, 2007, 857 p.

Claringbould I., Knoppers A., "Finding a 'normal' woman: selection processes for board membership", *Sex Roles*, 2007, 56, pp. 495-507.

Clark A., "What makes a good job? Evidence from OECD countries", in S. Bazen, C. Lucifora, W. Salverda (eds.), *Job Quality and Employment Behaviour in Europe*, Basingstoke, Palgrave, 2005, pp. 11-30.

Coates, D., *Models of Capitalism: Growth and Stagnation in the Modern Era*, Cambridge/Oxford/Boston, Polity, 2000.

Cohen-Charash Y., Spector P.E., "The role of justice in organizations: a meta-analysis", *Organizational Behavior and Human Decision Processes*, 2001, 86, pp. 278-321.

Collins H., "Flexibility and stability of expectations in the contract of employment", *Socio-Economic Review*, 2006, p. 139.

Collins H., "Legal Responses to the Standard Form of Contract of Employment", *Industrial Law Journal*, 2007, p. 2.

Collins H., *Employment Law*, Oxford, OUP, 2010.

Conseil Pontifical Justice et Paix, *Compendium de la doctrine sociale de l'église*, Paris, Les éditions du Cerf, 2008, 531 p.

Council of the European Union, Presidency Conclusions, Brussels, 23-24 March 2006, 7775l/06.

Coursier P., "La notion de travailleur salarié en droit social communautaire", *Droit Social*, 2003, p. 305.

Cropanzano R., Greenberg J., "Progress in organizational justice: tunnelling through the maze", in Cooper C.L., Robertson I.T. (eds.), *International review of industrial and organizational psychology*, New York, Wiley, 1997, pp. 317-372.

Cropanzano R., Bowen D.E., Gilliland S., "The management of organizational justice", *Academy of Management Perspectives*, 2007, 21, pp. 34-48.

Cropanzano R., Goldman B., Folger R., "Deontic justice: the role of moral principles in workplace fairness", *Journal of Organizational Behavior*, 2003, 24, pp. 1019-1024.

Cropanzano R., Rupp D.E., Mohler C.J., Schminke M., "Three roads to organizational justice", in J. Ferris (ed.), *Research in personnel and human resources management*, Greenwich, JAI Press, 2001, pp. 1-113.

D'Onorio J. B., "Le Concile Vatican II et le droit", in *Le deuxième Concile du Vatican (1959-1965)*, Actes du colloque organisé par l'École française de Rome en collaboration avec l'Université de Lille III, l'Istituto per le scienze religiose de Bologne et le Dipartimento di studi storici del Medioevo e dell'età contemporanea de l'Università di Roma-La Sapienza (Rome 28-30 mai 1986), Rome, École française de Rome, 1989, pp. 651-688.

D'Antona M., "Limiti costituzionali alla disponibilità del tipo contrattuale nel diritto del lavoro", *Argomenti di diritto del lavoro*, 1995, p. 63.

Dahl S.A., Nesheim T. and Olsen K., "Quality of work. Concept and measurement", in A.M. Guillén, S.A. Dahl (eds.), *Quality of work in the European Union. Concept, Data and Debates from a Transnational Perspective*, Brussels, P.I.E. Peter Lang, 2009.

Davidov G., "Three Axes of Employment Relationships: a Characterization of Workers in Need of Protection", *University of Toronto Law Journal*, 2002, p. 402.

Davies P., "The Emergence of European Labour Law", in McCarthy W. (ed.), *Legal Intervention in Industrial Relations: Gains and Losses*, Oxford, Blacwell, 1992.

Davoine L., "Are quantity and quality of jobs correlated? Using, interpreting and discussing the Laeken indicators", *CEE Working paper*, 2006, p. 59.

Davoine L., *La qualité de l'emploi: une perspective européenne*, Thèse, Université Paris 1 Panthéon-Sorbonne, 29 novembre 2007.

Davoine L., Erhel C., Guergoat-Larivière M., "Monitoring quality in work: European Employment Strategy indicators and beyond", *International Labour Review*, Vol. 147, No. 2-3, Geneva, 2008, p. 163-198.

Davoine L., Erhel C., "La qualité de l'emploi: une mise en perspective européenne", *La qualité de l'emploi*, Centre d'études de l'emploi, Paris, La Découverte, coll. Repères, 2006, p. 16.

De Brouwer A., *Le Parti Populaire Européen: son identité et son nécessaire élargissement*, Working Paper No. 33, Barcelona 1991, 28 p.

De Munck J., "A Capability for Voice in Restructuration Context? Learning from VW-Brussels", Research Report, *Capright*, 2010.

De Val Tena A.L., "La polìtica de empleo en la Uniòn Europea: de la estretegia de Lisboa a la estrategia 'Europa 2020'", *Temas Laborales* 106/2010, p. 99.

Deakin S., "Capacitas: Contract Law, Capabilities and the Legal Foundations of the Market" in Deakin, S. & Supiot, A. (eds.), *Capacitas*, Oxford and Portland, Hart Publishing, 2009, p. 1-30.

Deakin S. & Supiot A. (eds.), *Capacitas*, Oxford and Portland, Hart Publishing, 2009.

Debusscher, P., "Mainstreaming gender in European Commission development policy: conservative europeanness?", *Women's Studies International Forum*, 2011, 34, 39-49.

Deery M. & Jago L.K., "The core and the periphery: an examination of the flexible workforce model in the hotel industry", *International Journal of Hospitality Management*, Vol. 21, No. 4, 2002, p. 339-351.

Degryse C., Natali D. (eds.), *Social developments in the European Union 2010*, Brussels, Ose-Etui, 2011.

Delmas-Marty M., *Trois défis pour un ordre mondial*, Paris, Seuil, 1998.

De Schutter O., "Le rôle de la Charte sociale européenne dans le développement du droit de l'Union européenne", in De Schutter O. (ed.), *La Charte sociale européenne: une constitution sociale pour l'Europe*, Brussels, Bruylant, 2010.

Deumer J., "Flexicurité et qualité de l'emploi: le cas du travail à temps partiel", *Courrier hebdomadaire du CRISP*, 2010, 29/30, No. 2074-2075.

Dickens L., "Problem of Fit: Changing Employment and Labour Regulation", *British Journal of Industrial Relations*, 2004, Vol. 42, No. 4.

Diller J., "Responsabilité sociale et mondialisation: Qu'attendre des codes de conduite, des labels sociaux et des pratiques d'investissement?", *Revue internationale du travail*, No. 2, 1999, p. 107-139.

Dorssemont F., "Le sentenze Laval e Viking e l'esercizio del diritto all'azione collettiva in Europa", in Cilento M. (ed.), *I Percorsi della Solidarietà Lavoro, mercato e diretti nell'Unione europea*, Rome, Edizioni Lavoro, 2009.

Dorssemont F., "Industrial Relations and Collective Labour Law in Papal Encyclicals: The Case of the Social Teaching of the Holy Roman Catholic Church", in *Labour Law between Change and Tradition, Liber Amicorum Antoine Jacobs*, Bulletin of comparative labour relations, No. 78, 2011, p. 59.

Dorssemont F., "The right to take collective action v. fundamental economic freedoms in the aftermath of *Laval* and *Viking*", in M. De Vos, *European Union Internal Market and Labour Law: Friends or foes*, Antwerpen, Oxford, Intersentia, 2009, 45-104.

Dorssemont F., "La (non)conformité du droit belge relative à l'action collective par rapport à la Charte sociale européenne", X. *Actualités du dialogue social et du droit de grève*, Kluwer, Waterloo, 2009, 167-202.

Douglas-Scott S., "A tale of two courts: Luxembourg, Strasbourg and the growing European Human rights acquis", *Common Market Law Review*, 2006, p. 629.

Douglas-Scott S., "Relations between international courts and community Courts: Mutual deference or subordination?", *Common Market Law Review*, 2005, p. 581.

Dovis P., Saraceno C., *I nuovi poveri: politiche per le disuguaglianze*, Turin, Codice, 2011.

Drobnic S., Guillén A.M. (eds.), *Work-Life Balance in Europe. The Role of Job Quality*, Palgrave Macmillan, 2011.

Drouin R-C., Duplessis I., "La régulation internationale du travail de 1998 à 2008: un Eldorado normatif ou un désert interprétatif?", in J. Charest, G. Murray, G. Trudeau (eds.), *Quelles politiques du travail à l'ère de la mondialisation?*, Québec, Presses de l'Université Laval, 2010.

Du Roy I., *Orange stressé. Le management par le stress à France Télécom*, Paris, La Découverte, 2009.

Duclos L., Kerbourc'h J.-Y., *Organisation du marché du travail et "flexicurité" à la française*, Conseil d'Orientation pour l'Emploi, Document de travail No. 10, Paris, 2006, 96 p.

Dufresne A., "Les grandes orientations de politiques économiques: un tournant institutionnel, quels changements substantiels", *Revue Belge de Sécurité Sociale*, 2001, p. 92.

Dufresne A., "La nécessaire européanisation du syndicalisme: enjeux et défis actuels", in Devos C., Faniel J., Gobin C. & Vandaele K. (eds.). *Syndicalisme: un mouvement pour le XXIe siècle*, Bruxelles, VUB-presses, p. 82-91.

Duplessis I., "Le vertige et la soft Law: réactions doctrinales en droit international", *Revue québéquoise de droit international*, Hors-série, p. 245.

Duplessis I., "La Déclaration de l'OIT relative aux droits fondamentaux au travail: une nouvelle forme de régulation efficace?", *Relations industrielles/Industrial Relations*, 2004, pp. 52-72.

Ebbinghaus B., "Trade unions' changing role: membership erosion, organisational reform, and social partnership in Europe", *Industrial Relations Journal*, Vol. 33, No. 5, 2002, p. 465-483.

Egger P., "Towards a policy framework for decent work", *International Labour Review*, Vol. 141, No. 1-2, Geneva, 2002, p. 161-174.

Eglise Orthodoxe Russe, *Les fondements de la doctrine sociale*, Paris, Les éditions du Cerf – Istina, 2007, 194 p.

Ellis E., "The impact of Lisbon Treaty on Gender Equality", in *Gender Equality Law Review*, European Network of Legal Experts in the field of Gender Equality, European Commission, 2010/1.

Esping-Andersen G., *The three worlds of welfare capitalism*, Princetown University Press, 1990.

Esteve R., "La nozione di lavoratore subordinato nel diritto comunitario e nel diritto nazionale", *Diritti Lavori Mercati*, 2004, p. 63.

European Commission (1996), *Communication from the Commission: Incorporating Equal Opportunities for Women and Men into All Community Policies and Activities*, COM(96) 67 final, 21 February 1996.

European Commission, *Report from the Commission to the European Parliament, the Council, the European Economic and Social Committee and the Committee of the Regions, 2010 Report on the application of the EU Charter of Fundamental Rights*, COM(2011) 160 final.

European Commission (2010a), *EUROPE 2020 A strategy for smart sustainable and inclusive growth*, Communication from the Commission, COM(2010) 2020 final, Brussels.

European Commission (2010b), *2010/707/EU: Council Decision of 21 October 2010 on Guidelines for the Employment Policies of the Member States*, Official Journal L 308, 24/11/2010 pp. 0046-0051, Brussels.

European Commission (2010c), *An Agenda for new skills and jobs: A European contribution towards full employment*, Communication from the Commission to the European Parliament, the Council, the European Economic and Social Committee and the Committee of the Regions, COM(2010) 682 final, Brussels.

European Commission (2010d), *Commission discussion note – Towards a more focused approach on job quality*, Discussion note for the Employment Committee Ad Hoc Group, ADHOC/12/170610/EN, Brussels.

European Commission (2010e), Communication from the Commission to the European Parliament, the Council, the European Economic and Social

Committee and the Committee of the Regions, *Strategy for equality between women and men 2010-2015*, COM(201) 491.

European Commission (2010f), Communication from the Commission, *Strategy for the Effective Implementation of the Charter of Fundamental Rights of the European Union*, COM(2010) 573 final.

European Commission (2010g), *Strategy for equality between women and men 2010-2015*. Publications Office of the European Union, 2011: Luxembourg.

European Commission, Communication from the Commission to the European Parliament, the Council, the European Economic and Social Committee and the Committee of the Regions of 21 February 2007, *Improving quality and productivity at work: Community strategy 2007-2012 on health and safety at work*, COM(2007) 62 final.

European Commission, *Promoting decent work for all: The EU contribution to the implementation of the decent work agenda in the world*, Communication from the Commission to the Council, the European Parliament, the Economic and Social Committee and the Committee of the Regions, COM(2006) 249 Final, Luxembourg.

European Commission, *Employment and Social Policies: A Framework for Investing in Quality*, Communication from the Commission to the Council, the European Parliament, the Economic and Social Committee and the Committee of the Regions, COM(2001) 313 final, Brussels.

European Foundation (EUROFOUND), *Quality of Work and Employment in Europe: Issues and Challenges*, Foundation Paper No. 1, European Foundation for the Improvement of Living and Working Conditions, Dublin, 2002.

European Foundation (EUROFOUND), *For a better quality of work: European Union presidency conference. (Summary)*, European Foundation for the Improvement of Living and Working Conditions, Dublin, 2006.

Euzéby A. et C., "Droit à la sécurité sociale et développement humain", *Actes du Colloque international sur le droit à la sécurité sociale*, papers from the international conference on the right to social security, Brussels, 17-18 February 2006.

Fagan C., Burchell B., *Gender, jobs, and working conditions in the European Union*. Luxembourg, European Foundation for the Improvement of Living and Working Conditions, 2002.

Faundez J., *Affirmative action: international perspectives*, Geneva, International Labour Office, 1994.

Faure E., *Learning to be: the world of education today and tomorrow*, Paris, Unesco, 1972.

Favennec-Hery F., "Les plans de départs volontaires autonomes", *La semaine juridique sociale*, No. 39, 2010, p. 1384.

Fields G.S., "Decent work and development policies", *International Labour Review*, Vol. 142, No. 2, Geneva, 2003, p. 239-262.

Fiske S.T., "Stereotyping, prejudice, and discrimination", in D.T. Gilbert, S.T. Fiske, G. Lindzey (eds.), *The handbook of social psychology*, New York, McGraw-Hill, 1998, pp. 357-411.

Folger R., "Distributive and procedural justice: Combined impact of 'voice' and improvement on experienced inequity", *Journal of Personality and Social Psychology*, 1977, 35, pp. 108-119.

Folger R., Cropanzano R., "Fairness theory: justice as accountability", in J. Greenberg, R. Cropanzano (eds.), *Advances in organization justice*, Palo Alto, Stanford University Press, 2001, pp. 1-55.

Fontanelli F., "I principi generali dell'ordinamento UE dopo Kucukdeveci. Riflessioni sull'efficacia indiretta orizzontale e sul principio di solidarietà", *Rivista italiana di diritto pubblico comparato*, 2010, p. 1145.

Frazer H., Marlier E., *In-work poverty and Labour Market Segmentation in the EU: Key Lessons*, Synthesis Report, 2010, p. 32

Freedland M., Kontouris N., "Toward a Comparative Theory of the Contractual Construction of Personal Work Relations in Europe", *Industrial Law Journal*, 2008, p. 62.

Fredman S., "The broken promise of flexicurity", *Industrial Law Journal*, 33(4), 2004, pp. 299-319.

Gallie D., *Employment Regimes and the Quality of Work*, Oxford, Oxford University Press, 2007.

Garabiol P., "La flexisécurité: une révolution européenne", *Questions d'Europe*, Fondation Robert Schuman, No. 73, 2007, 9 p.

Garcia A., "The general provisions of the Charter of Fundamental Rights of the European Union", *European Law Journal*, Vol. 8, No. 4, 2002, pp. 492-514.

García-Izquierdo A.L., García-Izquierdo M., "Discriminación, igualdad de oportunidades en el empleo y selección de personal en España", *Revista de Psicología del Trabajo y las Organizaciones*, 2007, 23, pp. 111-138.

García-Izquierdo A.L., Ramos-Villagrasa P.J., "Calidad de Vida Laboral (CVL): una perspectiva psicosocial", in A.M. Guillén, R. Gutiérrez, S. González (eds.), *Calidad del Trabajo en la Unión Europea: concepto, tensiones, dimensiones*, Pamplona, Thomson-Civitas, 2009, pp. 189-212.

García-Izquierdo A.L., Aguinis H., Ramos-Villagrasa P.J., "Science-practice gap in e-recruitment", *International Journal of Selection and Assessment*, 2010, 18, pp. 432-438.

Gazier B., *Tous "sublimes": vers un nouveau plein-emploi*, Paris, Flammarion, 2003.

Ghaï D., "Decent work: Concept and indicators", *International Labour Review*, Vol. 142, No. 2, Geneva, 2003, p. 113-145.

Ghailani D., "How cant rade union rights and economic freedoms be reconciled in the EU? The Laval and Viking cases", in Degryse, P. Pochet (eds.), *Social Development in the European Union 2007*, Brussels, ETUI-OSE, 2008.

Ghailani D., "The Rüffert and Luxembourg cases: is the European social dimension in retreat?", in Degryse (ed.), *Social Development in the European Union 2008*, Brussels, ETUI-OSE, 2009.

Gilliland S.W., "The perceived fairness of selection systems: An organizational Justice perspective", *Administrative of Management Review*, 1993, 18, pp. 694-734.

Gilliland S.W., "Effects of procedural and distributive justice on reactions to a selection system", *Journal of Applied Psychology*, 1994, 79, pp. 691-701.

Gilliland S.W., Chan D., "Justice in organizations: theory, methods, and applications", in N. Anderson, D.S. Ones, H. Kepir Sinangil, Ch. Viswesvaran (eds.), *Handbook of Industrial, Work, and Organizational Psychology*. London, Sage, 2001, pp. 143-165.

Gineste S., *"Flexicurity": contribution to the EEO Autumn Review 2006*, European Employment Observatory, 2006, 12 p.

Giubboni S., "La nozione comunitaria di lavoratore subordinato", in *Il lavoro subordinato*, S. Sciarra, B. Caruso (eds.), Giappichelli, Torino, 2009.

Giubboni S., "La protezione dei lavoratori non-standard", *Rivista giuridica del lavoro*, 2011.

Goldman B., Gutek B.A., Stein J.H., Lewis K., "Employment discrimination in organizations: antecedents and consequences", *Journal of Management*, 2006, 32, pp. 786-830.

Gomel B., "Politiques publiques et qualité de l'emploi", *La qualité de l'emploi*, Centre d'études de l'emploi, Paris, La Découverte, coll. Repères, 2006, p. 105.

Gómez Heredero A., *Social security – Protection at the international level and developments in Europe*, Editions of the Council of Europe, Paris, 2008.

Gottardi D., "Tutela del lavoro e concorrenza tra imprese nell'ordinamento dell'Unione europea", *Giornale di diritto del lavoro e delle relazioni industriali*, 2010, p. 509.

Griffin G., *Women's employment, women's studies and equal opportunities 1945-2001: reports from nine European countries*, Hull, University of Hull, 2002.

Groussot X., Pech L., *Fundamental Rights Protection in the European Union post Lisbon Treaty*, Policy Paper No. 173, Fondation Robert Schuman, 2010.

Guillén Ana M., Dahl S. A. (eds.), *Quality of Work in the European Union Concept, Data and Debates from a Transnational Perspective*, Brussels, P.I.E. Peter Lang, 2009.

Gust G.A., *Equality at work*, Manila, ILO, 2006.

Hamermesh D., *The changing distribution of job satisfaction*, National Bureau of Economic Research, 1999.

Hassel A., "What does business want? Labour market reforms in CMEs and its problems", in Hancké B. *et al.* (eds.), *Beyond Varieties of Capitalism: conflict, contradiction, and complementarities in the European economy*, Oxford, Oxford University Press, 2007, p. 253-278.

Hennion S., Le Barbier-Le Bris, Del sol M., *Droit social européen et international*, Paris, Presses universitaires de France, 2010.

Hillaire Y. M., "Une doctrine sociale régulièrement mise à jour", *Communio*, No. XXXIV, 3-4, 2009, p. 41-49.

Höpner M., "Corporate Governance in Transition: Ten Empirical Findings on Shareholder Value and Industrial Relations in Germany", *MPIfG Discussion Paper*, Vol. 1, No. 5, 2001.

Huiskamp R., Vos K., "Flexibilization, Modernization and the Lisbon Strategy", *International Journal of Comparative Labour Law and Industrial Relations*, 23 (4), 2007, pp. 587-599.

International Labour Organisation (ILO), *Decent work – Report of the Director-General*, 87th session of the International Labour Conference, 1-17 June 1999, Geneva.

International Labour Organisation (ILO), *ILO Resolution and Conclusions concerning social security*, 89th Session of International Labour Conference, 2001.

International Labour Organisation (ILO), *From Pilot to Decent Work Country Programme – Lessons from the Decent Work Pilot Programme*, 2006, Geneva.

International Labour Organisation (ILO) (2008a), *ILO Declaration on Social Justice for a Fair Globalisation*, adopted by the International Labour Conference at its 97th Session, 28 May-13 June 2008, Geneva.

International Labour Organisation (ILO) (2008b), *Chairperson's report*, Tripartite Meeting of Experts on the Measurement of Decent Work, Geneva, 8-10 September 2008, International Labour Office, Geneva.

International Labour Organisation (ILO) (2008c), *ILO Decent Work Country Programmes – Bringing Focus to ILO Country-level Contributions: A Guidebook for Developing and Implementing Decent Work Country Programmes*, Version 2, July 2008, Geneva.

International Labour Organisation (ILO) (2009a), *Guide to the new Millennium Development Goals Employment Indicators – including the full set of Decent Work Indicators*, International Labour Office, Geneva.

International Labour Organisation (ILO) (2009b), *Decent Work Country Profiles – Austria*, International Labour Office, Geneva.

Joblin J., "Quatre-vingts ans de présence jésuite au BIT", *Choisir*, 2003, p. 13-17.

Kahil-Wolff B., Greber P.Y., *Sécurité sociale: aspects de droit national, international et européen*, Brussels, Bruyant, 2006, p. 127

Kahn-Freund O., "A note of status and contract in British Labour Law", *Modern Law review*, 1967, p. 635.

Kalleberg A., Vaisey S., "Pathways to good job: work quality among the machinist", *British Journal of Industrial Relations*, Vol. 43, No. 3, 2005, pp. 431-454.

Kalleberg A.L., "Precarious work, insecure workers: Employment relations in transition", *American Sociological Review*, Vol. 74, No. 1, 2009, p. 1-22

Kantola J., *Gender and the European Union*, Basingstoke, Palgrave Macmillan, 2010.

Keune M., "Flexicurité: le nouveau remède aux problèmes du marché européen du travail", *Bilan social de l'Union européenne 2007*, Brussels, ETUI-REHS, 2008, p. 175.

Keune M., Jepsen M., *Not balanced and hardly new: the European Commission's quest for flexicurity*, ETUI Working Papers, WP 2007.01, Brussels, European Trade Union Institute.

Koukiadaki A., *Case Law Developments in the Area of Fixed-Term Work*, in *Industrial Law Journal* 2009, p. 89.

Kravaritou Y., "Les Chartes de l'Union européenne et les droits sociaux", in Aliprantis N. (ed.), *Les droits sociaux dans les instruments européens et internationaux. Défis à l'échelle mondiale*, Brussels, Bruyant, 2009.

Kravitz D. A., "Attitudes toward affirmative action plans directed at Blacks: Effects of plan and individual differences", *Journal of Applied Social Psychology*, 1995, 25, pp. 2192-2220.

L'Horty Y. (ed.), *La qualité de l'emploi*, Centre d'études de l'emploi, Paris, La Découverte, coll. Repères, 2006, 123 p.

Lallement M., *Sociologie des relations professionnelles*, Paris, La Découverte, 2008

Lattès J.-M., "Doctrine sociale chrétienne et droit du travail: tradition et modernité", in *Mélanges P. Le Tourneau*, Paris, LGDJ, 2008, pp. 611-624.

Lattès J.-M., "Doctrine sociale chrétienne, catholicisme social et droit du travail", *Bulletin de littérature ecclésiastique*, BLE CIX/3, 2008, pp. 255-264.

Lercler D., *Rapport sur le projet de loi relatif aux droits et devoirs des demandeurs d'emploi*, Rapport Parlementaire No. 400, Sénat, 18 juin 2008.

Leschke J., Watt A., Finn M., *Putting a number on job quality? Constructing a European Job Quality Index*, WP 2008.03, ETUI-REHS Research department.

Leventhal G.S., "What should be done with equity theory? New approaches to the study of faimess in social relationships", in K.J. Gergen, M.S. Greenbers, R.H. Willis (eds.), *Social Exchange: Advances in Theory and Research*, New York, Plenum, 1980, pp. 27-55.

Levêque A., *Le développement d'un cadre d'indicateurs relatifs à des transitions positives et à la flexicurité dans le contexte des relations individuelles de travail*, University of Liege, 2010.

Levy J., *The State After Statism: New State Activities in the Age of Liberalization*, Harvard University Press, 2006.

Liff S., Ward K. "Distorted views through the glass ceiling: the construction of women's understandings of promotion and senior management positions", *Gender, Work, and Organization*, 2001, 8, pp. 19-36.

Lozano E., *Comments on the conceptual paper of the task force: "Towards international quality of employment framework"*, Joint UNECE/EUROSTAT/ILO Seminar, 18-20 April 2006, Geneva, http://www.unece.org/stats/documents/2007.04.labour.htm.

Macours J.-F., "La flexicurité: panacée européenne à la crise de l'emploi?", *Actualités en droit social européen*, Brussels, Larcier, 2010, p. 111-124.

Manca Governatori, Mascherini, Towards a set of Composite Indicators on Flexicurity: a Comprehensive Approach, European Union, 2010.

Mangan J., *Workers without Traditional Employment: An International Study of Non-standard Work*, Cheltenham/Camberley/Northampton, Edward Elgar Publishing Ltd., 2000.

Manning A., "We Can Work It Out: The Impact of Technological Change on the Demand for Low-Skill Workers", *Scottish Journal of Political Economy*, Vol. 51, No. 5, 2004, p. 581-608.

Marlier E., Natali D. (eds.) with Rudi Van Dam, *Europe 2020: Towards a more social EU?*, Brussels, P.I.E. Peter Lang, 2010.

Maupain F., "Le renouveau du débat normatif à l'OIT – De la fin de la guerre froide à la mondialisayion", *Bulletin de droit comparé du travail et de la sécurité sociale*, 2001, p. 3.

Maupain F., "Revitalization not retreat: the real potential of the 1998 ILO declaration for the universal protection of workers' rights", *European Journal of international Law*, Vol. 16, No. 3, 2005, pp. 439-465.

Maupain F., "Nouvelle fondation ou nouvelle façade? La déclaration de l'OIT sur la justice sociale pour une mondialisation équitable", *Droits fondamentaux*, No. 7, 2008.

McCann D., *Regulating Flexible Work*, Oxford, Oxford University Press, 2007.

Michaud V., *Welfare and the Labour Market in the EU*, ENEPRI paper, No. 7, 2004.

Minnerath R., *Doctrine sociale et bien commun*, Paris, Beauchesne, Coll. Le point théologique, 2010, 178 p.

Moreau M.-A, *Normes sociales, Droit du Travail et mondialisation*, Paris, Dalloz, 2006, 418 p.

Moscoso S., García-Izquierdo A.L., Bastida M., "Reactions toward affirmative action measures for women", *Revista de Psicología del Trabajo y de las Organizaciones*, 2010, 26, pp. 211-221.

Müller D., "Le principe protestant de l'éthique et la substance catholique de la morale", in Gavric A. et Sienkiewicz G. (eds.), *État et bien commun*, Berne, Peter Lang, 2008, pp. 247-263.

Nayer A. *et al.*, *Le droit à l'épanouissement de l'être humain au travail: Métamorphoses du droit social*, Brussels, Bruylant, 2007, p. 223.

Nickless J., *European Code of Social Security*, Editions of the Council of Europe, 2002.

Nogler L., *The concept of "subordination" in European and Comparative Law*, Quaderni del Dipartimento di Scienze giuridiche, Università di Trento, 2009.

Nogler L., "Rethinking the Lawrie-Blum Doctrine of Subordination: A Critical Analysis Prompted by Recent Development in Italian Employment Law", *International Journal of Comparative Labour Law* 2010, p. 83.

Ostner I., Lewis J. (1995). "Gender and the evolution of European Social policies", in Stephan Leibfried and Paul Pierson (eds.), *European Social Policy: Between Fragmentation and Integration*, Washington, DC, Brookings Institution, pp. 159-93.

Peccoud D. (ed.), *Le travail décent. Points de vue philosophiques et spirituels*, Genève, BIT, 2004, 187 p.

Peña-Casas R., *Quality of Work and Employment in EU Policy Arena: Conceptual Frameworks and Monitoring Indicators*, Paper for the RECWOWE Network, 2007.

Peña-Casa R., "Monitoring Quality of Work and Employment in the European Union. Conceptual Frameworks and Indicators", in Guillén, Ana M., Dahl S.A. (eds.), *Quality of Work in the European Union Concept, Data and Debates from a Transnational Perspective*, Brussels, P.I.E. Peter Lang, 2009.

Perulli A., *Economically dependent/quasi-subordinate (parasubordinate) employment: legal, social and economic aspects*, Report for European Commission, Directorate-General for Employment and Social Affairs, 2002.

Perulli A., "Per uno Statuto del lavoro autonomo", *Diritto delle relazioni industriali*, 2010, p. 621.

Pochet P., *What's wrong with EU2020?*, ETUI Policy Brief, Issue 2/2010.

Pochet P., *EU 2020. Social impact of the new form of European governance*, ETUI Policy Brief, European Social Policy, Issue 5/2010.

Pollack, M.A., Hafner-Burton, E. "Mainstreaming gender in the European Union", *Journal of European Public Policy*, 2011, 7, 432-456.

Quadruppani S., "Restructurations et résistance chez Fiat", in *Le Monde diplomatique*, No. 684, 2011, p. 10

Ralle P., "Introduction", *La qualité de l'emploi*, Centre d'études de l'emploi, Paris, La Découverte, coll. Repères, 2006, p. 7.

Ramonet M., *Les cellules de reclassement*, Rapport au Conseil économique, social et environnemental, 2010, 106 p.

Raoul-Duval I., Perrin V., "Les cellules de reclassement", *Les cahiers du DRH*, 2010, p. 164.

Razzolini O., "Beyond the Contract: 'Economic' and 'Bureaucratic' Dependence in Personal Work Relations", *Comparative Labour Law and Policy Journal*, 2010, Vol. 31, p. 1011-35.

Reich R.B., "The challenge of decent work", in *International Labour Review*, Vol. 141, No. 1-2, Geneva, 2002, p. 115-122.

Ritter J.A., Anker R., "Good jobs, bad jobs: Workers' evaluations in five countries", *International Labour Review*, Vol. 141, No. 4, Geneva, 2002, p. 331-358.

Roccella M., *Lavoro subordinato e lavoro autonomo, oggi*, WP C.S.D.L.E. "Massimo D'Antona", It. 65/2008.

Rodotà S., "Il Codice civile e il processo costituente europeo", *Rivista Critica di Diritto Privato*, 2005, p. 19.

Rodrìguez-Pinero y Bravo-Ferrer M., "La reforma laboral y el dinamismo del contrato de trabajo", *Relaciones laborales*, 2010, No. 21-22, p. 1.

Ryan A.M., Ployhart R.E., "Applicants' perceptions of selection procedures and decisions: A critical review and agenda for the future", *Journal of Management*, 2000, 26, pp. 565-606.

Ryan M.K., Haslam S.A., "The glass cliff: evidence that women are over-represented in precarious leadership positions", *British Journal of Management*, 2005, 16, pp. 81-90.

Ryan M.K., Haslam S.A., "The glass cliff: exploring the dynamics surrounding the appointment of women precarious leadership positions", *Academy of Management Review*, 2007, 32, pp. 549-572.

Salais R., "La politique des indicateurs. Du taux de chômage au taux d'emploi dans la Stratégie européenne pour l'emploi", in Zimmermann, B. (dir.), *Les sciences sociales à l'épreuve de l'action: le savant, le politique et l'Europe*, Paris, Maison des Sciences de l'Homme, 2004, p. 287-331.

Schein V.E., "The relationship between sex role stereotypes and requisite management characteristics", *Journal of Applied Psychology*, 1973, 57, pp. 95-100.

Schein V.E., "The relationship between sex role stereotypes and requisite management characteristics among female managers", *Journal of Applied Psychology*, 1975, 60, pp. 340-344.

Schein V.E., "Women in management. Reflections and projections", *Women in Management Review*, 2007, 22, pp. 6-18.

Schmid G., *Non-Standard Employment and the New Standard Employment Contract: Reflections from a Transitional Labour Market Point of View*, paper presented to the IIRA European Congress 2010 in Copenhagen, 28-30 June.

Schmidt F.L., Ones D.S., Hunter J.E., "Personnel selection", *Annual Review of Psychology*, 1992, 43, pp. 627-670.

Schmitt N., Gilliland S.W., "Beyond differential prediction: Fairness in selection", in D.M. Saunders (eds.), *New approaches to employee management: Fairness in employee selection*, Greenwich, JAI Press, 1992, pp. 21-46.

Schneider R., *Quality counts*, OECD Observer, No. 248, March 2005.

Schulze Buschoff K., Protsch P., "(A-)typical and (in-)secure? Social protection and 'non-standard' forms of employment in Europe", in *International Social Security Review*, Vol. 61, 4/2008, p. 51.

Sciarra S., *Il tempo determinato nella giurisprudenza della Corte di giustizia europea. Un tassello nella "modernizzazione" del diritto del lavoro*, WP C.S.D.L.E. "Massimo D'Antona", Int. 52/2007.

Sciarra S., Davies P., Freedland M., *Employment Policy and the Regulation of Part-time Work in the European Union: A comparative Analysis*, Cambridge, Cambridge University Press, 2004.

Sen A., "Work and rights", *International Labour Review*, Vol. 139, No. 2, Geneva, 2000, p. 119-128.

Sen A., *Development as Freedom*, Oxford, Oxford University Press, 1999.

Sen A., *Éthique et économie*, Paris, PUF, 2003.

Sen A., *The Idea of Justice*, Cambridge Mass., The Belknap Press of Harvard University Press, 2009.

Sennett R., *The Corrosion of Character: Personal Consequences of Work in the New Capitalism*, New York, W.W. Norton & Co., 1999.

Sepùlveda Gòmez M., "Responsabilidad social de las empresa y efficacia en la calidad en el empleo", in *Eficacia de las normas laborales desde la perspectiva de la calidad en el empleo*, J. Cruz Villalòn (ed.), Tirant lo Blanch, 2011, p. 298.

Servais J.M., "Globalization and decent work policy: Reflections upon a new legal approach", *International Labour Review*, Vol. 143, No. 1-2, 2006, pp. 185-207.

Servais J.M., *International Labour Law*, Kluwer, 2008.

Sheridan A., Milgate G., "She says, he says: women's and men's views of the composition of boards", *Women in Management Review*, 2003, 18, pp. 147-154.

Smith M. *et al.*, "Job quality in Europe", *Industrial Relations Journal*, 2008, pp. 586-603.

Somavia J., *Decent jobs for all in a global economy; an ILO perspective*, document submitted to the Third WTO Ministerial Meeting, 30 Nov.-3 Dec. 1999.

Stone-Romero E. F., Stone D.L., "How do organizational justice concepts relate to discrimination and prejudice?", in J. Greenberg, J.A. Colquitt (eds.), *Handbook of Organizational Justice*, Mahwah, Lawrence Erlbaum, 2005, pp. 439-467.

Supiot A., "A propos d'un centenaire, la dimension juridique de la doctrine sociale", in *Droit Social*, 1991, p. 916.

Supiot A., *Les notions de contrat de travail et de relation de travail en Europe, Rapport pour la Commission des Communautés Européennes*, Bruxelles, 1992.

Supiot A. (ed.), *Transformation of labour and future of labour law in Europe. Final report*, Report for the European Commission, 1999.

Supiot A. (dir.), *Au-delà de l'emploi*, Paris, Flammarion, 1999.

Supiot A., *Critique du droit du travail*, Paris, PUF, 2002.

Supiot A., *Le droit du travail*, Presses universitaires de France, Coll. Que sais-je?, 2004.

Supiot A., "La place de la sécurité sociale dans le système des normes internationales du travail", *Semaine sociale Lamy*, Supplément, No. 1272, 2006, p. 7.

Supiot A., "En guise de conclusion: la capacité, une notion à haut potentiel", in Deakin, S. & Supiot, A. (eds.), *Capacitas*, Oxford and Portland, Hart Publishing, 2009, p. 161-71.

Supiot A., "Justice sociale et libération du commerce international", *Droit social*, 2010, p. 133

Supiot A., *L'esprit de Philadelphie, La justice sociale face au marché total*, Paris, Seuil, 2010.

Thelen K. & Kume I., "Coordination as a political problem in coordinated market economies", *Governance*, Vol. 19, No. 1, 2006, p. 11-42.

Tippins N.T., "Adverse impact in employee selection procedures from the perspective of an organizational consultant", in J.L. Outtz (ed.), *Adverse Impacti*, New York, Taylor & Francis, 2010, pp. 201-225.

Trubek D., Trubek L., "Hard and Soft Law in the Construction of Social Europe: the Role of the Open Method of Coordination", *European Law Journal*, Vol. 11, No. 3, 2005, pp. 343-364.

United Nations – Economic Commission for Europe (UNECE), *Potential indicators for measurement of quality of employment*, Note by the secretariat for the Fifty-eighth plenary session of the Conference of European Statisticians, Paris, 8-10 June 2010, Geneva, UN.

Vandamme F., "Problème du jour – "Flexicurité": qui est concerné?", *Revue du Marché commun et de l'Union européenne*, No. 511, 2007, p. 482-485.

Vandenbroucke F., Hemerijck A. and Palier B., *The EU Needs a Social Investment Pact*, OSE Paper Series, Opinion paper No. 5, May 2011.

Vanhercke B., "Is the 'Social Dimension of Europe 2020' an Oxymoron?", in *Social developments in the European Union 2010*, C. Degryse and D. Natali (eds.), Brussels, Ose-Etui, 2011.

Vecerník J., "Skating on Thin Ice: A Comparison of Work Values and Job Satisfaction in CEE and EU Countries", *International Journal of Comparative Sociology*, Vol. 44, No. 5, 2003, pp. 444-471.

Vielle P., *Flexicurité: redéfinir la sécurité des citoyens européens*, OSE Policy Paper No. 1, Brussels, October 2007.

Vielle P., "How the Horizontal Social Clause can be made to work: the lessons of gender mainstreaming", in *The Lisbon Treaty and Social Europe*, N. Bruun, K. Lörcher, I. Schömann (eds.), Oxford, Hart Publishing, 2012.

Vielle P., Pochet P. & Cassiers I. (dir.), *L'État social actif: vers un changement de paradigme?*, Brussels, P.I.E. Peter Lang, 2005.

Walker A., Taylor P., *The Ageing Workforce: Employers' Attitudes Towards Older Workers, Work, Employment and Society*, Vol. 8, No. 4, 1994.

Walker A., *Towards Active Ageing in the European Union*, paper for the Millennium Project Workshop, – *Towards Active Ageing in the 21st century*, The Japan Institute of Labour, 2001.

Widmer F., "Institutional Investors, Corporate Elites and the Building of a Market for Corporate Control", *Socio-Economic Review*, 2011, Vol. 4, p. 671-697.

Wilpert B., "Organizational behavior", *Annual Review of Psychology*, 1995, 46, pp. 59-90.

Wilson F., "Women in Management in the UK", in M. Davidson, R.J. Burke (eds.), *Women in Management Worldwide: Facts, Figures and Analysis*, Aldershot, Ashgate, 2004, pp. 99-114.

Wisskirchen A., "The standard-setting and monitoring activity of the ILO: Legal questions and practical experience", *International Labour Review*, Vol. 144, No. 3, 2005, pp. 253-289.

Wynn M., Leighton P., "Will the Real Employer Please Stand Up? Agencies, Client Companies and the Employment Status of the Temporary Agency Worker", in *Industrial Law Journal*, 2006, p. 318.

Zappala L., "The Temporary Agency Work Directive: an Impossible Political Agreement?", *Industrial Law Journal*, 2003, 32, pp. 310-314.

Zappala L., "Abuse of the Fixed-Term Employment contracts and Sanctions in the Recent ECJ's Jurisprudence", *Industrial Law Journal*, 2006, 35(4), pp. 439-444.

Zappalà L., "I lavori flessibili", in *Il lavoro subordinato*, S. Sciarra, B. Caruso (eds.), Giappichelli, Torino, 2009.

"Work & Society"

The series "Work & Society" analyses the development of employment and social policies, as well as the strategies of the different social actors, both at national and European levels. It puts forward a multi-disciplinary approach – political, sociological, economic, legal and historical – in a bid for dialogue and complementarity.

The series is not confined to the social field *stricto sensu*, but also aims to illustrate the indirect social impacts of economic and monetary policies. It endeavours to clarify social developments, from a comparative and a historical perspective, thus portraying the process of convergence and divergence in the diverse national societal contexts. The manner in which European integration impacts on employment and social policies constitutes the backbone of the analyses.

Series Editor: Philippe Pochet, General Director ETUI-REHS (Brussels) and Digest Editor of the Journal of European Social Policy

Recent Titles

No.74 – *Quality of Employment in Europe. Legal and Normative Perspectives*, Silvia BORELLI & Pascale VIELLE (eds.), 2012, 978-90-5201-888-1

No.73 – *Renewing Democratic Deliberation in Europe. The Challenge of Social and Civil Dialogue*, Jean DE MUNCK, Claude DIDRY, Isabelle FERRERAS & Annette JOBERT (eds.), 2012, 978-90-5201-875-1

No.72 – *Democracy and Capabilities for Voice. Welfare, Work and Public Deliberation in Europe*, Ota DE LEONARDIS & Serafino NEGRELLI (eds.), 2012, 978-90-5201-867-6

No.71 – *Trajectoires des modèles nationaux. État, démocratie et travail en France et en Allemagne*, Michèle DUPRÉ, Olivier GIRAUD et Michel LALLEMENT (dir.), 2012, ISBN 978-90-5201-863-8

No.70 – *Precarious Employment in Perspective. Old and New Challenges to Working Conditions in Sweden*, Annette THÖRNQUIST & Åsa-Karin ENGSTRAND (eds.), 2011, ISBN 978-90-5201-730-3

No.69 – *Europe 2020: Towards a More Social EU?*, Eric MARLIER & David NATALI (eds.), with Rudi VAN DAM, 2010, ISBN 978-90-5201-688-7

No.68 – *Generations at Work and Social Cohesion in Europe*, Patricia VENDRAMIN (ed.), 2009, ISBN 978-90-5201-647-4

No.67 – *Quality of Work in the European Union. Concept, Data and Debates from a Transnational Perspective*, Ana M. GUILLÉN & Svenn-Åge DAHL (eds.), 2009, ISBN 978-90-5201-577-4

No.66 – *Emerging Systems of Work and Welfare*, Pertti KOISTINEN, Lilja MÓSESDÓTTIR & Amparo SERRANO PASCUAL (eds.), 2009, ISBN 978-90-5201-549-1

No.65 – *Building Anticipation of Restructuring in Europe*, Marie-Ange MOREAU (ed.), in collaboration with Serafino NEGRELLI & Philippe POCHET, 2009, ISBN 978-90-5201-486-9

No.64 – *Pensions in Europe, European Pensions. The Evolution of Pension Policy at National and Supranational Level*, David NATALI, 2008, ISBN 978-90-5201-460-9

No.63 – *Restructuring in the New EU Member States. Social Dialogue, Firms Relocation and Social Treatment of Restructuring*, Marie-Ange MOREAU & María Esther BLAS LÓPEZ (eds.), 2009, ISBN 978-90-5201-456-2

No.62 – *Jobs on the Move. An Analytical Approach to "Relocation" and its Impact on Employment*, Béla GALGÓCZI, Maarten KEUNE & Andrew WATT (eds.), 2008, ISBN 978-90-5201-448-7

No.61 – *Les nouveaux cadres du dialogue social, Europe et territoires*, Annette JOBERT (dir.), 2008, ISBN 978-90-5201-444-9

No.60 – *Transnational Labour Regulation. A Case Study of Temporary Agency Work*, Kerstin AHLBERG, Brian BERCUSSON, Niklas BRUUN, Haris KOUNTOUROS, Christophe VIGNEAU & Loredana ZAPPALÀ, 2008, ISBN 978-90-5201-417-3

No.59 – *Changing Liaisons. The Dynamics of Social Partnership in Twentieth Century West-European Democracies*, Karel DAVIDS, Greta DEVOS & Patrick PASTURE (eds.), 2007, ISBN 978-90-5201-365-7

No.58 – *Work and Social Inequalities in Health in Europe*, Ingvar LUNDBERG, Tomas HEMMINGSSON & Christer HOGSTEDT (eds.), SALTSA, 2007, ISBN 978-90-5201-372-5

No. 57 – *European Solidarities. Tensions and Contentions of a Concept*, Lars MAGNUSSON & Bo STRÅTH (eds.), 2007, ISBN 978-90-5201-363-3

No. 56 – *Industrial Relations in Small Companies. A Comparison: France, Sweden and Germany*, Christian DUFOUR, Adelheid HEGE, Sofia MURHEM, Wolfgang RUDOLPH & Wolfram WASSERMANN (eds.), SALTSA, 2007, ISBN 978-90-5201-360-2

No. 55 – *The European Sectoral Social Dialogue. Actors, Developments and Challenges*, Anne DUFRESNE, Christophe DEGRYSE & Philippe POCHET (eds.), SALTSA/Observatoire social européen, 2006, ISBN 978-90-5201-052-6

Kolibri 360 GmbH
Ferdinand-Jühlke-Straße 7
99095 Erfurt, Deutschland
produktsicherheit@kolibri360.de